Dr Dennis Townhill, 1982

Photo by Murray Donald of Edinburgh

The Imp and The Thistle

The story of a life of music making

DENNIS TOWNHILL

Dennis Townhill

G. H. SMITH & SON,
Easingwold, York, England

ISBN 0-9538823-0-6

Publisher: Dr Dennis William Townhill, OBE
Printed from Author's disk by G. H. Smith & Son, Easingwold, York, England

Cover design by Nick Waters
Colour Box Design Co. Ltd., 33 Bishopthorpe Road, York, England

Contents

Preface

"Not another one" would be an understandable comment on the appearance of yet one more book of reminiscences. My only justification is that a number of people encouraged me to have it published.

It all began by spending occasional spare moments looking through scrapbooks I have kept since childhood and jotting down recollections of events and activities that have occurred during my life. They have reminded me of many people that I have met and the great debt of gratitude I owe to some of them. Many others have pursued a similar musical career and with much greater distinction, nevertheless I hope readers may find some features of interest in the book.

I am indebted to many people in its preparation, in particular to Dr Francis Jackson, OBE for kindly writing a foreword, to members of the Executive Committee of the Federation of Cathedral Old Choristers' Associations for their advice and support - to Canon Allan Maclean, Margaret Horner and Derek Sutton who have kindly read, pruned and corrected the proofs and David Horner who guided me through some of the mysteries and pitfalls of publication. The book would not have appeared at all but for the generous help and skill of Frank MacRae in deciphering and preparing the text from my often almost illegible handwriting. I accept responsibility for any inaccuracies and omissions.

Finally to my wife for her patience, tolerance and support throughout my career.

It is my hope that the book will generate funds for the FCOCA whose aims and membership are very close to my heart.

Edinburgh
April 2000

Dennis Townhill

4

Foreword

Dr Francis Jackson OBE Organist Emeritus, York Minster

By way of reply to the question - frequently asked of one who has reached mature years - "Are you writing your reminiscences?" it is perhaps a natural reaction to say, "Oh, but there's nothing worth writing about". That may be a truthful statement on the spur of the moment but, given a little thought and some reflection, could prove to be wide of the mark in some degree. For, the human brain being such a marvellous apparatus, the wonders it can perform are, to say the least, remarkable; once it can be given its head and allowed to get into its stride, the memory part of it can throw up all kinds of thoughts and events that had been entirely forgotten.

Happily, Doctor Townhill has responded to the call in full measure, giving us the benefit of his rich store of memories - the result of a full life devoted to church music and the diversity of situations connected with it.

The list of his involvements, which is formidable, leads one to speculate on the sheer practicability of discharging the assignments accompanying them and one is forced to the conclusion that only someone with a complete dedication to the cause - and to his fellows - could accomplish such a daunting task. And with such complete success.

Perhaps a clue to this success lies in his obvious belief in those he has to work with, and the consequent response this attitude engenders in them. An even-tempered optimist such as he is can only inspire confidence and elicit the best efforts from anyone who enters his field of activity.

To mention one aspect among many - not invidiously, I hope - his heroic work in the development of St Mary's Music School, supported, of course, by his wife Mabel's sterling help, is an achievement of immense significance and great pride to the Cathedral, all this despite setbacks and frustrations which normally attend such an enterprise - one which moreover can scarcely be said to lie in the ordinary course of a sensitive musician's life and work or in any part of his training. But Doctor Townhill did achieve all this triumphantly, and it can be counted among his greatest achievements: a lasting testimony to his love of the church and its music, which was plain to witness in the day to day singing of the choir under his inspired direction. This was his first love and his principal raison d'être as Organist and Master of the Choristers of St Mary's.

But his other activities, so many and varied, were deployed with the same enthusiasm and dedication, to the great benefit of the many who have been (and happily still are) privileged to know him and to work with him. We who read this book are indeed fortunate that he has found time and used his literary skills to enable us to share in the recall of so many aspects of a remarkably happy and productive life, which even now continues and in which he has our warmest good wishes for the future.

To my wife, Mabel and our family

Chapter 1 - The beginnings (1925-1934)

"The Little Imp"

The ancient City of Lincoln, in the East Midlands of England, stands on a hill about two hundred feet above the surrounding countryside. The hill is part of a limestone ridge that stretches for some sixty miles through the countryside of Lincolnshire. It was along this route that the invading Roman Legions marched north from London after landing in England in the year 43 AD. The river flows through a gap in the ridge and widens into a pool, still there and called Brayford. There is evidence of an even earlier settlement in this area, Lindon or Lindune, meaning a lake, as in the Welsh *Llyn*. The Romans built their fortress on the north side of the gap at the convergence of two main roads, Ermine Street from the south and the Fosse Way from the south west. These roads were built by 47 AD. The city known as Lindune Colonia (hence Lincoln) became the capital of one of the four provinces of Britain and achieved an eminence that it has never maintained since.[1]

It was in this city that I was born on 29 May 1925, the anniversary of the Restoration of the Monarchy in 1660. It was known as Oak Apple Day, as a reminder that King Charles II escaped from Cromwell's soldiers by hiding in an oak tree. I remember, as a small boy, chanting with other children, "29th of May, Royal Oak Day - if you don't give

Ted, Gladys, Becky and Minnie in Chaplin Street, Lincoln.

1. Ref. A Short History of Lincoln (1979), Sir Francis Hill.

us a holiday we'll all run away". It was no longer a public holiday but it was the custom to wear a sprig of oak leaf on your clothes to mark the anniversary. Anyone not wearing it was chased and stung with nettles.

The Lincoln of my childhood was a modest and rather sleepy county town with a population of some sixty-seven thousand people. There was a clear division between uphill and downhill. In general terms, the wealthier and more professional classes lived uphill, in the area of the ancient Roman city.

With the development of industry in the nineteenth century, the population spread below the hill to the south. It was in this area that factories were built and houses to accommodate the workers in those factories. No 1 Chaplin Street in which I lived and grew up was at the top end of a street of terraced houses off the main road from the south, or High Street, below the hill. It was named after Sir Henry Chaplin, a former Member of Parliament for Lincoln.

At the top of the street on the south side stood the large Hannah Memorial Chapel and on the north side there was a garage and saleroom for Ford cars. Few people in Lincoln owned cars before the Second World War and I remember being fascinated by the promotional films shown in the saleroom from time to time. Most people travelled to work on foot or on bicycle and in the early morning, at midday and early evening the High Street seemed full of an endless stream of humanity. I lived with my grandparents for the first twenty-three years of my life and their house stood next door to the Ford garage. It was large compared with those in the rest of the street and had three stories as well as a cellar. At the side of the house there was an archway leading through a covered yard to workshops behind the house.

My grandfather was a blacksmith, farrier and wheelwright and carried on his own business in these premises. The forge was in one of the workshops and another was leased to a joiner. A third area was used for storing tools, iron and steel bars and other equipment. For some years my grandfather trained racing pigeons and there were lofts in the yard where they were kept and fed. It seemed miraculous that the birds could be sent long distances from their home and yet unerringly find their way back. My grandfather was a stocky, muscular man of considerable strength. I clearly remember as a small boy watching him heating strips of iron in his forge and then shaping the red hot metal into horseshoes or hoops for cart wheels. He wielded both a seven pounds and a fourteen pounds hammer with ease, one handed and two handed respectively. The middle finger of my left hand still bears a small scar which was the result of his accidentally striking it! No doubt I had unthinkingly put my hand on the anvil but fortunately no permanent damage was done.

Large cart horses were regularly brought through the archway into the yard to have new metal shoes nailed into their hooves. The horses were not always quiet and well behaved and I watched with some alarm as my grandfather strove to control the rearing and kicking animals. Another of his jobs which fascinated me was the fitting of iron hoops on to cart wheels. This involved bringing the red hot hoops from the forge into the yard and hammering them around the wheels. They were then dropped into a large bowl of cold water with resulting loud hissing and clouds of steam. The metal contracted as it cooled and gripped tightly round the wooden wheel-frame.

To return to my family origins. My grandfather, John Edward Townhill, was born on 20 October 1882. He was the third of the seven children of William Townhill, (born 7 February 1855) and Ann Bunniss (born 8 October 1849). William was a skilled bricklayer who held the local record for laying the largest number of bricks in a working day. He was no mean craftsman in other ways for the round dining table he made on his marriage still serves us well in our kitchen at the present time! I was told that I spent many happy hours as a small child sitting on its base under the table top playing with saucepans by taking the lids off and putting them back on again.

John Edward married Agnes Oram in 1903 and they had one child, Minnie, my mother. Agnes died soon after giving birth to her daughter and thus John Edward found himself a widower at the age of twenty-one. He did not remain alone for long for he remarried. Rebecca Agnes Meanwell was the eldest of a family of fourteen children and was born on 30 July 1872. She clearly remembered the celebrations of Queen Victoria's Golden Jubilee in 1887. As I write these reminiscences, it is bewildering to think of the immense changes that took place during my grandparents' lifetime, including the development of the railways, the invention of the internal combustion engine and motor car, electricity and electric lighting, the aeroplane, the wireless, television, mechanically operated washing machines, vacuum cleaners, gas and electric cookers, refrigerators, cameras, cinema, to mention but a few of the features of our lives today which we take for granted but which did not exist in my grandparents' younger days.

Becky, as she was known to family and friends, was a small lady with a large and generous heart. She worked *in service* before she married and rose to the responsible position of cook in a large house. Although small in stature, she had plenty of spirit. She told the housekeeper that she would not start work until she had been given breakfast. On the housekeeper asking who she thought she was in laying down conditions, Becky retorted, "I'm Bouncing Bess from Buggery and I'm not starting work until I've had my breakfast." On another occasion before she was married, my grandfather, commonly known as Ted, called for her at the house where she worked. On being invited inside he was asked if he would like a glass of beer. He said "I don't mind" to which the housekeeper replied, "Well, I don't mind either," and Ted did not receive his glass of beer. Becky was furious and told him he should always say "Yes please," when he was offered anything whether he wanted it or not.

My mother died of tuberculosis at the age of twenty-three when I was two and a half years old. The only memory I have of her is a photograph and that I called her "Giggie". She fell in love with a musician in the seaside resort of Skegness where both were working during the summer holiday season. Unhappily, they never married and she was abandoned by him and returned to Lincoln. I was unaware of these facts until later in my life and accepted Ted and Becky as my mother and father, sharing their surname. Looking back over my life, I can only be immensely grateful for the love and care they gave me. The beginnings could hardly have been less auspicious for I was a small, thin baby not expected to survive infancy. But survive I did, despite a mastoid operation at the age of two and bouts of such common childish ailments as mumps, measles and chickenpox. These are but a faded memory and small incidents in a carefree, secure and happy childhood.

No 1 Chaplin Street contained features which were typical of their time but very different from those enjoyed today. There were three rooms on the ground floor - kitchen or scullery, dining room and front room or sitting room. The kitchen had a stone-flagged floor with a small fireplace on one side and a deep sink facing a window on the other. Cooking and washing of clothes was all done in this area. Before we had hot water pipes installed, water was heated in pans on the fire or on the gas cooker. Clothes were placed in boiling water in a large container or "dolly-tub" and stirred round by hand with a wooden pole which had prongs or feet attached. They were then scrubbed by hand on a board at the side of the sink with soap. After rubbing in the sink the clothes were placed in a mangle to squeeze most of the water out. The mangle had two wooden rollers held in an iron frame and was operated by turning a handle at the side. The clothes were dried outside in the small enclosed back yard. There were two out-houses in the yard, one for storing coal and wood and the other was the lavatory. The dining room and front room also had fireplaces. Those in the kitchen and dining room had iron side-ovens which were used for heating and cooking food. Coal was the sole source of fuel for heating in the house and lighting was provided by gas until electricity was installed. There were no gas lights in the bedrooms when I was small and candles were used. Although there were fire places in the bedrooms I do not remember them ever being used and in the winter the rooms were very cold! Undressing was a hurried operation and cuddling the hot-water bottle inside one's bed was sheer bliss!

There were four bedrooms on the first floor until one of them was converted into a bathroom when a hot water system was installed. It must have been about this time that the house was wired for electricity. For many years our house was the only one in the area to have the luxury of an indoor bathroom. Prior to that, washing and bathing was done in the kitchen standing or sitting in a large metal wash tub. We never had an inside lavatory and a chamber pot under the bed provided the necessary facility. The contents had to be disposed of in the lavatory in the back yard.

As far as I can remember, there were two rooms in the third floor attic. One was a bedroom occupied by a long-standing lodger whose name I have forgotten. The other was a large room which I used for playing with my toys. It was a perfect setting for my Hornby clockwork railway set of which the Flying Scotsman engine was a pride and joy. Below the ground floor there was a cellar, reached via stone steps. It was always cold and an ideal place for storing perishable food at a time when there were no domestic refrigerators.

Ted and Becky had a daughter Vera, who, like my mother died at the early age of twenty-three years. She developed appendicitis whilst on holiday and this turned into acute peritonitis. I have often marvelled at their resilience in the face of so much misfortune. Vera was musical and had learnt to play the piano. There was an upright piano in the front room and the sound of her playing evidently fascinated me. As a small child I constantly tried to make sounds on it, standing on tip-toe to reach the keys. Vera gave me some rudimentary tuition from the age of three or four years old and I had more formal lessons from a Mr Henderson when I was aged six years.

We lived in the Parish of St Peter-at-Gowts and I was baptised in the church by the Vicar, Canon Townroe. The church had a Saxon tower and was one of the few to survive intact after the Civil War in the mid-17th century. It was in the district of Wigford and took its name from the Great Gowt and Little Gowt. These were spurs or drains flowing under the High Street from the river Witham into the Sincil Dyke. St Peter's was within easy walking distance from Chaplin Street and stood on the same side of the High Street. The church schools for infant and primary age children were a little further down. I attended these schools from the age of five to nine years. I remember nothing of the first infant years but do recollect something of the last year in the primary department. The Headmaster was called Mr Hawes and there were three assistant teachers. The senior teacher was a Mr Dickinson nicknamed "Dickie" and the other two were Mr Deighton "Dido" and Miss Marshall "Moggy", in whose class I was a pupil. There was a bicycle shed in the playground which served as a goal for football games supervised by Dickie. Mr Deighton's son, George, became a friend in later years when we were fellow members of the First Xl football team at The Lincoln School. Miss Marshall's parents were friends of my grandparents. She occasionally visited the house, much to my embarrassment for I feared that my knowledge of her school nickname might be revealed. I am sure that she was well aware of what we called her.

I also attended St Peter-at-Gowts Church Sunday School and this proved to be a major influence in determining the future course of my life. The Sunday School Superintendent was Miss Allison, a tall lady who wore a long black dress with an embroidered white collar round her neck and black lace-up boots. I sat next to her in church during the services. Miss Allison told my grandparents that I had a promising singing voice and that they should do something about it. She suggested that they should ask the church organist, Miss E M Pollard, for advice. This they did, and she said that she would recommend me for a chorister place in the Cathedral choir. I was duly summoned for audition with fourteen other boys to compete for three vacant places.

The audition was held in the Cathedral Song School, a room above the choristers' vestry on the south side of the building. It was reached by a narrow winding stone staircase whose uneven steps had been worn away by successive generations. Inside the Song School there were wooden desks facing one another for the choristers to stand behind and behind these, benches and wooden music desks for the men (lay vicars). There was a grand piano between the desks and a number of photographs hanging from the stone walls of former organists and of the Cathedral choir. There was also a framed copy of the Preface to William Byrd's *Psalms, Sonets & Songs of Sadnes and Pietie*. William Byrd (1543-1623) was the greatest composer of his period and Organist of Lincoln Cathedral from early 1563 to late 1572. Whilst I did not read the Preface at the time of my audition, it is worth reproducing here as a convincing list of "Reasons (as Byrd writes) briefly set down by th'auctor, to perswade every one to learne to sing."

1. First it is a knowledge easely taught, and quickly learned where there is a good Master, and an apt Scoller.
2. The excercise of singing is delightful to Nature & good to preserve the Health of Man. (Certainly true in Byrd's case since he lived to the ripe old age of eighty!)
3. It doth strengthen all the parts of the brest & doth open the pipes.
4. It is a singular good remedie for a stutting & stammering in the speech.
5. It is the best means to procure a perfect pronunciation to make a good Orator.

6. It is the only way to know where Nature hath bestowed the benefit of a good voyce; which guift is so rare, as there is not one among a thousand that hath it; and in many that excellent guift is lost, because they want Art to expresse Nature.

7. There is not any musicke of Instruments whatsoever, comparable to that which is made of the voyces of Men, where the voyces are good, and the same well sorted and ordered.

8. The better the voyce is, the meeter it is to honour and serve God therewith; and the voyce of Man is chiefly to be employed to that ende. Omnis spiritus laudet Dominum.

Since singing is so good a thing
I wish all men would learne to sing.

They are not quite ten commandments for the musician, but Byrd certainly hit a few nails on the head! I was reminded of this many years later when in conversation with Yehudi Menuhin. He said that singing was so important and that all musicians should sing.

But to return to my audition for entry to the Cathedral choir. The Organist and Master of the Choristers was Dr Gordon Archbold Slater, a tall, well built man who succeeded the redoubtable Dr G J Bennett in 1931. Sitting beside him at the piano was the assistant organist, Clifford Hewis. He had been a Lincoln chorister and pupil of Bennett. His whole musical career was spent in Lincoln and he remained assistant continuously for over fifty years broken only during the World War of 1939-45 when he served in the Armed Forces. I was asked to sing scales and arpeggios to various vowels, to test the quality and range of the voice. Then followed a series of unrelated notes played in succession which I was asked to sing as quickly as I could. This was presumably to test speed of reaction and ability to pitch notes accurately. Then to sing the middle or lower notes of three-part chords and sing a short melody from memory after it was played twice. After being asked to read part of a psalm I was given a hymn to sing which I had prepared in advance. Slater played the tune through and he was highly amused when I told him that he had played a wrong note and also played the hymn in a different key from that printed in the book. He had no doubt done this deliberately and he then asked me to name some random notes on the piano to test that I really did have perfect pitch.

Happily I was successful and was awarded one of the three probationer places. The other two were won by Philip Dobby and John Cotton and we duly began our duties in September 1934 when the choir resumed after the summer holidays. Thus a chance remark by a Sunday School superintendent opened doors which led to a lifetime's service to the Church and its music.

" The Imp flew into the Cathedral"

The Cathedral in which I was to spend so much of my life for the next fifteen years stands at the top of Lindum Hill and dominates not only the city but the whole of the surrounding countryside. On a clear day it can be seen forty miles away and seems to soar into the heavens. It is widely considered to be the finest cathedral in England and its three towers give an effect of majestic splendour. Whilst there was probably an earlier cathedral in Lincoln, the present building was begun in 1073, after the Norman Conquest. Due to various catastrophes, such as fire, earthquake and collapse of the central tower, the Cathedral has undergone rebuilding and restoration over the years and this accounts for the variety of architectural styles in the building. Obvious features of the original massive and imposing Norman west front remain in the three great rounded arches and lateral recesses. One of the glories of the Cathedral is the Angel Choir in which most of the choral services take place. The rebuilding of the Cathedral was begun in 1192 during the episcopate of Bishop Hugh of Avalon who was later to be canonised. The work was continued by one of his successors, Bishop Robert Grosseteste (lit. Big Head!) and the Angel Choir was completed during his period in office to house the shrine of St Hugh. It takes its name from the carved figures of angels with outspread wings which fill the spandrels of the triforium arches and has been described as "one of the loveliest of human works". Not all the carved figures are so angelic for at the convergence of two of the arches in the south choir aisle there is a little grotesque figure widely known as the Lincoln Imp. Legend has it that the Imp flew into the Cathedral and created a disturbance during Divine Service and was promptly turned into stone! It has been adopted as a mascot by the people of Lincoln. The City football team is known as "The Imps" and its image is reproduced on the badge and tie of the Cathedral Old Choristers' Association.[2]

THE LINCOLN IMP

2.   Ref. The Pictorial History of Lincoln Cathedral, Colin Dunlop.   *Photo © by Judges Postcards Ltd., Hastings*

And so in September 1934, I began the first of almost daily journeys by bus, by bicycle or on foot from my home in Chaplin Street, through the High Street, up Lindum Hill to the Cathedral. The routine was a busy one and more demanding in terms of time than that of today's cathedral choristers. Each weekday, except Wednesday which was a *dumb day,* we rehearsed in the Song School at 8.45am to 9.45am followed by Choral Mattins on Tuesday and Friday. Mattins was replaced by Choral Eucharist on Major Saints' Days. After practice or service, we made our way down Wragby Road to the Lincoln School where all the choristers were educated after the closure of the Cathedral Choir School in 1919. Lincoln School at this time was a boys' grammar school with a prep. department taking pupils from the age of seven. Boys entered senior school at the age of eleven after taking a qualifying academic test and remained until the school leaving age of sixteen with the option of staying until eighteen. Choristers seem to have been given an automatic transfer into the senior school for, with hindsight, I am sure not all of them would have reached the required standard. Afternoon school ended at 3.30pm and choristers had to put a move on to get to the Cathedral by 3.45pm for a short rehearsal before Evensong at 4pm. Senior choristers ensured that smaller ones did not dawdle and I clearly remember being led by the ear on many occasions by Jack Daniels, one of the head boys. On Sundays, there was a rehearsal at 9.45am followed by Mattins at 10.30am. The choristers went out during the sermon for a bun and a glass of milk in the Song School. Suitably refreshed we were ready to sing for Choral Eucharist which began at 11.45am. This usually ended between 12.45am and 1 pm when we made our way home for lunch. This was a fairly brief interlude for we had to be back in the Song School for a rehearsal before Evensong which began at 3.45pm ending at about 4.45pm. The rest of the day was our own! As school classes were held on Wednesday and Saturday mornings there was not much free time for a chorister. School games (soccer and cricket) were played on Wednesday and Saturday afternoons. The only opportunity for a chorister to play was on a Wednesday unless you were unfortunate enough to be put in detention for misbehaviour!

In addition there were annual extra-liturgical musical performances of Handel's Messiah or Bach's Christmas Oratorio at Christmastide and a shortened version of Bach's St Matthew Passion before Easter. For these, the Cathedral choir joined the Lincoln Musical Society Chorus and Orchestra and professional soloists. The latter included some of the best-known singers of the day such as Elsie Suddaby, Isobel Baillie, Kathleen Ferrier, Norma Procter, David Galliver, Wilfred Brown, Stanley Clarkson, Thomas Hemsley and Gordon Clinton. We did have some choir holidays but they did not always coincide with school holidays especially at Christmas and Easter. We sang at morning and afternoon services on Christmas Day and also at services on the Feast Days that followed on 26, 27 and 28 December, the Sunday after Christmas, 1 January and 6 January. By the time we got a rest from choir duties we had resumed school! Eastertide was not much better for we were, of course, singing up to Easter Day. The summer holiday began after the first Monday in August which at that time was a Bank Holiday. That coincided with the annual reunion of old choristers and the leaving ceremony for those whose time in the choir had come to an end. We resumed early in September.

The foregoing schedule seems something of a dog's life and it could be asked whether the demands made upon a chorister's time and concentration at such an early

The Cathedral Probationer (1934) in "bumfreezer"

Photo by Harrison of Lincoln

age are a deprivation or an experience of lasting benefit. My eldest grandson, Richard, was one of my choristers at St Mary's Cathedral, Edinburgh, and he was interviewed by a national newspaper about his memories of his time in the choir. He was studying biology at the University of St Andrews at the time and expressed his views without any prompting from me! He said that he remembered a close-knit environment which he had left with regret and that he had gained a lot. Singing in a cathedral choir, often practising for several hours a day, he explained, instilled a discipline which was a valuable tool in life; "all the ex-choristers I know have gone on to be successful," he said.

It is undisputed that a chorister's training creates a sense of teamwork and is one of the few activities in which children work alongside adults to the highest professional standards. Added to this is the experience of the contact with beautiful music and beautiful language, in inspiring, awesome buildings. This creates a recipe for confidence, reliability and integrity: former choristers often achieve excellence, not only in music but also in other professions. This has been my experience too and I count myself very fortunate and privileged to have been part of this ancient and ongoing tradition. It provided me with spiritual, musical and scholastic education and even clothes! During the week, the choristers wore school blazers and school tie but on Sunday we wore Eton suits, white stiff collars and mortar boards. The jackets were short and what we called "bum-freezers" as they did not cover over bottoms! The collars were starched and uncomfortable and they tended to chafe the skin. My grandparents found it difficult to afford school and choir clothes and I wore second-hand outfits handed on from more affluent families.

Before recounting chorister and school days, a few people and events come to mind from earlier childhood. Whilst my grandparents had a good many relatives, they only seemed to keep regularly in touch with a few. On most Sunday afternoons and evenings we visited my Aunt Sarah, the widow of Frank, one of my grandfather's brothers. She lived not far from Chaplin Street in a small terraced house with her two sons Ralph and Walter. Her daughter Gladys lived on the opposite side of the same street. She was married to Joe Teft, a sailor, of whom I saw little as he was most often away at sea. They had two children, Marjorie and Leslie, and they were usually visiting Aunt Sarah on Sunday afternoons as well! There was a piano in the front room at her house and this provided a regular excuse for me to arrange impromptu concerts. Marjorie wrote out the programmes and after tea everyone was press-ganged into the front room to listen to my solo recital whether they wanted to or not! I loved Aunt Sarah and found frequent excuses to visit her. She was always so obviously pleased to see me and invariably produced delicious home-baked jam tarts and cakes which were an added attraction. Her eldest son Ralph was an apprentice to my grandfather and worked alongside him in the forge in Chaplin Street for many years. His brother, Walter, was a sensitive man and always well dressed. He liked music and took a close interest in my activities and progress. When I reached teenage he was deputed to tell me what he knew of my origins and also the facts of life. Both Ralph and Walter married when they were in their late thirties or mid-forties and neither of them had any children.

There were a number of children in Chaplin Street with whom I played happily in my early childhood. For some inexplicable reason, most of them lived on the same side of the street. The houses on our side were small and each pair shared a common passageway and each had a small backyard. The Belcher family lived next door to us at No 3. They had five children - a large number for such a small house. The eldest girl, Marjorie, eventually married and lived a few houses further down the street. The eldest boy, Billy, was some years older than me and so I had little do with him. He always seemed to be sitting on the step outside the house so I can only think he was unemployed. His younger brother Frank and his still younger sisters Hilda and Lucy were among those who played together in the street. Reg and Harold Hillman were also in our group.

The houses on the opposite side of the street were more superior for they had bay windows and a small garden area at the front. I do not remember having much to do with children from those houses but Betty and Hazel Harmston and a boy called Neil Lovely were familiar. Hazel was unexpectedly to reappear much later in my life as the wife of Pat Hewis, a fellow chorister. As there was very little traffic in the side streets we were safe to play our ball games, hopscotch, whipping tops or simply to run races around the adjoining streets. Horse-drawn vehicles were common and coal and milk were delivered to the houses from these. From time to time, in the summer, an ice-cream cart came round and travelling tinkers offering to sharpen kitchen knives. One day a car drove down the street and a group of us decided to run across the road - hopefully before the car got to us. Unfortunately, I left my bid too late and the car knocked me down. Happily, I was not hurt badly and just received a bump on the head and grazed knees. The driver stopped, and, I suppose wishing to cheer me up and pacify me, put me in the passenger seat of the car and drove me round the next street and then took me home. The only other time that I remember being struck on the head was some years later in a school cricket match when I failed to catch the ball! Friends said I've never been normal since!

Among other occasional visitors to No 1 Chaplin Street were a Mr and Mrs Frank Saddington and Mr and Mrs Harris. Frank Saddington was a commercial traveller who came to take orders for iron and steel from my grandpa. Sometimes he brought his wife with him and they would stay for a cup of tea. Frank Saddington was a small, dark-complexioned man, whilst his wife was a very large lady indeed. I believe she weighed over twenty stones and no chair in the house was large enough to accommodate her! The story was told that Frankie arrived home one day, somewhat inebriated. "Where have you been?," asked his wife. "I've been having a little drink with my friends," was the reply. "Well now you can have a little drink with me, you bounder!" and his wife picked up a soda syphon and squirted the contents in the face of her errant husband!

Mr Harris was a prison warder and he and his wife were friends of my grandparents. They had a physically disabled son called Billy who was mentally retarded and confined to a wheelchair. He would be in his twenties, I imagine, and was a very large lad and seemed immensely strong. He had a cheerful and friendly nature and liked to grasp your hand; unfortunately, he was reluctant to let go-he had a grip like a vice! Billy was restricted to a limited diet and I have clear memories of my grandma cooking tripe and onions with a white sauce and mashed potatoes for him. Fortunately we all liked the dish, although it is many years since I had any.

My closest friend from early childhood to manhood was Michael Freeman. He lived at 95 Sincil Bank, not far from Chaplin Street and also in the Parish of St Peter-at-Gowts. We began school together in the Infants at the age of five years and our school

Lincoln Minster The West Front
Photo © by Judges Postcards Ltd., Hastings

careers ran in tandem almost until school leaving age. Our paths diverged for two years when I became a chorister and transferred to the Lincoln School. Mike passed the entrance exam at eleven years and we joined up again in the senior school. We were very much the long and the short of it, for he grew to a height of six feet three inches and I only achieved five feet seven inches. The disparity was most evident in photographs in which we appeared together, for example, in the school First Eleven football team where we stand side by side. We also played in the school First Eleven cricket team for which I became vice-captain. Michael's father, "Jack" Freeman, was captain of the bellringers at St Peter-at-Gowts Church and Master of the Ringers at Lincoln Cathedral. His elder son, John, commonly known as "Bill" had also been a pupil at Lincoln School. Both boys learnt to ring both tower bells and handbells although Bill was the more enthusiastic and proficient. He became even more widely known as a

ringer than his father and was a member of the Central Council of Change Ringers. He had the distinction of being one of the team invited to ring the first peal on the newly installed bells in Washington Cathedral, DC, in the USA. I was a frequent visitor to the Freemans' house and during the war of 1939-1945 I spent almost every Sunday evening there. After supper, handbells were brought out and we spent an hour or two ringing. I never learnt to ring in the tower for fear of damage to my fingers, but I did become reasonably proficient with handbells. I tended to wear gloves to protect my fingers and acquired the nickname of the "gentleman" handbell ringer! Together with Bill and Michael Freeman and Ken Croft (another former Lincoln School pupil and Cathedral ringer) we rang a peal in Lincoln School library. Disaster nearly ensued when Jack Green, the school caretaker, came in and began to talk to us! Fortunately we managed to convey to him that he was not wanted, continued ringing successfully and completed the peal. Jack Green's amiable nature was sometimes exploited by us school pupils. During the war (1939-1945) seniors took turns to sleep at the School on firewatch duty in the cloisters. Mike Freeman, "Flier" Canner and myself formed one such group. Unfortunately, there were only two bunks for the three of us. Canner was well over six feet tall like Mike, so I was very much the squashed "piggy in the middle!" Philip Robinson, a boarder, sometimes joined us for a chat in the evening. On one occasion, Jack Green was doing his rounds carrying a bag of chips. Robinson promptly helped himself to some without a murmur of protest from the caretaker!

My friendship with the Freeman family led to invitations to join them on ringers' outings from time to time. On more than one occasion we visited the small village of Surfleet, near Spalding in South Lincolnshire. Here lived a market gardener called Rupert Richardson who was also a well-known campanologist. He was no doubt a man of some substance for he and his wife Mary and daughter Enid, lived in a large house within its own considerable park. The house and grounds were situated on the banks of the river which flows through the village. On the other side, the village church, with its leaning tower, is clearly visible through the trees. The Richardsons frequently had week-end house parties to ring in the village church. There were twelve bells in this small church, more than twice as many as in most villages - indeed more than in many much larger churches and cathedrals.

My role was to play the organ for the Sunday services and join the handbell ringers in the house. Sunday lunch was a sumptuous meal. Rupert Richardson sat at the head of his large dining-table, carving slices from the largest joint of roast beef I have ever seen. He was a very big man and it was highly amusing to hear him call to his small domestic cat in a high-pitched voice, "Toots, tiny Toots" whilst offering it scraps of food from the table. We were a lively lot! On one occasion we travelled by car, on a beautiful summer day from Lincoln to Surfleet. The sunroof and side windows were open. Bill Freeman was supposedly driving but from time to time he stood up with his head above the roof of the car waving his arms at approaching motorists and shouting "Look, no hands." Meanwhile, his brother kept control of the steering wheel from the passenger seat. Fortunately, there was little traffic on the roads.

After the diversion into the ringing fraternity it is necessary to fill in some of the details of chorister and school days. Looking back over my life, I am continually amazed at how a chance meeting or remark have proved a major influence or turning point. One of these happened at a fellow chorister's house during a birthday party. Always keen to try the piano if there was one available I duly played. It so happened that a piano-teacher friend of the family was present. Unknown to me he said to the chorister's parents, "that boy plays musically but he needs a good teacher!" This comment was passed on to my grandparents who immediately went to see the piano teacher. By a stroke of good fortune he lived in the next street to us and agreed to take me as a pupil. I was nine years old. His name was George Fountain, LRAM and I owe an immense debt to him for his teaching skill and interest in my musical development. Although he was blind from birth he seemed to have an unerring sense of direction and walked about the city without guidance. He studied piano under Frederick Jackson, another Lincolnian, and organ with Arthur Balfour at the Royal Academy of Music in London. He won several prizes at the RAM and also qualified as a piano tuner. One of his prizes was a beautiful gold pocket watch with a striking mechanism which enabled him to tell the time. He was a very sensitive pianist and inspired me by the beauty of tone which he drew from the piano. He was a very demanding teacher and would not allow any technical error to go uncorrected. On one occasion, a passage in the piece I was learning involved a leap from B to F which I muffed. "B F" he shouted at me - BF - bloody fool that's what you are, boy!" He also used to tap the pulse on the top of the piano whilst I was playing. If there was any unevenness he would tap even more firmly and say "Feel the pulse in your bones boy, damn you!" I do not remember feeling any animosity towards him, only a determination to show him that I was not such a bloody fool as he thought. He frequently walked round to No 1 Chaplin Street and listened outside the window of the room in which the piano was kept. If he could not hear it being played, he would knock on the front door and ask my grandparents where I was. On being told that I was out playing with my pals he insisted I was brought in to practise. It seemed grossly unfair at the time but no doubt was in my best interest.

When I was about thirteen years old and big enough to reach the pedals, George began to teach me to play the organ. At that time, he was organist of the church of St Mary-le-Wigford in the High Street, very near to the LNER station. The instrument had two manuals, tracker action, straight pedal board, lever swell pedal and was blown by hand. It cost half-a-crown ($12^1/_2$p) an hour to pay a lad to pump the wind for practice. Soon after I began lessons, George was appointed organist at St Michael-on-the-Mount. The church stood at the top of Steep Hill, not far from the Theological College. The two-manual organ in this church was built (I think) by the local firm of Cousans. Tonally, it was a very pleasant instrument with electric action, balance swell pedal and a radiating, concave pedalboard. It was a joy to play and I made rapid progress. Students from the Theological College were taught singing in the church on a Monday morning by Brother Edwin from Kelham Monastery. George Fountain was a very neat organist and his virtually silent pedalling was impressive. It did not take him very long to locate the stop jambs on any unfamiliar instrument and he was able to draw the stops by hand with unerring accuracy. My first two instruction books were The Organ by John Stainer and The First Year at the Organ by P C Buck. These are somewhat out of fashion nowadays but they provided a good grounding in some aspects of organ playing. George was friendly with Dr Willis Grant, assistant organist at the Cathedral when I was a probationer. He subsequently became organist of Birmingham Cathedral and then Professor of Music at Bristol University. He also took an interest in my musical progress during my early years and later on in my career.

George Fountain steered me through the LRAM piano diploma whilst I was still at school, at the age of seventeen. After that, formal lessons from him stopped but he continued to help me expand my piano repertoire.

He married when he was in his early forties and it was interesting to note that he lost the ability to find his way around the city unaided. His wife escorted him and he became reliant upon her. It has always been a source of sadness and regret that I failed to see him and his wife before leaving Lincoln to take up my first full-time musical appointment in Louth. I did try to contact him, without success, to say farewell. Perhaps I did not try hard enough. I never saw him again. Alas he died soon afterwards in his late forties. George was also responsible for getting me a new piano. He told my grandparents that their old upright instrument was inadequate. My grandpa asked him where a suitable instrument could be obtained. The result was that the three of us walked up the High Street to Rose's Music Shop where pianos and sheet music were sold. George recommended we should buy a new Broadwood rosewood upright piano which was on display. I did not believe that my grandpa could afford such an expensive item but, characteristically and without hesitation, he agreed to buy it. My memory may be imperfect but I believe it cost £150 which was a great deal of money in the 1930s. It was a beautiful instrument with lovely singing treble notes and a sonorous bass register. It was a joy to play and no doubt provided an extra incentive to practise. It served me well for about forty years.

George Fountain did not enter his pupils for graded examinations such as those organised by The Associated Board of The Royal Schools of Music. He considered that the time spent preparing for these exams prevented the exploration of a wide repertoire of music.

My chorister days were almost unadulterated joy except for the first year when I was a probationer and not allowed to sing during the services. I found this very frustrating and frequently went home tearfully complaining to my grandparents. Of course, this probationary year soon passed and indeed it seemed no time at all before I became a *cope boy* and then finished singing treble at the age of fifteen. We sang a wide range of music from the 16th century to the 20th century. The music of William Byrd, of course, figured prominently and we sang the Masses for four and five voices, the *Short* service, the *Second* service and on special occasions, the *Long* or *Great* service. Choristers tend to find Tudor and Renaissance music boring and I was no exception. However, of the many anthems by Byrd that we performed, a few such as *Sing joyfully* and especially *Laudibus in sanctis* I found thrilling. I suppose the most memorable were the settings and anthems of the 19th century of which we sang a good many. The settings and anthems by Stanford, S S Wesley, Walmisley, Wood and Harwood remain vividly in the memory. Those with independent accompaniments such as Stanford in A *Evening Service*, Harwood, *O how glorious*, Wesley, *The Wilderness*, Parry, *Hear my words* and *I was glad*, Bairstow, *Blessed city, heavenly Salem* come readily to mind. Extracts from Oratorios were also in vogue during my chorister days and we greatly enjoyed solos and choruses from Handel's *Messiah*, Haydn's *Creation*, Brahms' *Requiem* and Dvorak's *Stabat Mater*. All of these were sung in English as was the opening chorus from Bach's Cantata *Wachet auf!* on the Sunday next before Advent.

Music by contemporary church music composers was introduced by Slater and whilst this posed no special problems for the choristers, the elderly lay vicars seemed to have great difficulty with the more advanced melodic and harmonic idiom. I can remember quite clearly their struggle to master the *Evening Service* in G by Herbert Howells and their obvious dislike of the music. Herbert Howells was a regular visitor to Lincoln, mostly as an adjudicator, and I got to know him quite well. His son, Michael, (immortalised by the hymn tune of that name) died at the age of ten years. This sad loss had a profound effect on Howells and I have always imagined, perhaps erroneously, that he took special interest in me as a small boy of about the same age as his son. Whatever the truth of this, our paths crossed a good deal during the next forty years or so. During my time as a chorister, Howells adjudicated me many times as a competitor at the Lincoln Competitive Music Festival. I have to confess that I did not always come first in the piano classes! To my chagrin, I was sometimes beaten by a girl called Christine Vickers, a pupil at South Park High School in the city. Norah Kimpton, also a South Park pupil, was another regular and successful competitor. Like me she eventually became one of the Lincoln Festival official accompanists and a professional musician. For most of her working life she was on the staff of The Bishop Grosseteste Teacher Training College in Lincoln. Her brother Geoffrey was a pupil at Lincoln City School and also very musical. He was a string player and composer and had a distinguished career as a professional musician. Both Norah and Geoffrey became life-long friends and may well be mentioned again in this narrative. Their parents were lovely people and staunch church members. Their father was a licensed lay reader in the Church of England and their mother a committed member of the Methodist Church.

Choristers in a cathedral choir become a very closely knit group and strong friendships are formed which last a lifetime. Singing, playing and mixing together almost every day of the year creates a bond that is not easily broken. Certainly, I have found this to be so and my fellow choristers remain vivid in my mind. There is a tendency to remember most clearly those who were more senior rather than the small fry below. Of these, Geoff Broxholme was a head chorister when I was a probationer. He possessed a hard-backed hairbrush which descended upon the head of any probationer caught talking in the Vestry before a service. He sang the treble solo in Wesley's *Blessed be the God and Father* on the day he left the choir at the age of seventeen! Treble voices lasted, on average, much longer in those days before the war and Geoff left the choir not because his voice had broken but because it was time for him to find employment. After the war, boys and girls matured much earlier and few boys continued to sing treble after the age of thirteen. It is said that better nutrition is responsible. Geoff's father, "Brocky", worked alongside my grandfather in one of the iron and steel foundries in Lincoln and so the family were well known to me. Sydney Brewer was another excellent solo boy and his confident rendering of *I know that my Redeemer liveth* from Handel's *Messiah* made a lasting impression upon me. Sydney's father worked in the booking office at the LNER station with Harris Ellingworth who was destined to become my father-in-law. Roy Bryan was the outstanding solo singer of my generation. He was from Chesterfield and boarded with Mr Newborne, the Head Verger. My favourite solo was the final section of S S Wesley's anthem *The Wilderness* - "And sorrow and sighing shall flee away", although *The Magnificat* from Stanford in G with its spinning-wheel accompaniment ran it a close second. My grandparents had friends in Birmingham whom they visited occasionally by train. On one such visit, during the return journey late at night, I inflicted the Wesley upon the passengers in our compartment much to the embarrassment of my grandparents.

Numbered among choristers senior to me were Norman Curran, Dana Duckles, the brothers Harry and Ronny Sargent, Ted Brookes, Peter Harker, Phil Popham, Tom Laidler, Dick Rollett, Richard Scott and Ted West. Harry Sargent became an agent for an insurance company and sold me my first life policy; Ted Brookes' father worked in a wet fish shop in the High Street and not unnaturally was nicknamed "Fishy". Peter Harker emigrated to Canada in adult life and became an eminent geologist. Philip Popham was a big and rather intimidating lad who, I believe, became a taxi driver. Dick Rollett's parents owned, or managed, a grocery shop in Bailgate, whilst Ted West's family owned a garage in the High Street not far from Chaplin Street. Tommy Laidler was very musical and played the piano and the organ admirably. I believe he considered pursuing a career in music but decided against it, perhaps wisely. His father was one of the alto lay vicars in the Cathedral choir. He had a steady flute-like voice of beautiful quality but his enunciation was never very clear. Richard (Dick) Scott became a successful businessman and a member of the MCC. Watching cricket was a priority in his adult life and seemed to take precedence over most of his other activities.

Of my immediate contemporaries in the choir, Gerald Esam was one of my best friends and remained so throughout our subsequent lives. His boyhood nickname was "Sos" although I neither knew nor understood how or why he acquired it. Indeed, many nicknames seem completely irrational. Why, I have often wondered was Ray Dring, captain of the Lincoln School first eleven football team called "Bummer" and why was I always known as "Baggy"? Gerald Esam lived in the village of North Hykeham, a few miles south of Lincoln. His parents were lovely people who lived in a typical country cottage with a fairly large garden. They had some apple trees and the fruit seemed like nectar to my boyhood palate. Our house was roughly halfway to the Cathedral from North Hykeham and Gerald often called for me especially on a Sunday. On one occasion in the winter, the snow was so deep that it was impossible to travel by any other means than on foot. Completely undeterred, Gerald trudged to Chaplin Street and then together we completed the journey to the Cathedral in time for choir practice and the Sunday services. Such determination and devotion to duty are not so common these days. Gerald had a very distinguished career in banking, beginning in the most junior post at the National Provincial Bank in Lincoln and reaching the dizzy heights of Executive Director for the City of London in the National Westminster Bank. As Executive Director he was provided with a chauffeur-driven car and I always felt a special thrill on the occasions that I was given a ride in the car with him. Gerald married Mary Vinter, a Lincoln lass from a musical family. One of her relatives was Gilbert Vinter, a Lincoln old chorister and a very distinguished orchestral composer and conductor. Other fellow choristers of my generation and subsequent ones were John Benson, Basil Clarke, David Clifford, Brian Cundill, John Drury, Alan Fanthorpe, Graham Garton, David Harris, Billy Heck, John Hollingworth, Alf Kelsey, John Kershaw, Graham Patman, Ray Roberts, Denys Talbot and Alan Valley, some of them re-appeared later in my life and will no doubt be mentioned.

The Lincoln choristers wore blue cassocks under white surplices and white neck ruffs. The four senior boys also wore black copes over their other robes fastened with a clasp. A unique situation arose a few years after I had left the choir when the *cope boys* were two sets of identical twins - Peter and Michael Rushton and David and John Taylor. The gentlemen of the choir or lay vicars as they were called at Lincoln seemed mostly elderly to me and of variable quality. They were nine in number - three of each voice, alto, tenor and bass. I do not suppose they were paid very much and they needed other employment which would fit in with their daily Cathedral duties. There was no retiring age and they therefore tended to continue singing long after their voices had passed their best. Of the altos, Tom Laidler has been mentioned. Cantoris alto was John Ramsay. He had a beautiful and expressive voice but sang most of the time with his elbow propped on the stalls and the palm of his hand resting on the side of his cheek. It looked as if he was bored with it all, and of course, he might well have been! I thought it very strange that he became an ordained priest later in his life. John Render and Fred Booth were two good tenors. Fred Booth was small, round and bald. He used to wear a skull-cap to protect his head from the cold draughts and freezing temperatures in the winter for there was no heating in the building. Indeed, even on the hottest summer days it was cold but at least there was a welcome relief in those circumstances. Fred was sometimes required to sing the Evangelist part in the St Matthew Passion, which he did very effectively and he was also a good bassoon player.

The basses were Messrs Woodward, Endersby and Fieldhouse. Mr Woodward's son, Reg, was a chorister who left the choir just before I joined as a probationer. He eventually became ordained and served as Precentor of St Mary's Cathedral, Edinburgh and headmaster of the Choir School 1946-53, with great distinction. Woodward's bass colleague on Cantoris was Mr Endersby who had the loudest voice I had heard at that time. His interpretation of extended solo passages in anthems such as "Say to them of a fearful heart" from S S Wesley's *The Wilderness* was very dramatic and operatic in style. To a small boy, the effect was electrifying and the whole building seemed to shake. Cathedral choirs were rarely conducted at this time, except in unaccompanied music. The Organist and Master of the Choristers usually accompanied from some distance with the result that the ensemble was often untidy and unpredictable. The Litany was sung at Mattins on Friday mornings. The suffrages were sung by two lay vicars from the kneeling desk in the middle of the Choir. The combination of one of the altos and "Thunderguts" Endersby produced a very odd musical effect.

Memories of my time at Lincoln School are almost entirely happy, although I believe I was a trial to some of the teachers in early teenage years. A chorister's life was a busy one and involved missing one or more lessons each day. As a part compensation, choristers did not take Latin as a school subject. A strange choice since we sang a good deal of church music in Latin. It also meant difficult choices when Certificate examinations approached. It was common for choristers to fall behind in schoolwork until they left the choir and then for them to rapidly catch up. My school reports in the Secondary Department reflected this and I languished in the bottom half of the form lists. Despite this, the headmaster's remarks were always encouraging and expressed his belief that I could and would do better!

This proved an accurate prediction for after I left the choir at the age of fifteen, my position in the form lists improved dramatically from the bottom three to the top three! For the purposes of the School Certificate examinations, pupils were placed in either Remove Modern or Remove Classical groups. The syllabus for the former included the more scientific subjects of maths, physics and chemistry whilst the latter included Latin and Greek. Although my strengths lay in the more classical subjects, I was placed in the modern set because I had studied no Latin. Fortunately, we had a superb maths teacher affectionately known as "Shrubby" Plant who successfully guided me through the requirements of the Ordinary papers of algebra, arithmetic and geometry. However, I did not aspire to the Advanced Syllabus which included calculus and co-ordinate geometry. Chemistry posed few problems but physics was something of a struggle. The teachers for those two subjects were named Dollery and Stollery and they operated in adjacent laboratories. When it came to complicated calculations and equations in chemistry lessons, Mr Dollery frequently popped into the physics lab and returned with the solutions! Dollery was a keen cricketer. His brother was a professional player with Warwickshire and both County Captain and a member of the England team. Since I played for the school teams at

Under 14, Under 15 and First Eleven, Dollery took a special interest in my progress in chemistry as well as on the sports field. Similarly, I got on well with Mr Stollery as he had a great interest in the organ music of J S Bach!

I have often reflected upon the important influence that teachers have upon their pupils and been grateful for the windows they opened and the enthusiasms they kindled.

Head Chorister 1939 - 1940

Photo by Harrison of Lincoln

Often a chance remark is sufficient to effect a remarkable change. Our senior English teacher was Mr John Phillips, affectionately known as "Johnny Pips". Like most boys I went through a phase of reading magazines such as *The Hotspur* and *The Champion* which were full of unlikely stories in colloquial language and liberally sprinkled with cartoon pictures! "Johnny Pips" found me reading one of these magazines one day and casually said, "It's time you stopped reading that sort of thing - try this" and he put a copy of *The Flight of the Heron* into my hands. This led me to avidly explore some of the marvellous corpus of English literature, both novels and poetry. At this stage it was mostly the writings of the 19th-century authors such as the Brontë Sisters, George Eliot, Jane Austin, Anthony Trollope, Charles Dickens and Thomas Hardy that were my staple fare. I still recall the overwhelming effect of *Wuthering Heights* and *Tess o'the D'Urbervilles* the first time I read them. Thomas Hardy was a favourite author until I worked my way through most of the novels and reached *Jude the Obscure*. The frustrating misfortunes which befall the principal characters and intense sadness in that final novel caused me to reject Hardy for some years. My grandfather possessed the complete set of novels of Charles Dickens and had read most of them. This seemed remarkable considering he left school at the age of eleven. He also kept his own accounts and had the capacity to add up long columns of figures with unerring accuracy. His handwriting, too, was beautifully neat and legible. Whilst I have not been able to emulate him in reading all of Dickens' novels, many of them have become familiar and for many years I have read *A Christmas Carol* at the appropriate season.

Our modern languages teacher was "Jigger" Shepherd and he advised me to get out of Lincoln, otherwise, he said, I should end up as organist and choirmaster of Wragby Parish Church (a small village near Lincoln). In due course, I took his advice. Our religious education teacher was The Revd J Lee, commonly known as "Jazzy" Lee. On his retirement, he told us that he had been at Lincoln for nineteen years. He said it took at least twenty years to become accepted by Lincoln people so he was getting out before they did!

As well as being reasonably good at soccer and cricket, I was also quite a good sprinter and eventually became captain of the School athletics team. 100, 220 and 440 yards races were my best distances although I did also run for the school at 880 yards. We had annual competitions with athletics teams from grammar schools in Newark and Grantham. On one occasion, my fellow competitor for Lincoln School in the 880 yards race was a lad called Eddie Dwane. As Eddie had won this race in the previous year, I was told to run alongside him as he knew how to pace the distance and when to make the final sprint for the finishing tape. Disaster ensued as we tagged along at the back of the pack of runners from the beginning. Eddie showed no signs of making any effort to improve our position and we finished the race as we began - in the last two places!

My sporting abilities put me in the good books of our Housemaster, Bill Bailey, although our relationship became strained on one occasion. Bill was the school woodwork and metalwork teacher, practical activities for which I had little natural aptitude. However, I did develop some skill at turning wood bowls on the lathe and quite enjoyed making them. The woodwork shop looked out on to the school playground and the lathe was situated near one of the leaded glass windows. We were told never to switch the lathe on to its quickest speed. Stupidly, I did so and the block of wood, which I was given to shape into a bowl, split with a loud bang. One piece shot through the window into the playground and the other landed at the far end of the room! Fortunately I had moved away from the lathe to get a chisel otherwise I might well have been badly injured. From that moment I was banned from the woodwork shop and told never to darken its doors again.

Other teachers of whom I have happy memories were J A Baxter, "Weary" Williams, Peter Baker and "Bosky" Wood (Sixth-form Master). There was little importance placed upon music at Lincoln School in my time and it was very much a fringe subject. No instrumental music was taught within the school timetable and only one weekly period of class singing. It was considered a parental responsibility to provide their children with instrumental lessons and to pay for them!

Inevitably a few pupils emerged with musical talent and went on to study music seriously and then to enter the profession. Steve Race, the distinguished jazz pianist and broadcaster was held up to young aspirants such as me as an example of what might be achieved. Neville Marriner was another former Lincolnian to achieve even greater eminence in the musical profession as a violinist and then as a conductor. His father was an amateur violinist who played in the Lincoln Symphony Orchestra. Neville left school at the age of sixteen to take up a place at the Royal College of Music in London. During the holidays, he and I played through many of the well-known pieces in the violin repertoire including sonatas by Mozart, Schubert, Beethoven and Brahms. The piano parts were often more technically demanding than the violin and I especially remember struggling through the César Franck Sonata. Neville shared digs with Antony Hopkins, a fellow RCM student who eventually became well known as a pianist and a popular presenter of radio programmes. They lodged in Baron's Court which is conveniently situated three stops away from South Kensington station on the London Underground, near to the College. I stayed in the same house on two or three occasions with them in London to take Diploma exams. The owners were a very ill-assorted couple who spoke with broad, cockney accents. The wife was a lady of ample proportions who seemed completely to dominate her much smaller husband. He cleaned our shoes each morning whilst she served us with beans on toast as the regular breakfast menu. Antony Hopkins claimed to have invented a new shaving method. He had a lethal looking cut-throat razor which he wielded from side to side on his beard rather than the usual up and down movement. It all looked far too dangerous to me!

After leaving the Cathedral choir at the age of fifteen, I took on a succession of Sunday organ jobs. The first was at Glentham, a village some distance from Lincoln. I caught a bus at 8.30am on the Sunday morning and returned home in the evening by the 8pm bus. I was given lunch and tea at the vicarage and as I was studying for School Certificate Examinations I took the opportunity of doing some homework in between services. On arrival at the church on the Sunday morning I conducted a rehearsal of the village church choir in the west gallery where the organ was situated. It was a small, two-manual instrument with mechanical action and blown by hand. At the side of the organ seat there was a large wooden chest, filled with indifferent organ music, mostly by Victorian composers and a considerable number of dead flies. The Vicar and his wife were charming people with a large number of children. There were at least seven and there could have been as many as ten but my memory is uncertain. Many years later, I received a letter from one of the children, recalling the days we spent at Glentham. He had been given my address by a mutual acquaintance. Unhappily, he was suffering from cancer and died soon after our exchange of letters.

After nine months at Glentham, I was invited to become organist at Burton Parish Church, a village a few miles north of Lincoln. This only involved playing for the evening service and was much more convenient. The organ had two manuals and was tonally very pleasant but there were no pedals. I used to travel out to Burton by bus and was given tea by a charming old lady called Miss Elsmere, a member of the congregation. Her brother had been a professional musician and she very kindly gave me his copies of most of J S Bach's Clavier works in the Peters edition. They were inscribed as a gift to Mr E C H Elsmere - "From the Committee of The Lincoln High Street Circuit Eisteddfod 1926 as an appreciation of services rendered as adjudicator." The copies were in an almost pristine condition and had hardly been used. I had them covered with cardboard and they have been invaluable additions to my collection of keyboard music despite the accretion of 19th-century editors such as Czerny and Griepenkerl.

After only six months I moved to the Church of St Mary-le-Wigford where I had begun my organ lessons. The services here were very "High Church" and the Vicar, Father Butolph, insisted that the organist made his confession regularly. He was a large, jolly parson with whom I got on well but he was very put out when I refused to play the melody of the well-known Victorian ballad *Home Sweet Home* as a hymn tune. From there I moved to the church of St Mary Magdalen as organist and choirmaster. The church was situated very near to the Cathedral and next door to the White Hart Hotel. The Vicar was The Revd C T H Dams who also held the position of Succentor at the Cathedral. He subsequently became Precentor of Westminster Abbey. The organ console in the church was in a loft above the vestry and was reached from a winding staircase. Access was from a door at the bottom of the staircase and the key was kept on a hook at the side of the door. I was in the habit of staying behind after the morning service to practise on the organ. On one occasion the church wardens inadvertently locked the door and I was trapped. In order to attract attention from outside the church, I piled all the hymn books on to the organ keys and drew all the available stops. The resulting loud and very dissonant sounds, I thought, were sure to make a passer-by investigate and I stood hopefully looking over the organ loft to the door at the back of the church. Eventually the door opened and a lady peered in. Hurriedly pulling the books off the keys I shouted "Oi! let me out!" A startled look of fear came over her face and she fled from the church. Putting the books back on the keys I waited again for a rescuer. Not long afterwards a man came through the door and looked around. This time, I called out less forcefully and was released. On leaving the church, I saw a man cleaning his car outside and expressed surprise that he had not reacted to the hideous noise coming from inside. "Oh, I just thought you were practising!"

The church had quite a good adult choir which enabled regular anthems to be sung. One Sunday morning a new anthem was to be performed and I had the temerity to tell one of the men who had not attended rehearsal that he would not be allowed to sing. He informed me that he had been a member of the choir for umpteen years and was not going to take instructions like that from an arrogant teenager. Furthermore, he intended to leave the choir immediately and promptly stormed out of the church!

Chapter 3 - Student Years   (1943-1949)

"When I was bound apprentice in famous Lincolnshire"

After gaining good results in the School Certificate examinations (the equivalent of today's GCSE) I moved up into the Sixth Form Classical, specialising in French, English and history. The Headmaster, G F Franklin, commonly known as "The Gaffer", had always been supportive and interested in my progress. He suggested that I should compete for an organ scholarship at Cambridge University but Gordon Slater, the Cathedral organist, insisted that it would be better for me to study with him as an articled pupil-assistant. This was the time-honoured method of training as a cathedral organist and choirmaster. It was a musical apprenticeship which provided not only a thorough knowledge of the repertoire and the liturgical framework of the services but also an awareness of the administration and personal relationships involved in a cathedral context. It provided the opportunity to attend and observe the daily training, rehearsals and singing of the services by the choir as well as seeing and hearing, at first hand the accompaniment and directing of the music. It had never seriously occurred to me that I should pursue any career other than in cathedral music and so I was more than happy when "The Gaffer" suggested I should leave the Grammar School at the end of my first year in the Sixth Form and accepted Gordon Slater's suggestion. This enabled me to devote all my time and attention to the study and practice of cathedral music and prepare for the appropriate professional qualifications. And so I resumed my daily journeys to the Cathedral and began taking organ and paperwork lessons from "Gassy"Slater whose nickname was derived from his initials GAS. At my first organ lesson he said, "Well Dennis, you needn't expect me to tell you that your playing is good but, by golly you'll know about it if it isn't!" He never did tell me personally that anything was good but I know he was privately pleased with my subsequent achievements. After his death in 1979, I was given some of his personal vocal scores including one of Bach's B minor Mass. Inside the front cover was a programme of the performance I had conducted in Grimsby Parish Church in 1961 and which Slater and his wife attended. On it he had written, "A very fine performance - I was proud of him". It was very moving to read his comments.

This period between leaving school and taking up my first full-time appointment was a very busy one. As mentioned earlier, I had obtained the LRAM Diploma for Piano and went on to successfully take the Associate and Fellowship Diplomas of the Royal College of Organists. For the Associate Diploma I was awarded *The Read Prize* for gaining the highest marks in all sections of the exam during that year. Concurrently, I studied for the Bachelor of Music degree of Durham University and completed it in 1947. At this time it was possible to study for the degree externally so I had to travel to Durham in successive years to sit the written papers. The Professor of Music was Sir Edward Bairstow, Organist of York Minster. He was a marvellous musician but impatient and abrasive. As the candidates assembled in the examination room he swept in and brusquely said, " Well, get sat down, we haven't all day to waste." On one occasion I travelled from Durham to York on the train with him and Gordon Slater. On alighting from the train at York we walked to the station entrance where he was expecting to be met by his wife. She had not arrived and without waiting a second he hailed a taxi and went home. A few seconds later, Lady Bairstow drove up having been delayed by heavy traffic.

The results of the examinations were posted on University notice boards the following day and it was with a good deal of trepidation that the list was scanned. Whilst I was never very confident of passing, but did, an older fellow candidate was quite sure he had failed and did! He told me that he had been taking the exams unsuccessfully for a number of years. On asking why he bothered to subject himself to this repeated failure he said that it was a perfect alibi for spending a week away from his wife! Bairstow was taken ill during the summer of 1946 and it was said he marked the Mus. B. papers in hospital. After his death, Ernest Bullock, a former pupil of Bairstow, acted as the interim professor and was one of the three examiners to pass the string quartet which I submitted for the required exercise to complete the degree. The others were Herbert Howells and H K Andrews, Director of Music at New College, Oxford. Bullock was a fairly regular visitor to Lincoln and a number of things remain in my mind. On one occasion Slater asked me to play the piano for Bullock when I was in my early teens, presumably to get his opinion on my potential. Some years later the BBC broadcast a programme of Bullock's church music in a Choral Evensong from Lincoln. Bullock played the organ for the service and I had the privilege of turning the pages for him. The introit was *O most merciful*, the canticles in D major and the anthem *Give me the wings of faith*. His sensitive accompaniments and easy control of the organ were a joy to see and hear. Successively organist of Exeter Cathedral and Westminster Abbey, Bullock became the Joint Professor of Music at Glasgow University and Principal of the Royal Scottish Academy of Music and Drama. I believe he greatly missed being involved in church music. Coincidentally, Ernest Bullock's daughter Mary and I graduated as Bachelor of Music from Durham University and received the degree at the same congregation in 1947. Dr H "Ken" Andrews was also an occasional visitor to Lincoln. He was a leading authority on Palestrina and 16th-century sacred music and contrapuntal technique and had a dry and caustic sense of humour. On one visit to Lincoln he sat, or rather he sprawled, for he was a very tall man, next to Slater at the piano in the Song School during a rehearsal of an anthem by William Byrd. He told people afterwards that the performance was not very good and that Slater had turned to him and said, "You will not often hear a performance like that." Andrews said that he felt bound to agree with him!

1943 was the four hundredth anniversary of the birth of William Byrd (1543-1623). To mark the anniversary, the BBC broadcast a series of programmes of his sacred and secular music from the Cathedral. The programmes were devised and introduced by The Revd Dr E H Fellowes, a minor Canon of Windsor and a leading authority on English cathedral music. It was a revelation to hear some of the verse-anthems performed with a consort of viols and also the string Fantasias and keyboard music. I found the anthem, *Have mercy upon me, O God* and the *Cradle Song* for treble voices particularly memorable.

Apart from helping with the training of the choristers, taking occasional rehearsals of the full choir and playing for some of the services, I was called upon to play the *Continuo*

Dennis Townhill (Mus.B)

Photo by Harrison of Lincoln

(on a grand piano!) for the annual performance of Bach's St Matthew Passion with orchestra. The solo parts were sung by professional singers and selected lay vicars from the Cathedral choir. The local orchestral society had a stiffening of professional players including Frederick Mountney, the Leader, from Nottingham and a double-bass player from Huddersfield by the name of Mr Herbert Bottomley. The latter was positioned next to me by the piano and invariably arrived at the rehearsal after the opening chorus had begun. By this time, Slater's beat had developed into a series of horizontal, sweeping gestures invariably causing Bottomley to whisper in his broad Yorkshire accent, "Ow many bloomin' beats in a bar does 'e mean to beat?" Slater also conducted the Lincoln Orchestral Society, a large amateur body which as well as accompanying the annual performances of *Messiah* and *St Matthew Passion* in the Cathedral, gave a programme of secular music in the Corn Exchange. This building also served as an occasional cinema and concert hall. From time to time this involved my playing extra percussion instruments such as cymbals, triangle and tambourine - a good exercise in counting and concentration. It also served as an introduction to some of the standard secular choral and orchestral works. Slater gave an annual series of illustrated lectures on the History of Music for the Extra-mural Department of Hull University. These took place in the Usher Art Gallery at the bottom of Lindum Hill and were an invaluable source of information and instruction for me. He also arranged a series of chamber concerts in the Gallery, accompanying most of the visiting soloists himself. The performance by Peter Pears and Benjamin Britten made an immense and lasting impression, especially the newly written arrangements of folk songs. I have never forgotten the emotional intensity they generated in *The Bonnie Earl of Moray* and its heart-rending effect.

Concerts were also held in St Swithin's Church below Lindum Hill. The church had a good grand piano and quite a good pipe organ. There I heard some of the leading artists of the time such as Moiseiwitsch, Solomon and Myra Hess. The organist Douglas Fox gave a brilliant recital including J S Bach's Prelude and Fugue in D major (S 532) and it seemed unbelievable that he could achieve such results with only one hand and his feet. It was only afterwards that I learned of his disability.

During this period of study and apprenticeship, I continued to live at home with my grandparents. As far as I can remember I did not pay them anything towards my food and lodging nor did they ask or expect me to do so. However, I did earn a little money from taking a few private piano pupils and a little teaching at De Aston Grammar School at Market Rasen and the Girls' High School at Brigg. Both were small towns within easy reach of Lincoln by bus. I also taught a few young bandsmen at the army barracks in Lincoln. On one occasion I was invited to deputise as the pianist in their dance band at a Saturday night ball in the Drill Hall. This was a completely new experience and enjoyable until it became necessary for me to improvise a solo. Without any music in the score to play from I was foxed and could only lamely vamp some chords until the rest of the band jumped in and rescued me! A school friend, George Maile, was a good jazz musician, playing double-bass in a local band. In return for giving him some piano lessons he introduced me to some of the popular music of the time. The music of Duke Ellington, Billy Mayerl and George Gershwin had a particular appeal for me not to mention Bill "Count" Basie.

32

Another pupil was the young son of John Phillips, my English Master at Lincoln School. He did not practise in between lessons as much as he should have done. At one lesson, in exasperation, I said to him, "And how old are you?" to which he replied, "Eight, Sir." "Why you will soon be as old as me," I said. "Shan't," was the answer. "Well, how old do you think I am?" "Between forty and fifty." "Goodness, that's as old as your Daddy." "Well you're bald anyway," to which there was no further response as I had indeed begun to lose my hair in my early twenties.

About this time I was invited to give courses in Appreciation of Music for the Extra-mural Department of Nottingham University. This involved travelling weekly by car to nearby towns during the winter months. As I did not have my own transport, I was driven by a couple of brothers who were only too pleased to be able to get extra petrol coupons and some small payment. During the war, and for some years after, petrol was rationed, as was food. On one journey a large hare ran into the path of the car. As it seemed to be dead, but not damaged too much, the driver picked it up and put it in the boot. When, after the lecture, we arrived back in Lincoln, he opened the boot and got a shock when the hare jumped out, having been stunned and not killed! It was one occasion when a Lincolnshire poacher was not successful!

In 1947, I was appointed Conductor of Brigg Choral Society and official accompanist of the newly-revived North Lincolnshire Competitive Music Festival. Both were invaluable opportunities in conducting and sight-reading as well as experience in rehearsing amateur music-makers and exploring the repertoire of standard secular choral works. Brigg Festival was one of the oldest in the country. It had been founded by the singer, Gervase Elwes, whose family lived in the nearby Elsham Hall. The folk-song Brigg Fair was sung at a Festival by a local farmer called Joseph Taylor. The tune so impressed the adjudicator that he passed it on to the composer Frederick Delius who used it as the basis for his orchestral rhapsody Brigg Fair. On my visits to Brigg, I stayed with Miss Felicia Taylor, a committee member. She was a close relative of Joseph Taylor, perhaps a granddaughter, and I subsequently discovered that he was related by marriage, to my grandfather. Concurrently, I was one of the official accompanists for the Lincoln Competitive Music Festival of which Gordon Slater was the Chairman. This brought me into contact with many of the leading adjudicators of the time such as Herbert Howells, Maurice Jacobson, Sydney Northcote, Thomas Armstrong and Michael Head. Slater did a fair amount of adjudicating too and in 1948 made a tour of the Canadian Festivals. Accompanying amateur singers without prior rehearsal or prior sight of the music in a Festival class was something of a nightmare. They often had little sense of time or rhythm and sometimes produced a scruffy, almost illegible, manuscript copy of their own choice song with a request to transpose it into another key.

In 1946-1947, my earnings totalled £100 and in the following year increased to £180 15s. 0d. The balance sheet for 1947-1948 is recorded in my cash book:-

Earnings	£	s.	d.	Expenses	£	s.	d.
Church Salary	30	0	0	Life Insurance	12	10	11
Lectures	37	10	0	Heating (Coal)	3	19	2
Choral Class (Brigg)	15	15	0	Lighting		8	6
Pupils	90	0	0	Proportion of Rates	1	18	0
Teaching Band Boys	7	10	0	Tuning of Piano	1	5	0
				Cleaning of Room	13	0	0
Total	180	15	0	Total	33	1	7

Income in 1948-1949 increased further to a total of £288 17s 6d whilst expenses remained almost the same at £33 19s 1d. My bank savings account was beginning to show a healthy balance.

Life was not entirely taken up with work and study. Our local parish church, St Peter-at-Gowts had a flourishing Youth Fellowship, to which I belonged, and eventually became its Chairman. Activities included table tennis, lawn tennis and a football team of which I became captain. A highlight was competing in the Lincoln Youth Organisations' cup final played on the Lincoln City Football Club ground which we won 3 - 2! The Vicar of St Peter's, Canon Gilbert Houlden, a keen sportsman himself, gave a good deal of encouragement to the young people of his congregation.

The church had a strong link with the Theological College and ordinands were seconded to visit the church and to help in the various organisations. One of these was Basil Moss who had a profound influence on us. He had a very lively and extrovert personality and later became successively, Sub-warden of the College, Secretary of ACCM, the Churches Committee for the selection of ordinands and Provost of Birmingham Cathedral. The staff of the Theological College were regular visiting preachers. The Warden of the College at this time was Canon Eric Abbott, later to become Dean of Westminster Abbey. He was a quiet, scholarly man and one of the few people I have known who could hold the attention of a congregation in a sermon lasting up to forty minutes. Canon T R Milford, sometime Chancellor of Lincoln Cathedral and subsequently Master of the Temple Church in London, was another compelling preacher who had the capacity to make a congregation laugh audibly during his sermons. He was a tall man with a bald pate and untidy hair sticking out from the sides of his head and strongly resembled the actor, Alistair Sim. His brother, Robin Milford was a professional musician and composer. One of Milford's predecessors as Chancellor was Canon J H Srawley, an internationally renowned theologian. He seemed to be somewhat forgetful. On one occasion, he set off from his stall towards the lectern to read the first lesson only to find when he got there that his path was blocked by the bulky frame of the Precentor! Nonplussed, he returned to his stall. The Precentor during my time at Lincoln was The Rt Revd Arthur Grieves, also the Suffragan Bishop of Grimsby. It is not surprising that he was known as the "Fish Bish", considering that Grimsby was a great fishing port.

The Bishop of Lincoln was The Rt Revd Nugent Hicks - a large, and to my young eyes, quite one of the ugliest men I had ever seen! After preparation from Canon Scott, the Succentor, I was confirmed by the Bishop in the Cathedral, together with other fellow choristers. One of the Priest Vicars was The Revd G B Bentley, later to become residentiary

Canon of St George's Chapel, Windsor. It was the priest vicar's duty to sing the cantor's part in the versicles and responses at Mattins and Evensong, and to intone the Collects. Bentley obviously thought that he could pitch the opening "O Lord open Thou our lips" without being given a note from the organ. On his Lincoln debut he set off on a much higher note than he should have done, so that the even higher intonation required for the second versicle was impossible for him and the choir. After a strangulated attempt he gave up and the choir collapsed in scarcely concealed hysterics. We had little contact with Dean R A Mitchell other than seeing and hearing him at the services. The Sub-Dean, Canon A M Cook, could certainly be heard and seemed unable to control the volume of his voice. I believe he had some impediment which prevented his projecting quietly. The first time he read a lesson the choristers nearly jumped out of the stalls as he explosively announced the reading. Canon Hubert Larkin, Sub-Dean of Lincoln before Canon Cook, was a model railway enthusiast. He had a hole made in the wall of one of the rooms in his house so that the trains could run from one to the other! The Archdeacon of Lincoln, Canon Kenneth Warner, subsequently became the Bishop of Edinburgh. Little did I dream as a probationer that our paths would cross again later in my life.

To return to the activities of the members of St Peter-at-Gowts Youth Fellowship. The Vicar's interest and influence led to the fostering of vocation to the Ministry. Three of my contemporaries applied to ACCM for training. Jack Talent, son of a local newsagent and Michael Freeman, previously mentioned, were accepted but Arthur Talbot, son of a local dentist was unfortunately unsuccessful. Jack Talent was a pupil at Lincoln School and was very fastidious in his dress. It was a source of some amusement to us all that he had a handkerchief in the sleeve of his jacket. But it was also a source of admiration that, unlikely as it seemed, he spent most of his ministry in South Africa working amongst a predominantly black and poor community. He became Archdeacon of Kuruman and rode around the Diocese on horseback visiting his flock. Michael Freeman began his ministry in the Lincoln Diocese before moving to Warwick where he eventually became leader of the team ministry there and a Canon in the Diocese of Coventry. Of course, the young people of the Fellowship formed relationships with those of the opposite sex. In my case, I was fortunate to fall in love with one of the members who eventually returned my affection. Mabel Ellingworth lived near to the parish church, in Vernon Street and attended regularly as well as joining in the activities of the Youth Fellowship. We became engaged on her twenty-first birthday, 4 February 1947. Harris Ellingworth, her father, was a quiet, good-humoured man with a handsome wife who had a much more extrovert character. They had three children, Tony the eldest, who died in early manhood and two girls, Dorothy, and Mabel the youngest. Dorothy married Flight Sergeant Derek Williams in St Peter's Church in April 1945. Derek hailed from Brierfield, near Nelson in Lancashire and was stationed at the RAF camp in Waddington. Lincoln was surrounded by airfields so that a considerable number of RAF personnel came into the city in their free time. Although there were munitions factories in the city, Lincoln suffered very little from the bombing raids by the German air forces. Whilst there were many warnings from air-raid sirens, I only remember one occasion when some fire-bombs fell. Happily, little damage was done and the Cathedral, which must have been a landmark, mercifully escaped unscathed. Growing up during the war was an interesting experience, to say the least. Food and clothing were rationed and all lights had to be blacked-out in houses and all public buildings during the hours of darkness. Street lights were minimal and headlamps of buses and cars were reduced to small strips of light. Despite these restrictions, we seemed to lead a contented life and the plainer food provided a more healthy diet.

After the Wedding Service (1949)

Chapter 4 - First Full-time Appointment   (1949-1956)

"We shall have to get married!"

1949 was a momentous year in my life. The appointment of Organist and Choirmaster at the Parish Church of St James, Louth, coupled with the position of music master at the town's Boys' Grammar School became vacant. Clifford Hewis, assistant organist at the Cathedral, and recently returned from war service in the RAF, applied and was offered the job. He decided that he did not wish to leave Lincoln and Gordon Slater said, "Well, you had better go, Dennis." After interviews with the Rector of Louth and the Headmaster of the School, I was offered and accepted the joint appointment, in April, at the age of twenty-three and took up duties on Whit Sunday. The organist was provided with accommodation in a side wing of the 18th-century Rectory for a modest rent. This precipitated matrimony, for as Mabel remarked, "we shall have to get married now because you will need someone to feed and look after you!" Happily, she has been feeding and caring for me ever since and I have never ceased thanking God that she has. We were married in the Parish Church of St Peter-at-Gowts, Lincoln, by the Vicar, Canon Gilbert Houlden, on 21 May 1949. My lifelong friend, Michael Freeman, was my Best Man. Mabel wore a white veil over her face on arriving at the church but the Vicar told her to lift it over her head to allow her face to be seen, remarking that he would not mind if Dennis wore a veil but she was worth looking at! After a short honeymoon in Stratford-on-Avon, we took up residence in St James' Lodge, Louth.

The ancient market town of Louth, with a population of about 11,000 people, nestles in the Wolds of Lincolnshire and has been described by the poet, John Betjeman, as "the loveliest country town in England." The spire of the present 15th century church, the tallest on any parish church in England, is a dominant feature of the surrounding countryside and rises to a height of two hundred and ninety-five feet feet. The spacious nave has an unusually wide central aisle, formerly occupied by short benches for those who did not rent a pew and for pupils of local schools. The church records reveal that there was an organ in the building before 1500. The present fine instrument of three manuals and pedals was totally rebuilt in 1911 by the firm of Norman and Beard, retaining much of the original pipework of the organ installed by Gray and Davison in 1857. In the one hundred and seventy-eight years between 1768 and 1946, the church had but four organists. Since then, there has been a much more rapid succession.[3]

Churches abound with stories of the eccentric behaviour (sometimes scandalous) of organists and clergy and Louth was no exception. George Porter, commonly known as "Old" Porter, served as organist from 1866 to1897. He was in the habit of slipping unseen out of a side door behind the organ chamber, during the sermon, into the Wheatsheaf Inn for a pint (or two) of ale. Unfortunately, he failed to return in time to play the hymn after the sermon on one occasion and was summarily dismissed.

3.   Ref. St James' Church, Louth (1989).

Louth Parish Church

Photo by Derrick Furlong

My immediate predecessor was Harold Dexter (1946-1949), who moved from Louth to Holy Trinity Church, Leamington Spa and from there to Southwark Cathedral, as Organist and Master of the Choristers. He was a fine musician and his youthful enthusiasm and forthright manner proved a severe cultural shock to the community after the long reign of Owen Price, who served as organist from 1897 to 1946.

Dexter apparently had a capacity for expressing himself in colourful language. It was said that he would kneel between the choristers' stalls during services and vehemently whisper, "Sing, you little beggars, sing" and that he once told the sopranos of the Town Choral Society that they sang like "a lot of porpoises in labour!" He and his wife also had colourful tastes in the house. When we moved into St James' Lodge we found that the outside of the bath was painted bright red! He was very helpful prior to our move to Louth and handed over a well-drilled church choir and a well organised and ambitious curriculum at the Grammar School.

The Rectory stood in its own grounds opposite the church, separated by a narrow cobbled lane so that it could not have been more convenient for both Rector and organist. St James' Lodge was more than sufficient for our needs as newly-weds and we had saved sufficient money to furnish it modestly. After buying a necessary wrist watch to ensure punctual attendance for the various duties and commitments, we began the first week of our married life with the princely balance of five shillings (25p). At least, we were not in debt. The Lodge had a large stone-flagged kitchen, a large dining-cum-sitting room and a small stone-flagged study, where our piano was installed. It also served as a music room for teaching private pupils. The bedrooms and bathroom were upstairs.

The Rector of Louth at this time was Canon Humphrey Burton. He was a large and pleasant man, but somewhat shy, and our relationship was rather formal. However, he gave me a free rein over the musical contents of the services and was generally supportive. He was sympathetic towards the place of music in worship but not very musical himself. I discovered that if tenor G was played on the organ he either thought it was an intonation for the opening versicle, " O Lord, open Thou our lips" or, an indication that the National Anthem was to be sung!

Humphrey Burton had been President of the Union at Cambridge and was very diplomatic in his dealings with his parishioners. He agreed to my request that the choir should have new cassocks but not to my suggestion that the colour should be scarlet rather than black. He said that the Parochial Church Council was very unlikely to accept such a radical change if any at all. He thought that a dark purple might be more appropriate and told the PCC that the choir would be getting new cassocks and that the colour would be not quite black! There was no opposition . He was also sometimes absent-minded and forgetful. On one occasion I heard him telling Mr Wilson, the Verger, to "Clear it away, Wilson. Clear what away, Rector?" the verger replied. With an airy wave of his hand, the Rector said, "Oh just clear it away" and walked out of the Church! Wilson told me afterwards that he never did find out what the Rector wanted clearing away.

Humphrey Burton's wife had been in a psychiatric hospital for some years, and after her death he remarried. His second wife, Mrs Loft, JP, was a widow and had been the Rector's housekeeper. She was a handsome and very competent lady with two sons, one of whom trained falcons. The Rectory had a beautifully maintained garden with a tennis court. One part of the garden was devoted to growing vegetables, including an asparagus bed. Occasionally, we were given a bunch of asparagus when the Rector was intending to have some for a meal. Mr Thornley, the gardener, told us that the Canon would not have it cut until half an hour before the meal so that it had the maximum time to grow!

The other official part of my joint appointment involved teaching music at the King Edward VI Boys' Grammar School. It was a typical country school of about three hundred and fifty pupils drawn from Louth and the surrounding area. It had a small boarding house and a prep. department so that the age-range was from seven to eighteen years. The school stood in its own grounds and the classrooms were built round an open quadrangle. Hedley Warr, the Headmaster, had been a chorister at Westminster Abbey and was not only an enthusiastic and competent singer and musician but also a committed churchman. He insisted that every class in the school should receive two lessons of music per week. He sang in the school choir, encouraged other members of the staff to do the same and ensured the boys attended rehearsals regularly! Each day began with a school assembly and prayers in the school hall. Monday morning assembly began with a rehearsal of the hymns to be sung during the week. On Friday mornings a collection was taken in aid of a charity chosen by the school prefects. Whilst this was being taken, one of Bach's Forty-eight Preludes and Fugues was played by the Music Master on the grand piano which stood on the platform. The boys were expected to stand still and listen in silence until the piece was finished - and they did!

It was not only a compulsory lesson in musical appreciation for the pupils but also a challenge for the music master who had to prepare a different Prelude and Fugue each week. The school orchestra consisted of an odd assortment and ill-balanced group of instruments of a few violins, viola, 'cello, some recorders and one trumpet. Finding and arranging suitable music for them to play was a test of ingenuity to say the least! However, the general provision and support for music in the school could not have been much better and the junior classes were an ideal recruiting ground for parish church choristers with the encouragement of the headmaster. Friday afternoons were something of a trial for both teacher and pupils. Music classes were held in the art room which looked on to the school yard and had to compete with the stentorian commands being bellowed by Major Mead, Officer Commanding the School Army Cadet Corps, and the vigorous marching of the recruits. Mead had an "old banger" of a car. His method of persuading the car doors to open was to bang his fist on top of the roof, whereupon the doors sprang open with alacrity! The school possessed a very attractive sports field and was the arena for the annual cricket match between staff and boys in which I played. We never beat the school team but we did have more success against staff teams from neighbouring schools.

In addition, I spent an afternoon teaching at Fir Close Girls' Preparatory School, rehearsed and conducted the town Choral and Orchestral Society, and Brigg Choral Society, gave adult education lectures in Appreciation of Music during the winter months, and in 1954 was invited to take over as conductor of Grimsby Madrigal Society. Meanwhile, I had acquired a number of private pupils, mostly for piano and organ. Outstanding among them was John Edwards, son of a Methodist Minister in Louth and a pupil at the Grammar School. He was awarded the silver medal for gaining the second highest mark in the British Isles for Grade VIII Piano in Associated Board exams in 1954. His talents led the senior master at the school to suggest that he should be entered in music for the School Certificate and A-Level academic examinations.

Hitherto, music had not been included as an examination subject in the school curriculum but when the opportunity was presented, a number of boys opted to take the course as well as John Edwards. A small group of pupils from the Girls' Grammar School also joined in as their music mistress was not qualified to teach the requirements for Advanced level. The headmaster made space in the timetable; the venture was successful and raised the profile of music in the school even further. John Edwards also studied organ with me and went on to gain the organ scholarship at Gonville and Caius College Cambridge and to read music. He eventually became Head of Music at Bury Grammar School, Lancashire.

A number of other pupils of this period pursued music professionally and re-appeared unexpectedly later in my life. In 1987, whilst I was travelling by train to London an elderly couple got on at Newcastle and sat down in seats on the opposite side of the coach. The lady kept looking at me and eventually came across the aisle and said, "Excuse me, you're Dennis Townhill aren't you? You taught me to play the piano forty years ago and I've since been to music college and qualified as a teacher. I've always wanted to thank you." She smiled and I recognised her as Peggy Beavans, a pupil at Brigg High School, who used to travel the sixty miles return journey to Louth for her lessons. She and her mother sang in Brigg Choral Society. More recently, a Mrs June Holt wrote to me from Mansfield. She had sung on the Isle of Arran with a choral group and in a roundabout way had obtained my address. She was a Louth girl, sang in the Choral Society, had piano and theory of music lessons from me and then went on to Bretton Hall Teacher Training College. I remembered her as June Vamplew and replied saying that coincidentally I would be giving an organ recital in Louth Parish Church shortly. She and her husband, also a professional musician, attended the recital and she identified herself on a press photograph of a Louth Choral Society concert over forty years previously.

Hedley Warr was Chairman of the Choral Society and Alex Slack, the Vice-Chairman and enthusiastic bass singer. Alex was a fellow Lincolnian whose father Hedley Slack had a printing business in the city. Alex was a highly respected solicitor in Louth, a committed member of the church and a town councillor, eventually serving as Mayor of the Borough. The chief citizens were not always as well educated or discerning. After a concert in the Town Hall attended by another holder of the office, the Mayor greeted me with the words, " Mr Townhill, I think you're luvly." I knew that the comment was nothing to do with my personal characteristics! Alex Slack and his wife, Margaret, became good friends and two of their children were piano pupils. The Choral Society gave two or three concerts annually in either the Parish Church or Town Hall with soloists and orchestra. Handel's *Messiah* or Bach's *Christmas Oratorio* in December and standard secular choral works suitable for a group of about fifty singers were performed with rural enthusiasm. There was a nucleus of string players in the town which was augmented by players from nearby towns and area. There were some competent players but also one or two passengers. Our local elderly double bass player rarely placed his fingers in the right place and had to be shielded from exposed passages. On one occasion, during a performance of the Aria, *Slumber beloved*, from Bach's *Christmas Oratorio*, when he was being "rested", he nodded off to sleep and his bow could be heard tapping clearly on the side of his instrument - miraculously in time with the music! The Parish Church choir was also a mixed bag of twenty boys and twelve men, but there were some good singers and they were a loyal and willing group of above average standard for a small country town. The Church was affiliated to the Royal School of Church Music and on visits from Special Commissioners such as Alwyn Surplice (Winchester) and Stanley Vann (Peterborough) the choir received encouraging reports.

In Cassock and Surplice (1976) by a Lay Clerk

Louth Music Club held subscription concerts by leading artists and groups. These took place in the Grammar School hall where there was a suitable platform and a good Bechstein grand piano. It fell to me to accompany solo singers and instrumentalists. The concerts by Thomas Hemsley (baritone) and David Galliver (tenor) remain vividly in my mind for different reasons. Hemsley was pedantic over expressive details in his interpretation of songs, in particular of Lieder by Hugo Wolf and insistent, quite rightly, that the piano part should be equally matching. Some years later he sang the part of Christus for me in Bach's *St John Passion* and spent an inordinate amount of valuable rehearsal time in changing the English translation of his part. It created great problems and stress for the 'cello continuo player in particular and I vowed only to perform such works in the original language in the future. Galliver's recital posed different problems. He had a lapse of memory in Beethoven's Song Cycle *An die ferne Geliebte* and missed out a fair chunk of one of the songs. His accompanist desperately busked the piano part until the correct place was found. No one in the audience seemed aware of the problem and neither did the singer!

In many ways Louth was an ideal and idyllic place for an aspiring young musician to develop his skills and gain invaluable experience. It provided a wide variety of opportunities requiring a good deal of hard work and ingenuity to obtain and maintain an acceptable standard. Among many memorable events were a performance of Edward German's *Merrie England* in the Town Hall to mark the Festival of Britain in 1951; a special programme of choral, orchestral and organ music in the Parish Church to mark the bi-centenary of J S Bach in 1950; a concert in the Town Hall by three hundred Louth children in 1953 as part of the local Coronation celebrations; a performance of Dorothy L Sayer's play *The Zeal of Thy House* at the Grammar School in which Hedley Warr played the part of the architect, William of Sens; a recital in the Parish Church in 1954 in which I accompanied Neville Marriner and 1955 when Neville was soloist in Bach's *E major Violin Concerto* with Louth Orchestral Society; singing by the choir of an Ascension Day hymn from the base of the church spire at 8 am. to the surprise of the passers-by in the streets below! Some of the men could not face the prospect of climbing the steps but the oldest, Charlie Smith, who was fond of telling me that "I joined the choir in 1887, Sir." remained undaunted!

In 1954, I was invited to join the twenty-four business and professional men in the new Rotary Club of Louth and have remained a member of Rotary ever since. I was the youngest member and on returning for the twenty-fifth anniversary, discovered there were only four of the founder members still alive! A few other people and matters deserve mention before moving on from Louth. Sydney Smith, a local Ludensian, was a splendid solo baritone who was regularly engaged to sing for the Choral Society concerts. He had an engaging personality and modesty, and deserved to be much more widely known. Elizabeth Sharpley, a farmer's daughter, was another very talented Ludensian. She gave more than competent performances of Beethoven's Piano Concertos in B flat and E flat (*The Emperor*) with the augmented Louth Orchestral Society. The Girls' Grammar School, as the Boys', took a small number of boarders and one of these was a Grimsby girl by the name of Hortensia Vincent. She had a very promising soprano voice and was accepted as a pupil by Roy Henderson, the celebrated singer and teacher. With financial help, raised locally, she moved to London for her lessons. Although she could well have pursued a successful career in music, she felt a stronger vocation for nursing. Three fellow church musicians working in the county during this time became life-long friends. Ted Ball was organist and choirmaster at St Matthew's Parish Church, Skegness, and was one of the most dedicated and talented trainers of boys' voices I have known. He was a charming and favourite visitor to St James' Lodge and introduced us to the delights of French wine! Some years later he resigned his post on the arrival of a new vicar who had no interest in the flourishing choir and standard of music Ted was providing. Russell Missin at Holbeach, later to become the Master of Music at Newcastle Cathedral and Robert Munns at Gainsborough Parish Church, were the other two. Subsequently, Robert pursued a successful career mainly as a solo recitalist and Associated Board Examiner. Peter Fletcher was another Louth lad to make his mark in the music profession. He had been a pupil of Harold Dexter and just gone to Cambridge as an organ scholar when I arrived in Louth. However, he assisted me at the church during vacations and had some lessons from me in preparation for the FRCO Diploma. He became a prominent and distinguished Music Adviser in London and Leicestershire.

The most important events on the domestic front were the advent of our two children; Richard Vaughan was born in Louth and District Hospital on 29 March 1950 and Barbara Jane on 10 May 1953 at St James' Lodge. The night before Vaughan's birth, I arrived home in Elizabethan costume, after directing a small group of singers in a concert of madrigals, to be told that Mabel had been taken to hospital. After enquiring by phone, I was told to go to the hospital the following morning. Whilst in the waiting room a doctor appeared and muttered, "That *****y woman has just about broken my *****y back!" Fortunately he was not referring to Mabel and indeed was not our family doctor.

We bought our first car in 1950. It was a 1935 Morris Eight, for which we paid £150. It was a reliable little car which gave no trouble, except that it tended to need frequent topping up with oil. It had no heating system and was very cold in the winter especially when the windscreen had to be unscrewed open in icy and foggy weather in order to see where we were going.

It was a busy and happy time and we would have been content to stay in Louth except that I became increasingly frustrated by the limited musical abilities and standards of the choral and orchestral performers. A determination to seek a move was engendered by Canon Aidan Ward who had succeeded Humphrey Burton as Rector of Louth. Soon after his arrival he told me that I must leave Louth and that it was not in my best interests to remain much longer. In 1954, at Gordon Slater's instigation, I applied for, and was placed on the short list for, the post of Organist and Choirmaster of St Mary's Parish Church, Nottingham. David Lumsden was appointed and I had to wait a further eighteen months before another opportunity presented itself. This time I was successful and in December 1955 was appointed Organist and Choirmaster of St James' Parish Church, Great Grimsby, and Music Master of St James' Choir School.

Chapter 5 - Second Appointment - A Fishy Business (1956 -1961)

"You should stay for 5 years"

Although Grimsby was only seventeen miles from Louth and still within the same Diocese of Lincoln, it had a good many musical opportunities to offer which were not available in many places further afield. Grimsby was and is the largest town in the County of Lincolnshire, situated in the north-east corner on the banks of the River Humber. Together with its adjoining seaside resort of Cleethorpes, it had a population of nearly 130,000 people. At the time we moved there, the value of the fish landed at the port was the largest in the world. More importantly for me, it had many fine professional musicians and a thriving cultural life. The Parish Church of St James was a cruciform shape and a beautifully proportioned building. It had been damaged by aerial bombardment during the war, but by 1956 it was carefully and faithfully restored and contained some fine, modern stained glass windows. In 1952 a large, new, three manual organ was installed in a gallery at the west end of the church to replace the previous instrument which stood in the north transept. It had been intended that the choir should sit in the gallery but the congregation would not agree and insisted that it should remain in the chancel. This posed obvious problems of balance and co-ordination and the frustration caused by these was a factor in the resignation of Stanley Robson, the organist and choirmaster of some thirty years. He was a fine musician and teacher and was greatly admired and respected in the community. He was the founder and conductor of the Grimsby Madrigal Society - a group of between thirty to forty singers specialising in *a capella* secular and sacred music of the 16th to 20th centuries. On Robson's departure from Grimsby I was invited to take over the conductorship of the choir and thus knew, and was known by many of the musical fraternity there. This coincidence was mentioned by the Vicar in the church magazine on the announcement of my appointment as organist and choirmaster, adding that had I been a stranger amongst the fifty-four candidates who applied I would still have secured the appointment. My immediate predecessor was Eric Coningsby who had succeeded Stanley Robson in 1952. He had formerly been Organist of Llandaff Cathedral. After only four years in Grimsby, he sadly died in his mid-forties, thus creating the vacancy.

Grimsby is one of the very few parish churches to have a Choir School at which the choristers are educated. This provides the opportunity for more rehearsal time and the consequent possibility of achieving a high standard. To this end, I was able to introduce a daily morning practice in the church after which the boys processed the short distance to the school. In addition, a mid-week Choral Evensong was introduced. In order to overcome the problems of balance and co-ordination, the choir processed to the west end of the church and stood under the gallery for the performance of accompanied music. They then processed back to the choir stalls in the chancel!

The Vicar was Canon Gervase Markham, a very able and efficient priest whose father had also been Vicar of Grimsby before becoming Bishop of Grantham. There were still people in the congregation who remembered Gervase as a small boy in his father's reign. As Vicar of Grimsby he had responsibility and jurisdiction over St James' Parish

Grimsby Parish Church

Photo by The Revd P C Patrick

46

Church and also the daughter churches of St Luke, St Martin and St Mark. The priests-in-charge of these churches were his curates in addition to his assistant at the parish church. At first, I found Markham rather formal and distant, but gradually our relationship became less like employer and employee and more friendly and equal. We met in his Vicarage study monthly to plan the music for the services in advance and the words and tunes for each hymn were carefully scrutinised and discussed. The date and service when each hymn was sung was recorded in our hymn books. It was a simple but efficient way of preventing undue repetition.

Like many church musicians I had strong views on what were good and bad hymn tunes, but I did not always get my own way. At Louth, I had refused to use Arthur Sullivan's tune, St Gertrude for *Onward Christian Soldiers* much to the frustration of the Rector. Soon after our move to Grimsby, the annual Civic Service was held, attended by the Mayor and members of the Borough Council. The hymns were accompanied by the Grimsby Borough Brass Band and the first one was *Onward Christian Soldiers* to the tune St Gertrude! I remember thinking how splendid it sounded! The organist's annual salary at Louth was £100 and at Grimsby it was £120. However, there were a considerable number of weddings and funerals in Grimsby which helped to boost the earnings. At Louth, Harold Dexter had negotiated organist's fees of three guineas, four guineas (with choir) and five guineas (with choir, bells and red carpet). At Grimsby, the fees were fifteen shillings (organ only), one guinea (organ and choir) and one pound ten shillings (with choir, bells and red carpet). I never understood why the organist should receive more money when bells and carpet were included as neither was his responsibility. Naturally, I questioned the discrepancy between the level of fees in the two churches, especially as Grimsby was a more important appointment. The Vicar was sympathetic and was willing to put a request for an increase to the Parochial Church Council. He decided that this should not amount to as much as the Louth scale. His proposal was that the organist's fees should be one guinea, two guineas and three guineas respectively and that the Vicar's fees should be two, three and four guineas. The PCC agreed the scale for the organist but stated that the Vicar's fees should remain at the legal limit of 18s 9d!

In those days, couples marrying before 5th April received a tax rebate. Consequently, March was a peak month for weddings and there were regularly between four and eight weddings each Saturday. It was necessary to take a drink and snack to be consumed in the organ gallery or dash across the road to the nearby *Hole in the Wall* café. June and September were also popular months for "tying the knot" in church and there were few blank Saturdays during the year.

Looking forward to the advantage of a choir school, it was deflating to find that the school was in turmoil and parents up in arms over the dismissal of the headmaster for sexual offences against pupils. This led to withdrawal of pupils and problems of chorister recruitment. However, an excellent new headmaster was appointed and after a difficult period, the fortunes of the school revived and recruitment of choristers improved. Michael Lloyd proved a dynamic headmaster and he gathered round him a group of dedicated teachers including his wife, Jean, who was a brilliant mathematician. Another member of staff was a young man destined to make his mark in politics. Patrick Cormack has had a distinguished career as a long-serving Member of Parliament for a West Midlands constituency, receiving a knighthood in recognition of his work.

Part of my duties was to provide some classes in music appreciation at the school - not always easy with a group of fidgety teenagers. However, seeds sown often bear fruit in the most unlikely places. Some years after leaving Grimsby, I was revisiting the town by car and was stopped by a policeman. Wondering why I had been stopped, I wound down the window to be addressed by a formidable uniformed figure. "Hello Mr Townhill, I was thinking of you recently as I listened to Beethoven's Fifth Symphony. You introduced us to that at school." I remembered him as a rather loutish and inattentive lad!

No mention has yet been made of our domestic arrangements. Unlike Louth, no accommodation was provided for the organist in Grimsby and we therefore had to look for suitable housing. My grandmother, now aged eighty-three years, had been ill and was clearly struggling to cope with looking after the house in Lincoln, so we suggested that she and grandpa should live with us in Grimsby. They were not keen to give up their independence but agreed. We therefore looked for a house large enough for us all and eventually took out a mortgage on a property at 8 Lambert Road, within easy walking distance of the church and the school.

By this time, I was becoming increasingly involved in the work of the Royal School of Church Music and was appointed Area Representative for Lindsey, the northern part of the diocese. Whilst still in Louth, I had acquired the Royal College of Organists Choir Training Diploma (CHM) with the intention of taking the Archbishop's Diploma in Church Music (ADCM). In preparation, I attended a week's course at the College of St Nicholas in Canterbury organised by the RSCM. This proved as memorable for the personnel involved as for the content of the course.

Gerald Knight, Warden and later Director of the RSCM, was in charge, and the distinguished group of visiting lecturers included Dr Heathcote Statham, organist of Norwich Cathedral, Dr H. "Ken" Andrews, organist of New College, Oxford and Erik Routley, Congregationalist Minister. Statham, who had a pronounced stammer, lectured on music of the Restoration period, Ken Andrews on Tudor church music and Routley on Hymns and Hymn tunes. The Diploma required candidates to be communicant members of the Church of England, vouched for by three referees, including a clergyman and a professional church musician and to be holders of the FRCO and Choir Training Diplomas of the RCO. The syllabus required a knowledge of Liturgiology, the Prayer Book, the place of music in worship, church music from plainchant to the present day including hymns. As well as written papers, a viva-voce examination was carried out by two distinguished church musicians, one appointed by the RCO and one by the RSCM. In my case they were Dr Henry Ley, former Organist of Christ Church Cathedral, Oxford, and recently retired Precentor of Eton College (1955) and Dr. Frederick Wadely, Organist of Carlisle Cathedral. Ley was a large man with an untidy shock of white hair while Wadely was much thinner with less hair! My only memory of a friendly and amiable encounter is a request to describe the modulations in the penultimate section of S S Wesley's anthem, *The Wilderness*. All must have been satisfactory as I was awarded the Diploma in January 1957, together with Robert Joyce, Organist of St Matthew's, Northampton and later Organist of Llandaff Cathedral. The Diplomas were presented personally by Dr. Geoffrey Fisher, Archbishop of Canterbury, during Evensong at Lambeth Palace in July. Mabel

Ted and Becky in the garden of 8 Lambert Road, Grimsby

travelled with me and on our return a pleasant surprise awaited us at Grimsby Town Station. The robed parish church choir and the headmaster were there to greet us. After the choir sang an anthem, the head chorister presented Mabel with a bouquet of flowers.

Harold Dexter had invited me to act as a housemaster at the RSCM residential course at St. Elphin's College, Darley Dale, at which he was Master-in-Charge. This led to similar further invitations including two to assist at the largest RSCM Course which was held annually at Rossall School, near Fleetwood in Lancashire. These summer courses had been conducted by Hubert Crook, Chief Commissioner of the RSCM, from their inception. On his death, Gerald Knight, now Director of the RSCM, decided to take charge of the course in the following year and gathered together what he described as the best team of young church musicians available. Most of them became cathedral organists and among them were Harold Dexter (Southwark), John Sanders (Chester and Gloucester), Derek Holman (Professor of Music, Toronto), Roy Massey (Birmingham and Hereford), Peter Stevenson (Portsmouth), John Nourse and Malcolm Cousins. The last two held important parish church appointments. The daily services were held in the school chapel and some of the housemasters were invited to accompany the services on the organ. The console was placed in a loft on one side of the chapel above the choir stalls. When my turn came, Psalm 24 was down to be sung. It was set to a double chant in E major, by Joseph Barnby, in which each half begins with a unison phrase. This provided the opportunity for some free harmonisation. At the rehearsal, I decided to begin verse seven, "Lift up your heads, O ye gates" with a spectacular dissonance on full organ. There was an equally spectacular silence from the singers who clearly thought there must be a mechanical fault in the organ. Gerald Knight patiently called out for me to try again, which I did, repeating the same dissonance. Realising that the effect was deliberate he suggested that I should begin the chant with a plain chord! How boring, I thought, and not anything like as exciting. On my next visit to the Rossall Course, the Master-in-charge was Charles Bryars, organist of Chesterfield Parish Church (of crooked spire fame) and music master of King Edward VII Boys' Grammar School, Sheffield. He had assisted Hubert Crook on a number of courses and was a very competent choirmaster, if somewhat eccentric. He was a cheerful character with an idiosyncratic turn of phrase which was guaranteed to amuse and intrigue small boys. Our paths were to cross a number of times in later years. Fellow Housemasters on that course were Michael Nicholas, organist of St. Matthew's, Northampton and Clifford Hartley, Organist of Monkwearmouth Parish Church, Sunderland.

Meanwhile I had organised and conducted a number of combined church choirs' festivals and day schools in different parts of the Lindsey area. In addition to Grimsby, festivals were held in Market Rasen Parish Church, Gainsborough Parish Church and St Lawrence's Church, Scunthorpe, with numbers ranging from two hundred and fifty to four hundred and fifty singers. In 1959, I invited Gerald Knight to conduct the combined choirs from 24 different churches in the area, in St James' Church, Grimsby, for which I played the organ. The congregation overflowed into standing room.

In the same year, I initiated a three-day non-residential course for choristers at All Saints, Grimsby. Dr Alan Bunney, RSCM Special Commissioner and Director of Music at Tonbridge School in Kent, was in charge and I assisted at the organ. Some seventy boys attended from affiliated choirs throughout North Lincolnshire. The course proved so popular that it was oversubscribed the following year when it was conducted by Kenneth Beard, organist of Southwell Minster, with my assistance. A new dimension was added by the attendance, for the first time, of two girls. It is interesting to reflect that at all the RSCM choir courses and events described above, the treble choristers were almost entirely boys unlike the present situation.

Opportunities to promote and conduct choral and orchestral works increased rapidly at this period. The Madrigal Society held its principal annual concert in the Town Hall in January and engaged one or more distinguished soloists to attract a larger audience. These included April Cantelo (soprano) at that time, wife of the conductor, Colin Davis; Colin Horsley (pianist); Rohan de Saram ('cellist); Tessa Robbins (violinist); John Ogdon and

Clive Lythgoe (pianists). The latter was soloist in 1958 when disaster ensued. As there was no grand piano available in Grimsby, an instrument was hired from Lincoln. Because of thick fog between the two towns, the piano was late in arriving and faults in the action were not detected until the soloist began to play. He struggled gallantly through his pieces in the first-half but eventually had to abandon a Beethoven Sonata. He generously played the *Mephisto Waltz* by Liszt on the Town Hall's ancient "honky-tonk" upright piano which he said reminded him of his Air Force days! An embarrassing public apology was made with an invitation to Clive Lythgoe to return the following year when he was assured that an adequate piano would be provided. The adverse publicity aroused prompted the Town Council to launch an appeal for funds to buy a new grand piano. Happily, it was successful, as was the return visit of Clive Lythgoe. In 1961, the soloist was John Ogdon who had just recently won an international piano competition. He was a large "Teddy-bear" of a man whom we found to be delightful, but somewhat forgetful and unaware of what was going on around him. As with many of the visiting soloists, he was a guest in our house. As it was winter, we had lit a paraffin stove in the bathroom and when my wife went up, after breakfast, she found the stove was billowing out black smoke. When she apologised to John Ogdon he said that he had not noticed anything untoward! The accompanist for the Madrigal Society's Town Hall concerts was a young Grimsby professional pianist called Janet Cotterill, who also gave lessons to our two children. Her mother was a singing member of the Society and whose husband shared my interest and enthusiasm for soccer. They possessed a television set and to my delight I was invited each year to the house to watch the F A Cup Final - a ritual enhanced by tea and cakes.

Large-scale choral works were performed by the Grimsby Philharmonic Society in the Methodist Church Central Hall. The conductor, Alec Redshaw, a Cleethorpes man, also conducted Hull Choral Union. He was a very fine musician, singing teacher and prominent music festival adjudicator. He also conducted a semi-professional chamber choir named The Redshaw Singers. He invited me to play continuo parts, where appropriate, for the Philharmonic Society performances and to accompany The Redshaw Singers for a number of concerts in Grimsby Parish Church, some of which were broadcast by the BBC. One of the concerts given by the Singers took place in Beverley Minster which is a large and resonant building. The organ console was on the choir screen and seemed miles away from the singers who were on ground level in the nave. The only contact was via a small speaker by the organ console. Co-ordination was very difficult and not made any easier by the demanding organ parts of Kodaly *Missa Brevis* and Britten *Rejoice in the Lamb*.

Having organised and conducted oratorios in Louth, I was determined to do the same in Grimsby, and as a starter arranged annual performances of Handel's *Messiah*, Bach's *Christmas Oratorio* and *St. John Passion*. The combined voices of the Madrigal Society and Parish Church Choir formed the chorus, and professional soloists were engaged.

Among the soloists were many who gained national and international reputations. They included sopranos Margaret Asher, Patricia Clark, Elizabeth Harwood, (just beginning her distinguished career) Eileen Poulter and Rita Vernon; contraltos Jean Allister, Dame Janet Baker (just beginning her distinguished career) and Janet Fraser; tenors Ronald

Bristol, Wilfred Brown, Edgar Fleet, David Galliver, Andrew Gold and Cyril Hornby; basses James Atkins, Stanley Clarkson and the more local, Louth baritone, Sydney Smith who was by no means overshadowed.

The players for the orchestra were gathered from the area and supplemented by professionals as required. There was a nucleus of very good string players in the neighbourhood, notably the Campey family. Dorothea Campey was a fine professional 'cellist and her two daughters, Fay and Rosalind, were violinist and pianist respectively. Some years later, the family moved to Cheshire and Fay became the Leader of the Manchester Camerata whilst Rosalind was a distinguished accompanist and teacher. The woodwind and brass were gathered from young professional players in London by James Brown, son of a local doctor. After completing his training at music college in London, James became principal oboe in the English Chamber Orchestra and was therefore able to entice some of the best players of his generation to Grimsby. No doubt the generous private hospitality and opportunity for a relaxed break from the pressures of London were an added attraction.

Other choral works performed were Haydn's *Creation*, Handel's *Samson* for the bi-centenary in 1959, and smaller-scale pieces such as Arthur Somervell's *Passion of Christ* and Charles Wood's *St Mark Passion*. In December 1960 the review of a programme of "Music of Christmas" in the Grimsby Evening Telegraph noted "A generous selection of the unusual, the unfamiliar and the plain courageous - an excellent state of things and in itself a cause for congratulation." The programme included Corelli *Christmas Concerto*, Benjamin Britten *Ceremony of Carols*, Vaughan Williams *Fantasia on Christmas Carols* and Elizabeth Poston *Nativity*. Elizabeth Poston had been a pupil of Vaughan Williams and to my delight accepted the invitation to attend the concert and to help us prepare her newly published work. She was a delightful lady, unusually tall, and she kindly dedicated a short piano piece entitled *Lullaby* to me. Our paths were to cross again later.

A number of special services in the course of my period in Grimsby deserve mention. Soon after my appointment, the newly consecrated Bishop of Lincoln, The Rt Revd Kenneth Riches, paid his first visit to Grimsby including, of course, a service at the parish church. The Vicar showed a good deal of imagination in marking important festivals. On Palm Sunday, for example, he organised a procession through the Bull Ring to the church, depicting Christ seated on a live donkey with members of the congregation carrying large palm leaves and singing the hymn *All glory, laud and honour!* On Christmas Eve, he held an informal session of carol singing for the general public in the church before the Midnight Eucharist. People flocked into the floodlit church after the closure of the pubs and some were in an advanced state of inebriation. Markham skilfully emptied the church of those not really there to take part in the Eucharist by wishing the carol singers a "Happy Christmas" and declaring that a long and serious service was about to begin, and suggesting that it was an appropriate time for those not wishing to stay for it to leave. Another public procession through the streets of the town was made on, or near, 25 July, The Festival of St James, Patron Saint of the church. The combined choirs and congregations of the parish church and daughter churches joined forces to hold a short service at the ancient site of the former Church of St Mary before moving into the parish church for the main celebration, at which the Bishop of Lincoln preached. The choir also sang carols round the town

Dennis Townhill at the organ of Grimsby Parish Church

53

christmas tree after the official switch-on of the christmas lights by the current Mayor of the Borough. Carol singing in one of the town's largest stores proved a very lucrative source of raising money for the choir music fund, and the annual Ascension Day hymns sung from the church tower attracted a good deal of attention from the general public. Regular lunch-time organ recitals were arranged and drew good support, whilst a special recital in 1957, in aid of Lincoln Cathedral Organ Restoration Fund attracted a large audience. Gordon Slater played organ pieces and the choir's contribution included the first performance of two short anthems recently composed by him. On completion of the restoration, I had the pleasure of giving one of the special recitals in the Cathedral to mark its return to use.

After a successful audition, I was invited to broadcast an organ recital for the BBC on 7 July 1957, and this led to regular broadcasts from the church. The proximity of the railway line and the frequent regularity of fish trains from the docks posed an obvious hazard to broadcasts. My first programme included a perfect reproduction of a passing steam train! Most subsequent broadcasts were recorded late at night in order to avoid interference.

The producer was invariably Stephen Wilkinson, the distinguished conductor of the BBC Northern Singers, and he asked me to play Bach's Prelude and Fugue in G minor (S 535), a work unknown to me at that time. It was a favourite of his and he said, that as far as he knew, it had not previously received a broadcast performance. It is a very attractive work, showing clear influence of the style of Buxtehude and with a memorable fugue subject. The other pieces were the Chorale Prelude *Liebster Jesu, wir sind hier* (S 634) by Bach and the Arabesque and Postlude from Louis Vierne's *24 Pieces in Free Style*. On one occasion Stephen Wilkinson was three hours late in arriving for a rehearsal and recording, which, instead of beginning at 9pm, started at midnight and continued until the early hours of the morning!

Whilst in Grimsby, I began to receive invitations to adjudicate at competitive music festivals in the area. A notable one was The Lindsey Federation of Women's Institutes' Festival which took place every four years. Whilst the WI is traditionally associated with jam-making, embroidery and domestic activities, most branches at this time had a choral group and it was surprising what a good standard some achieved. After area heats and rehearsal, the final competitions took place in Louth Town Hall followed by a combined choirs' concert of some three hundred singers, conducted by the adjudicator. Another event, which remains in the memory is a Circuit Rally of Methodists in the village of Bardney. Here, the invitation involved giving a recital and accompanying the hymn-singing by a congregation of some two to three hundred people. It was an eye-opener or more accurately an "ear-opener", for I had never heard such thrilling and expressive congregational hymn-singing. The contrast between this singing and the half-hearted, feeble efforts of Anglican congregations was startling.

Thirty private pupils helped to swell the modest income from church and school whilst the membership of the District Organists and Choirmasters' Association and the Gramophone Society filled in a few more hours. In view of the present high profile of Andrew and Julian Lloyd Webber, it was interesting to find a press cutting in one of my scrapbooks of their father attending, as a special guest, the annual dinner of the Organists and Choirmasters' Association. Dr Lloyd Webber was the Principal of the London College of Music and organist and choirmaster at the Kingsway Hall, in the City. As in Louth, I was invited to become a member of Grimsby Rotary Club, and in 1960 joined the Freemasons' Lodge of St James.

A number of the congregation of the parish church were members and the choir sang carols at the Lodge annual Christmas social. Both Rotary and Freemasonry have been a lasting source of interest and pleasure, as well as a refreshing change from the daily round of professional music.

It had always been my hope that our son, Vaughan, should become a cathedral chorister and it was great delight when he was successful in gaining a place in the choir of Peterborough Cathedral in 1960. This involved his attending the King's School as a boarder and living away from home a good proportion of the year. The Organist and Master of the Choristers was Stanley Vann, one of the best choir trainers of the time, and for whom I had the greatest admiration and respect.

Vaughan did not get off to a very good start because, through no fault of his own or indeed of ours, the trunk containing all his clothes failed to arrive at the school. It had been sent in advance but instead of getting to Peterborough, it was found in a depot at Wellingborough, a nearby town!

It is invidious to select individuals for special mention but there were some who played an important part in our Grimsby days. Sydney Grice, a local wholesale grocer was an efficient and loyal assistant and John Colebrook, an organ pupil, was always at hand to help in any way required. John became a town councillor after we left Grimsby, and eventually served a term as Mayor of the Borough. The churchwardens were a supportive pair and both had sons in the choir. Joe Barnes-Browne died some time ago but Ted Wilkinson and his wife, Barbara, never failed to send us Christmas and Birthday cards for over forty years! The choirmen were a loyal group, most of whom had been trebles in the choir and a number also sang in the Madrigal Society.

A long-standing friendship began in the most unlikely way when a young stranger rang our door-bell at 8 Lambert Road. He said that the Archdeacon The Ven. Lisle Marsden had suggested that he should ask for my help. On being asked how I could help him, he bluntly replied, " I want to know how to train my village choir." I told him he was welcome to attend the choir practices at St James' as an observer, and I would advise him as well as I could and that I would not require payment. Shortly afterwards he turned up at the house again, this time carrying a brace of pheasants as a gift. Rather lamely, I told him that I did not know whether my wife would know how to deal with them as we had never had any pheasants before. As a look of dismay came over his face, I quickly thanked him and assured him that my grandma would be able to pluck the feathers and prepare the birds for cooking! A week or two later he asked me to record the accompaniment on the piano of the chorus "How lovely are Thy dwellings fair" from Brahms' *Requiem* so that he could rehearse his choir with it. A day or two afterwards, he brought another brace of pheasants, this time with the feathers plucked and ready prepared for the oven! Before I could thank him, he returned to his car and carried a sack of potatoes into the house!

Norman Finch had been a chorister at Grimsby Parish Church and a pupil at St James' Choir School. This had given him a love for music in general and church music in particular. He and his wife Pat live in the small village of Goxhill on the Humber bank, some twenty miles from Grimsby, and we have enjoyed their warm-hearted and generous hospitality for more than forty years. Of the many memorable and sometimes bizarre experiences we have shared, two are apposite at this point.

St Mark's in Grimsby was the first new church to be built in the Lincoln Diocese since the war, and was due to be consecrated by the Bishop on 21 June 1960. I was asked to advise on the acquisition of a suitable organ for the church. The parish church organ had been built by the firm of J W Walker and Sons and was maintained by them. Their Grimsby tuner, Mr Cooper told me of a good three manual and pedal organ that was for sale. It had been built by Walkers thirty years previously for a Mr John Houston of Rothley, near Leicester, who had it placed in a special music room added to his house for his own private use. He had recently died and his widow was willing to sell it at a pre-war price. Mr Cooper arranged for me to visit Rothley to inspect the instrument and I asked Norman Finch to accompany me and to drive his car.

We set off for Rothley early in the day, inspected and tried out the organ, and I decided to recommend that it should be bought for St Mark's. It was a bargain at the price being asked and would fit into the space allotted in the new church for an organ. Our return journey was not as uneventful as the outward trip, for we ran into thick and dense fog as darkness began to fall. It was midwinter and the fog was compounded by freezing temperatures. I had to wind down the passenger side window in order to see the road verge and guide my driver. Eventually, we found ourselves behind a bus and we were able to follow its rear lights and drive with more confidence. After a few miles, the bus turned left and stopped. We duly followed and found ourselves in Newark bus station! Thinking it was only a temporary halt, we remained in the car and waited for the bus to move off again. It failed to do so and we got out to enquire the time for its departure from the driver, whom we found in the bus station café! "I'm not driving anywhere in this weather!" he said, and so we had to resume the journey unaided. Our route took us through Lincoln and we decided to make a stop-off in Vernon Street where Mabel's parents still lived. After a very welcome break, and a bowl of hot soup, we resumed our journey. Thankfully, the fog cleared as we drove through the city and we arrived home, some hours later than anticipated, without further problems.

A second journey also concerned the search for an organ, this time for Goxhill Parish Church. An advert in the Church Times announced that the organ builders, Hele & Company of Plymouth had a good second-hand two manual and pedals instrument for sale. We decided to investigate this offer and to drive down to Plymouth on a Monday and to return the following day. Norman arranged to pick me up in Grimsby at 7am for the journey of some three hundred and fifty miles. Meanwhile, he set off from Goxhill at about 6am, with a farmer friend by the name of John Dee, who was to share the driving as far as London. Before leaving Goxhill, Norman drove round the village blowing the car horn outside various farm houses just to let his neighbours know he was leaving! The journey was hair-raising and I had never travelled at such fast speeds in a car before. John Dee drove as far as London with his right hand on the steering wheel and the thumb of his left hand stuck in his trouser belt, passing every vehicle in sight. We dropped him off in Hyde Park where we arranged to meet him the following day at about noon. Norman told me that John had a lady friend in London with whom he intended staying overnight!

I experienced a feeling of some relief when Norman took over the driving which however was quickly dispelled since he drove just as fast. Speed limits did not exist for either of them and it was a matter of good fortune that we were not pulled up by the police. We arrived safely in Plymouth, saw the organ and decided against putting in a bid for it - had a good meal and stayed overnight in a comfortable, small hotel. We set off at 7am next morning, hoping and intending to get back to Grimsby by 6pm as I had a commitment that evening. We got to London in good time, left the car in Hyde Park and decided to get something to eat before meeting John Dee as previously arranged. When we returned, neither the car nor John Dee was to be seen. I began to have a feeling of anxiety that we should not get back to Grimsby in time for my meeting but Norman seemed quite unconcerned. After a while, we heard a car horn repeatedly blowing and to my relief realised it was John Dee driving Norman's car. I did not know that he had a spare set of car keys. He had duly found the car parked illegally and noticing police in the vicinity decided to drive round the park until we arrived. The rest of the journey was equally hair-raising but we did arrive back in Grimsby in time for my meeting - just!

It had always been my intention and ambition to conduct a performance of Bach's *Mass in B minor* and I planned a performance for July 1961, little realising that it would be my swansong before leaving Grimsby. Three choirs combined to form the chorus - Grimsby Madrigal Society, Grimsby Parish Church Special Choir and Louth Choral Society. Weekly chorus rehearsals began two years before the date of the performance. The Louth group were rehearsed by Michael Nicholas, their conductor and organist and choirmaster at Louth Parish Church at that time. I decided that it was necessary to have a fully professional orchestra which regularly played together and which specialised in music of the period. Through the good offices of James Brown, the Philomusica of London was engaged. In order to pay for the orchestra, I persuaded the local Education Authority to sponsor a concert for schoolchildren and to cover the travel and accommodation costs. This left us with just fees to pay for the B minor Mass performance. The orchestra contained some of the finest players of the day such as Carl Pini (Leader); Joy Hall ('cello); Archie Camden (bassoon); Alan Civil (french horn); John Wilbraham, Dennis Clift, Clifford Haines (trumpets) and Hubert Dawkes (spinet). Carl Pini suggested that we should meet in London sometime prior to the performance in order to discuss details of interpretation so that parts could be marked and rehearsed in advance. It saved a lot of time at the joint rehearsal in Grimsby and also helped us to achieve a more polished performance. The vocal soloists were Patricia Clarke (soprano), Jean Allister (contralto), Edgar Fleet (tenor) and Sydney Smith (bass). They were all first class singers who had previously sung for me, and this also helped to ensure a sense of common purpose. It is interesting to note how relatively modest the fees were compared to those commanded today. They tended to range between five and fifteen guineas although we did also provide good accommodation and hospitality in private homes, which both singers and players enjoyed and appreciated.

I was unprepared for the problems that faced the chorus in learning the work, as few, if any, of the singers had any previous knowledge of the music. There is a great amount for the chorus to sing and they could not seem to retain what had been rehearsed.

Up to a month before the performance it seemed as if they would never absorb the notes, and I suffered constant sleepless nights and horrific dreams of a disastrous failure. Then, as if by magic, everything began to fall into place and we were able to concentrate on the details of interpretation. The performance proved an unqualified success. The church was full to overflowing, the soloists and orchestra were superb and the chorus were lifted on to a higher plane by their professional support. The press reports were unusually complimentary. They described the performance as "A triumph and one of those occasions that music-lovers store in their memories." After all the hard work and the frustrations, it was especially gratifying to read that, "This was a magnificent evening of choral singing by three excellent choirs under a conductor who knew how to get them to give of their best." But the comment I treasure most was made by Archie Camden, the distinguished bassoonist in the orchestra who came to me after the performance and said, "Congratulations, you must be feeling very pleased." I was indeed, and very moved that he should have taken the trouble to make the comment.

On a more mundane plane, I was also responsible for much of the practical matters involved in the performances such as engaging the soloists and the orchestra, arranging for their accommodation, preparing the programme notes and the printing and advertising material. As there was no platform readily available we hired a lorry load of unused fish boxes and covered them with carpets for the chorus to sit on. My grandfather, now in his late seventies, helped me to carry them into the church, and on the morning after to place them outside ready for collection. Whilst each box was not too heavy, by the time we had each carried fifty or sixty the arm muscles had begun to feel the strain. It all gave me an insight into the practicalities of concert management and the truth of the old Yorkshire saying "If yer want owt doing, yer mun do it thi' sen." I was also taught a salutary lesson in rehearsal technique by Wilfred Brown, one of Britain's best solo tenors. As we were walking back to the house, after a rehearsal prior to our evening performance, he said, "You really must learn to select what is important and necessary to rehearse and not insist on going through everything. Further, if you carry on working yourself, and everyone else, into such an emotional state at the rehearsal, no one will have any energy left to give of their best in the performance." I took his words to heart and was grateful that he was sufficiently honest and concerned to tell me.

And so I was poised to leave Grimsby and my native country. As with Louth, I was happy in Grimsby and was leading a rewarding musical life, although I had a yearning to return to the daily round of cathedral music and worship. An opportunity had presented itself only a year after I had moved from Louth. Dr Willis Grant, who had been assistant organist at Lincoln when I was a probationer, had been appointed Professor of Music at Bristol University after serving twenty years as Organist at Birmingham Cathedral. He wrote and suggested that I should apply for the post at Birmingham and that he would support me. He also said that although I had only been at Grimsby one year, my contract committed me to no more than three months' notice and likewise, the church could, if it wished, terminate my appointment in the same time span. So I wrote to Canon Markham asking for his support. His reply was terse and unexpected. "No," he wrote, "I would not be willing to support your application. In my opinion, you should prove that you can make a success of your present appointment before seeking another. Furthermore, I think you should remain in Grimsby at least five years." This was strong stuff and I felt there was something in his remarks. However, I did apply and was unsuccessful. Nearly four years later I noticed an advertisement in The Church Times for the post of Organist and Master of the Choristers at St Mary's Cathedral, Edinburgh. I once more asked Canon Markham if he would support me, reminding him that I had now served exactly five years at Grimsby Parish Church. He readily agreed, and I know that he gave me a very generous reference in my application. Some time after I had left Louth, the former Rector, Canon Humphrey Burton, wrote to me saying that he was sending me an unsolicited reference of my early years in Louth. He thought it might be of some help to me in the future. It was an unexpected but very kind gesture.

I was placed on the short list or "leet" (as used in Scotland) and attended for interview on 27 June 1961. The other candidates on the short list for the job were Charles Hutchings, Organist and Choirmaster of St Peter's Church, Wolverhampton and Malcolm Cousins, Organist and Choirmaster of Mansfield Parish Church. Both had long connections with the work of the Royal School of Church Music. It was a coincidence that I had assisted Charles Hutchings at an RSCM three-day residential course for choristers in Boston, Lincolnshire, in the previous January. It proved an eventful course for Charles was taken ill on the first day and was unable to take any further part. I was left to conduct all rehearsals and to accompany the forty-five boys at the services and have oversight of them during the course. The only other helper was The Revd Horace Spence, Clerical Commissioner of the RSCM and chaplain of the course. I did appeal for assistance from the organist of Boston Parish Church (commonly known as "The Stump") but he was either unable or unwilling to accept my "cri de coeur".

To return to the proceedings in Edinburgh, I was required to play a couple of contrasting pieces on the organ and the accompaniment to the Magnificat of Stanford's setting in A major. It must have been at least twelve years since I had played the latter as it was not in the repertoire at either Louth or Grimsby. It was quite a stiff challenge on a strange organ without previous preparation. I was also asked to improvise a coda to a hymn. After lunch, I attended an interview. The panel consisted of the Provost, The Very Revd Dr Reginald Foskett, Forbes Ormiston, Cathedral Lay Representative, Leslie Falconer, Clerk to the Cathedral Board and Sydney Newman, Reid Professor of Music at Edinburgh University. I returned home the following day and on Thursday, 29 June I received a telegram offering me the post which I accepted.

When I told Gordon Slater the news, he looked at me in disbelief and said that he had not been consulted. I told him that I had given his name as one of the referees to which he replied that he thought I might regret accepting the appointment. My apprehension increased when I received a letter from Cyril Dams, now Precentor of Westminster Abbey, who told me there had been problems at St Mary's Cathedral. He suggested that I should go down to London and have a chat with the Abbey Organist, Sir William McKie. I subsequently visited Sir William who asked me if I wished him to tell me about the problems. I told him that I had been very warmly received in Edinburgh and, whatever the past problems, someone had to go and do the job and I felt that I could cope. "Then I shall say no more, he said, and wish you the best of luck."

Slater had told me I should become a cathedral organist by the time I was in my mid-thirties as he had. I have often thought since that many cathedral organists obtain their appointments too soon and too young. There are, unfortunately, very few parish churches nowadays that provide a young church musician with the opportunities to learn his or her trade. A few years in training and recruiting an amateur church choir successfully is an invaluable experience. It is certainly a salutary contrast with the hothouse atmosphere of a university college or cathedral close! It also teaches a concern for, and sympathy with the majority of church worshippers who have to make do with limited musical resources and competence. Nothing is better for keeping high-flying feet firmly on the ground and for correcting potential professional arrogance!

My appointment in Edinburgh was due to start from 2 October 1961 and so there were three months left for commitments in Grimsby, and elsewhere, before moving north. These included a number of organ recitals. I was beginning to obtain invitations from outside Lincolnshire, and two memorable ones were to Doncaster Parish Church to play on the famous Schulze organ and Holy Trinity, Brompton, in London. Magnus Black was the long-serving organist in Doncaster and Robert Munns was at Holy Trinity, Brompton. My pages were turned by a young music student at Brompton. She later married David Gedge, subsequently organist of Brecon Cathedral in Wales. Both Robert Munns and David Gedge, and their respective wives, have been friends of many years' standing. Another distinguished musician and his wife who became good friends were Francis Jackson, Organist and Master of the Choristers at York Minster and his wife, Priscilla. He first stayed with us on the occasion of his visit to Grimsby in February 1961, to give an organ recital at St James' Parish Church. Another development during this interim period was an invitation from Dr Greenhouse Allt, Principal of Trinity College of Music, London, to join their panel of external Diploma examiners. This I accepted, and remained on the panel for a good many years. My successor at Grimsby was Martin How, who later became Headquarters Choirmaster of the Royal School of Church Music at Addington Palace, Croydon. He was an excellent choir-trainer and has written some very effective church music.

We had to find a house in Edinburgh as accommodation owned by the Cathedral was not suitable. Consequently, we arranged to spend a week there hoping we could find the sort of house we needed. Happily we were successful and bought a splendid family house in Leith, about three miles from the Cathedral. It looked over the Links - a former golf course - which made an attractive outlook from the front of the house. As in Grimsby, it was spacious enough for the old folks to have their own sitting room and bedroom. It belonged to a retired solicitor and his wife who clearly wished us to have the house and told us they would accept our offer. In Scotland, the system required the buyer to make an offer for the property, on or above the upset (asking) price. Once the offer had been made and accepted, the contract was binding on both parties. It is interesting to reflect that the price we paid for this large and substantial house with a garden at the rear and small front garden was £2,800 in 1961. Fourteen years later, we sold it for approximately £15,000!

Conveniently, Mabel's sister and family lived in Stirling at the time and we were able to stay with them. We had only once before been to Scotland and that was to spend a short holiday with our relatives in Stirling. After farewell recitals in Grimsby and Louth, and the presentation of gifts after our last Sunday services on 1 October, we prepared for the removal to Edinburgh the following day. Despite all our efforts to keep our cat indoors, whilst the house contents were being loaded, he managed to escape and we were unable to find him when we were ready to leave. We were very unhappy at his loss, but knowing that cats are more attached to places than people, we asked our neighbours to keep a look-out for him in the hope he would return. He was friendly with their cats, so we hoped he would come back. And so we set off in our small Morris car on the almost three hundred miles journey to Edinburgh with grandma (now aged eighty-nine) grandpa, Barbara and our tortoise! We travelled by the A1 to Scotch Corner and turned off on the B6275 to Piercebridge, where the road joins the A68. This is our favourite route to Edinburgh from the East of England in good weather. It is the shortest in mileage and wends its way through some lovely countryside, with spectacular views, especially across Weardale. It crosses the Border at Carter Bar, gently takes you through historic Jedburgh and Lauder and on reaching the top of Soutra Hill, the capital city is revealed. It is a wonderful sight.

Thistle and Cobweb

Photo by John McPherson,

Chapter 6 - Third Appointment - In the Land of the Thistle
(1961 - 1991)

"Don't worry, I shall change all that"

"Auld Reekie", as Edinburgh is popularly known, is one of the world's most beautiful cities, enhanced by its position overlooking the estuary of the River Forth. Its nickname reflects the pall of smoke which formerly hung over the city in the days when houses were heated by fossil fuels. The advent of gas and electricity have eliminated the smoke only to be replaced by the more insidious pollution of motor vehicles. The high ridge of rock upon which the Old Town was built was chosen for defensive reasons as its name implies. The Gaelic words "Din Eidyn" (Dunedin) mean Edwin's Fort and "Burg" is a stronghold or town. The New Zealand city of Dunedin takes its name from the Scottish capital - no doubt from the number of emigrants from Scotland who settled there. The ridge, on which houses and tenements were built descends from the Castle to the Palace of Holyrood and was known from medieval times as The Royal Mile. Many of the tenements were built up to a considerable height and before the advent of more sophisticated waste disposal, the cry of "gardyloo" was frequently heard as the inhabitants emptied chamber pots and unwanted material on to the street below and on to the heads of unwary passers-by! Perhaps "Auld Reekie" incorporated smell as well as smoke! The Royal Mile embraces the medieval Kirk (church) of St. Giles, the 17th-century Parliament Hall and the Scottish Law Courts. Further down, the street runs through the old burgh of Canongate with its post-Reformation parish church.

Major expansion of the city took place during the 18th and 19th-centuries made possible by the draining of the Nor' Loch. This gave access to land to the north and west of the Old Town. Bridges across the drained loch (now containing gardens and the railway line) connected the Old and New Towns.

The first New Town was begun in 1767 on plans drawn up by James Craig and was finished by the end of the century. It developed both north and west during the 19th century forming what has been described as the most extensive example of a Romantic Classical city in the world. The city boundaries now encompass the ancient Port of Leith, the fishing harbour of Granton and Newhaven together with the resort of Portobello and the "Honest Toun" of Musselburgh, all standing on the shores of the Firth of Forth. This serves for a population of approximately half a million inhabitants and it was into this elegant city, with its distinctive stone buildings, that we arrived on 2 October 1961.[4]

Our first week was hectic to say the least. After a journey of some six to seven hours, we established ourselves, as best as we could, in our new home at 20 Claremont Park. Our old folks had endured the journey without problems or complaints. Unloading of our furniture and other belongings began at 6am next morning. On the Wednesday morning I caught the 8.30am train to Glasgow to begin teaching part-time at the Royal Scottish Academy of Music and Drama. Although my appointment at the Cathedral required

---

4.   Ref. The Buildings of Scotland - Edinburgh. (1984).

commitment full-time, the annual salary of £700 was inadequate and regular income from other sources was imperative. Through the good offices of Lord Kilbrandon, a member of the Cathedral Board, I was offered the work at the RSAMD.

The Principal was Dr Henry Havergal OBE who had previously been Director of Music at Fettes College, Edinburgh and then held similar appointments at Haileybury School and Winchester College.

This involved travelling to Glasgow three times a week on Monday, Wednesday and Friday. Monday was a full day of seven hours teaching, whilst the others were half days of three and a half hours. I was part of the Academic Studies Department, teaching harmony, counterpoint and keyboard harmony which most students regarded as a boring but necessary chore! However, I enjoyed the change from the routine of cathedral music and the opportunities to meet and to mix with a wider variety of professional and would-be professional musicians. More of that anon. Meanwhile, back in Edinburgh, Barbara, now eight years old, started as a pupil at Leith Academy Primary School and Mabel retrieved our black cat. Our Grimsby neighbours had telephoned to tell us that the cat had re-appeared and that they had put him in a cat box and put him on the overnight mail train for Edinburgh. We duly went to Waverley Station to collect him, but he could not be found. I had to leave to catch my train for Glasgow, whilst Mabel was left to search for the cat. Eventually he was found amongst the mail bags and other luggage and set up a pathetic "yowling" cry when he heard her voice. We were all delighted and relieved to get him back.

As I still had some nine months of membership of Grimsby Rotary Club left, I was able to attend the Edinburgh Club as a visitor. One of the benefits and privileges of membership is the opportunity to visit clubs throughout the world and which also provides a means of making up attendance requirements. The Edinburgh club was the largest in the British Isles, at this time, with a membership of over two hundred of the most prominent business and professional men in the area. Whilst there is no automatic transfer I was fortunate in having my application for membership accepted. I have valued and enjoyed Rotary and its opportunity for "Service Before Self", as well as for the fellowship of a wide cross-section of the community. The Edinburgh Club in 1961 met in the North British Hotel at the east end of Princes Street, next to Waverley Station, and well placed to attract visitors. Thus I attended on the Thursday lunchtime of our first week in the city. In the pre-lunch gathering, a member greeted me and seeing the name on my visitor's label said, "Oh, you must be the new organist of St Mary's Cathedral." Wondering how he knew, he told me that he was an honorary bass lay clerk in the choir. His name was Jack Langdon and he insisted on paying for my lunch which I believe was something like six shillings (30p). I thought this was very generous and that not all Scots were as mean as was popularly supposed. The following week I attended the club again, sought out Jack and returned the compliment by paying for his lunch. What I did not know was that the price had been increased substantially! Jack Langdon was responsible for obtaining a splendid grand piano for us . His brother, Ralph, had recently died and his widow wished to pass on his Ibach piano, free, to someone who would value and use it. Although we had brought our Broadwood upright with us, there was ample room in our spacious house for the grand as well and I gratefully accepted the offer. Ralph Langdon had been a highly respected,

St. Mary's Cathedral, Spires and West Door

Photo by Peter Backhouse

professional musician in the city, head of music at one of Edinburgh's foremost schools and organist and choirmaster of St John's Church at the West End of Princes Street.

On the Thursday afternoon, 5 October I had meetings successively with the Provost and the Precentor and in the evening met the gentlemen of the choir over drinks at the Berisford Hotel. On Friday 6 October, I met with the full choir for the first time in the Song School at the regular evening rehearsal. I decided to sit in as an observer and let the assistant organist take the rehearsal. I remember thinking that there was a lot of work needed to bring the choir up to a high standard when I took over the direction of the music on Sunday 8 October, after an eventful week. My recollection was confirmed some thirty years later in an article written by Peter Hunt, one of the choristers at the time, for the magazine "Once a Chorister".

He wrote, "I was a relatively new chorister at the time and I remember vividly my first impression of that severe-looking (sic) Englishman, as he sat on the probationers' bench, during the Friday evening practice, to observe. Although he said nothing during the whole evening, his eyes said everything and my worst fears were confirmed the following Monday when he arrived to take his first practice............he told us that he was not impressed by our singing, or our general demeanour, but that we should not worry too much as he intended to change all this...........and he did!"

Many people south of the border have a sketchy idea of the distinctive traditions and history of Scotland, ourselves included, before we settled in Edinburgh. It does not take long to realise that the culture, atmosphere and institutions are not the same as those in England. For example, the legal system, the education system and the national church are all different. My concern was with the church and its music and consequently it was in this area that I found most interest. The Presbyterian Church of Scotland is the established church whilst the Scottish Episcopal Church is a small minority nonconformist sect. It is a part of the Anglican Communion and a sister church of the Church of England, sharing the same liturgical and musical tradition. The church has always recognised the importance and value of music in its worship and the tradition of cathedrals and their choir schools is well documented. In Scotland, it has a somewhat chequered history. It is recorded that at the time of James IV of Scotland (1515-1535), the foundation of the Scottish Chapel Royal consisted of sixteen canons, nine prebendaries and six boys. This was to be a brief flowering, with the Reformation radically altering forms of worship for the next four hundred years. However, the tradition continued fitfully during the next hundred years until James VI (James I of the United Kingdom at the Union of the Crowns in 1603). He was anxious to restore it to its former glory and ordered that choral services should be held in the repaired and refurnished Chapel at the Palace of Holyroodhouse, Edinburgh. His son, Charles I, maintained this establishment. It is recorded that the strength of the Chapel Royal at this time was sixteen men, an organist and six boys, "who all sang their psalms, services and anthems sufficiently at the first sight to the organ." In preparation for the King's Coronation, at Holyrood, Edward Kellie the Director of Music informed him by letter that the boys practised daily and that the men met twice a week, presumably for rehearsal. In the Chapel, the men wore black gowns and the boys wore what were described as "sad-coloured coats". The choir was seated antiphonally as in a Cathedral. Before the sermon, the choir sang a full anthem and afterwards, "an anthem alone in verses with the organ".[5]

Charles created Edinburgh as a city, and the Diocese of Edinburgh was founded in 1633, with St Giles as the Cathedral. This situation remained until 1689 on the accession of King William. This split the church in Scotland, for the Episcopalians remained loyal to the Stuart cause and refused to recognise William as their lawful king. The consequence was that the established church became Presbyterian and the Episcopalians were disowned, disestablished and subject to severe penal laws. St Giles no longer functioned as a cathedral and the ejected members of the congregation worshipped in an old woollen mill in Carubber's Close, near the site of Old St Paul's Church. It was not until the repeal of the penal laws in 1792 that the possibility of building a new cathedral to replace St Giles could be considered, and not until the middle of the 19th century that the dream could become a reality. The unmarried daughters of the Walker family bequeathed their Drumsheugh Estates to fund the building of the cathedral on the Easter Coates site. On the deaths of the two sisters, the Trustees chose Sir George Gilbert Scott to be the architect and on 21 May 1874 the foundation stone was laid. The Nave was opened for services on 25 January 1879, the peal of ten bells, gifted by James Montgomery, the first Dean, were dedicated on 29 October and the building was consecrated on 30 October. The Cathedral choir was augmented for the Consecration service by singers from the Cathedral choirs of York, Durham and Ripon, as well as from churches in the Edinburgh Diocese, making a total of about one hundred and fifty voices.

The twin western spires were not added until 1917 when they were dedicated and known as Barbara and Mary after the Walker sisters. The Cathedral is dedicated to The Blessed Virgin Mary and is considered to be Scott's finest achievement. It is sometimes called "The Lichfield of the North". Its three spires are visible from many parts of Edinburgh and the building dominates the skyline of the west end of the city. It is the second largest church in Scotland (only St Mungo's in Glasgow is larger) and was the first large Cathedral to be built in Britain since the Reformation, apart from St Paul's, London.

From the outset, it was the intention that music and a choir should play a major part in the worship and witness of the Cathedral. According to the first Precentor, The Revd R Mitchell Innes, in his report of 1882, "The Choir may be said to have begun on 24 September 1878, when the first practice was held by Mr Collinson (the first organist) in the Iron Church (a temporary building in the Cathedral grounds)." The choir at that time consisted of twelve boys and six men, the latter chosen by competitive trial. The boys attended daily practice and the men two practices each week. The Voluntary Choir, consisting of volunteer boys and men, commenced on 24 November 1878. Its function was to sing at the Nave Evensong on Sunday evenings. In later years, they sang when the regular choir was on holiday. In January 1880, daily Choral Evensong was introduced. The Precentor wrote, "it soon became apparent that no satisfactory choir organisation, which should include daily choral services, could be maintained without a Choir School." It is fascinating to read the report on the choir work in 1886 by the Precentor. It was published as a small booklet in 1887 with a Prefatory letter from Dr John Dowden, the Bishop. The letter is illuminating.

---

5.   Ref. Music and the Reformation in England (1967), Peter le Huray.

"My Dear Mr Usher,

Your valuable report ought to be of real interest, not only to members of our Church but to all those in Edinburgh who are lovers of the higher kinds of ecclesiastical music. You know the profound importance that, in my judgement, attaches to music in its religious and devotional aspects. You have recorded the leading musical works performed in the Cathedral. Here are represented Palestrina and our own Tallis and Farrant, Blow, Wise and the immortal Purcell...... an honoured place is given to the mighty giants of universal and undying fame, J S Bach, Handel, Haydn, Mozart, Beethoven, Spohr, Mendelssohn. Nor are the best composers of our time forgotten. There are, I am sure, many connoisseurs and lovers of music in Edinburgh who are not aware that every weekday evening, at five o'clock , they may enjoy a really artistic rendering of some interesting specimen of church music; while on Sundays at half-past three, they are sure of a still more stately and dignified performance. Irrespective of its spiritual uses, music like that of the Cathedral, which is the fruit and outcome of painstaking labour and admirable artistic skill, deserves support from every man of culture."[6]

In May 1880, the Choir School was opened for choristers in the Old Manor House of Easter Coates or Old Coates House within the Cathedral precincts, thus standing in direct line with the ancient Scottish "Sang Schules". The house now standing was built during the second decade of the 17th century within the grounds of "Cotes" which was then well outside the city boundary. The first owner was John Byres (1569-1629), a corn merchant with mills in the Dean Village on the banks of the Water of Leith. The pediment on the south-west dormer window has the date 1615 and the initials of John Byres and his first wife, Dame Margaret Barclay. The house and the lands of Coates and Drumsheugh were bought by William Walker in the mid-eighteenth century and remained in the possession of the family until the death of Mary Walker in 1870. The house was extended and restored during the 19th century and it was in this building that the choristers were educated. At the time when the cathedral was being built there were suggestions that the house should be occupied by the first Dean. This idea was not pursued and the Cathedral Organist (Dr T H Collinson) and his family lived there for a while. It is said that they were driven out by the gas fumes! One wonders how the choristers were able to cope with the conditions. The blowing plant for the organ was located at one end of the building and the sound of the motor gave rise to the legend that the ghost of Sir John Byres haunted the building![7]

The first schoolmaster was Mr Albert Edward Howard and his assistant, Mr John Keith. Their annual salaries were £120 and £70 respectively. John Keith eventually became schoolmaster and, in all, served the school for forty-eight years. He had a reputation as a strict disciplinarian. It is said on hearing that a former chorister, aged fifteen, was behaving badly to his widowed mother, he went to the house and meted out immediate corporal punishment to the boy!

The first school register lists the names of the boys admitted on 19 May 1880, with their date of birth, date of leaving, previous school (in some cases) and the occupations of

6.   Ref. Songs and Stones (1996), Philip Crosfield.
7.   Ref. Old Coates House (1989), Ishbel Gray with contributions by Allan Mclean.

St Mary's Cathedral Choir (1961)

Photo by A G Ingram of Edinburgh

their parents. The latter include music teacher, mason, turner, carriage painter, watchmaker, bookmaker, lamplighter, photographer, tailor and saddler. The Precentor describes the choir membership and routine as it was in 1886. There were thirty regular boys (i.e. full-time choristers attending the school), about fourteen voluntary boys and fourteen probationers. This arrangement changed to 36 regular choristers and the voluntary boys were phased out. The choristers were divided into two groups or Divisions - in my time they were named "Collinson" and "Head" after the first two organists of the Cathedral. This system enabled the choir to maintain daily and Sunday choral services throughout the year without a break.

In 1886, two-thirds of the boys sang at each of the Sunday services and the two divisions sang at the daily services in alternate weeks. They all received two to two and a half hours musical work every weekday plus a weekly practice, with the men, on Friday evenings from 7.30pm to 9.20pm and a practice on Thursday evenings with the voluntary choir. Jack Blair, chorister from 1918-1923 and subsequently alto lay clerk for over twenty-five years, recalls that at practices, the boys sang scales for voice training, were taught to count and to beat time under the music desks and were taught the rudiments of music. They were not allowed to sing if they had colds, but were given slates on which to make up tunes instead. In 1886, each boy received free education with books. Boys under twelve years were paid £4 per year and £6 over twelve, the money going to the parents. They had six weeks summer holiday from school, but only three weeks from choir duties. At Christmas, they had a fortnight off school and three or four days from daily services. They also had a rest after Easter and "an occasional holiday for skating etc." The men were expected to arrange their summer holidays so that the choir was sufficiently provided for whilst having two Sundays off duty. There were thirteen men for Sunday services, festivals and other special services. Three men, alto, tenor and bass, sang at the daily Evensong and were paid £60 each per annum. By 1961, when I arrived in Edinburgh, this had been increased to £75! They all attended practices on Wednesday and Friday evenings. The Organist and Master of the Choristers received £170 per annum and the assistant organist £60. There were also a number of apprentices, mostly ex-choristers, whom the organist trained for a musical profession.

In 1961, Choral Evensong was sung every day at 5.15pm by the boys and men except Saturday, when it was sung by trebles only. As before, the two divisions sang alternate weeks. Soon after my arrival, I introduced Choral Mattins on either Tuesday or Thursday at 9.30am sung by trebles. There was a wide range of services on Sunday: 8am Holy Communion (1662 rite) said; 9.15am congregational Sung Eucharist (1929 Scottish Liturgy) without choir; 11am Choral Mattins with full choir of men and both divisions of choristers; 12 noon Choral Eucharist (1929 Scottish Liturgy) with full choir, once a month; 3.30pm Choral Evensong with full Choir; 6.30pm Nave Evensong with one division of choristers and voluntary men. The choristers had an hour's practice before Evensong daily and full practice with the men on Friday evening from 7.30pm to 9pm. There was also a practice before and after Mattins on Sundays.

There were thirty-six choristers, three paid daily lay clerks, nine or ten honorary lay clerks who sang on Sundays and on special occasions. There was also a group of voluntary men as previously mentioned so that there was a corpus of about twenty men to call upon. On attending a service at the Cathedral, some years before my time, the late Dr H K Andrews is reported to have described the choir as "not so much a cathedral choir as a *****y choral society!"

The daily lay clerks were Jack Blair (alto), Harry Brashaw (tenor) and Bob Kidd (bass). They were all former choristers at St Mary's and all gave virtually a lifetime's service to the Cathedral and its choir. They were all sound musicians and good singers who knew the repertoire intimately. Bob Kidd was an organ pupil of Dr Robert Head, organist (1929-1957) and sometime assistant organist. He held the choir together during Dr Head's latter years, and through the apparent difficulties prior to my appointment. He had the distinction of being one of the few people to sing at two Coronation services in Westminster Abbey in 1937 as a treble and in 1953 as a bass. He was a great help to me in my early years at the Cathedral and I valued his support and advice. He told me that he would remain in the choir for three years to help me settle in and then he wanted to run his own choir. He kept his word and was appointed organist and choirmaster of St John's Church, Princes Street, where he built up and maintained a good choral tradition for many years.

Before 1961, the choir repertoire had mainly been Victorian and Edwardian with also an unusual amount of Tudor music. The latter was due to the enthusiasm for this period of Colin Dunlop, Provost of the Cathedral (1940-1944). It is not surprising that with such a large choir, extended anthems and settings by composers such as Sterndale-Bennett, G J Bennett, Henry Smart, Charles McPherson, Goss, Samuel and S S Wesley, Parry, Stainer, Stanford, Steggall, Walmisley and Wood figured regularly on the music list. I have to confess that I had never seen or heard some of them. One of the past favourites had been the Magnificat and Nunc Dimittis in A for double choir by G J Bennett of Lincoln. It had a long organ introduction which sounded more like a curtain-raiser for a Gilbert and Sullivan light opera! My preferences at this time were for music by earlier composers up to and including the Restoration period and contemporary 20th-century composers. I had little liking for 18th and 19th century church music by British composers.

It was an intolerant and arrogant attitude but I fancy it was not uncommon amongst my contemporaries. The same attitude applied to organ music. During my student days, I learnt the six Trio Sonatas by J S Bach concurrently with the six Sonatas by Mendelssohn. It was over twenty years later before I rediscovered and played the Mendelssohn again, whilst I regularly played the Bach Sonatas throughout my career.

During my thirty years in office at St Mary's, the liturgical repertoire was greatly expanded. I was made aware of some of the surviving music by pre-Reformation Scottish composers, such as Robert Johnson, David Peebles and John Black, by their publication in *The Music of Scotland* volume of *Musica Britannica*. The research for this volume had been done by Dr Kenneth Elliott, Lecturer in the Music Department of the University of Glasgow who also edited the volume. Offprints of some of the motets were available and the pieces incorporated into the services. Classical masses by Haydn, Mozart and Schubert were introduced, often accompanied by orchestra. After a service in which the choir sang the Mass in G by Schubert, the then Bishop, Alastair Haggart, told me that he felt reluctantly seduced by the loveliness of the music against his better judgement! Where previously, music by continental composers had been sung in English translations, I made it a normal

71

practice to perform the settings and anthems in the original language as written by the composers.

A good deal of music by mainstream 20th-century composers was also introduced. These included Benjamin Britten, Lennox Berkeley, Michael Berkeley, Herbert Howells, Gustav Holst, Francis Jackson, John Joubert, Kenneth Leighton, William Mathias, Elizabeth Poston, Frederick Rimmer, Gordon Slater, William Walton, R Vaughan Williams as well as the Scottish composers Cedric Thorpe Davie and Robin Orr. Continental composers of the 20th century such as Maurice Duruflé, Zoltan Kodaly, Jean Langlais and Matyas Seiber were also represented. A number of works were commissioned by the Cathedral or composed for the choir and its organist. These included composers based in Scotland such as David Dorward (BBC Producer), Geoffrey King, John McLeod, Peter Naylor and Frank Spedding (both on the Staff of RSAMD) and Kenneth Leighton, Professor of Music, University of Edinburgh.

There had been a long tradition of performances of extra-liturgical music. In 1887 a very large congregation assembled for Gounod's *Redemption* with orchestra, organ and two choirs. In 1889, Dr Collinson formed an amateur orchestra although there is little evidence that it took part in any concerts. Bach's *St Matthew Passion* was performed in Holy Week, 1897; Mendelssohn's *Elijah* in May 1899; Brahms' *Requiem* in 1903 and Handel's *Messiah* in 1907.

When I took over in 1961, I found a long-established tradition of Bach's *St Matthew Passion* on Passion Sunday and of Brahms' *Requiem* on Remembrance Sunday. These were sung by the Cathedral choir in place of Choral Evensong with the solo parts taken by members of the choir. A shortened version of *St Matthew Passion* in English was used, in the edition prepared for St Paul's Cathedral, London, and accompanied on the organ. Brahms' *Requiem* was also sung in English, usually accompanied by organ and timpani but sometimes with the addition of strings. At this time, the string players used were members of the Edinburgh Chamber Orchestra conducted by Hans Gál who rehearsed them prior to the performance. I carried on this tradition but only used the Chamber Orchestra once. They were well drilled but most of the players had seen better days and I found their intonation unreliable. After a rehearsal with the orchestra, Hans complimented me on my conducting. Coming from such a distinguished musician, his remarks were greatly appreciated and treasured. He was born in 1890 and became a Lecturer at the University of Vienna. To quote from the fourth edition of Grove's Dictionary of Music, "As a composer, Gál may be considered one of the most distinguished representatives of the Vienna School." His career may have burgeoned further but for the rise of Fascism under Hitler and Hans Gál fled to Britain just before the onset of the second world war. He settled in Edinburgh where he obtained an appointment at the University. He was a wonderful musician and composer and although he was turned seventy when I got to know him, he lived for over another twenty-five years and continued active music-making. We became good friends and among many happy memories of him are a performance of his Concertino for Organ and Strings in the University Chaplaincy Centre, which he conducted and for which I played the solo part. The other was the party which was held to celebrate the sixty years of marriage between him and his wife, Hanna. There were over a hundred guests at the party and it was a delight to hear a trio played by Hans at the piano, his daughter Eva playing violin and his eight year old grandson on the 'cello. Age difference was irrelevant!

Eventually, I felt the need to vary the Remembrance Sunday programmes and introduced a performance of Fauré's *Requiem* in alternate years. Having conducted choral works in Louth and Grimsby with orchestra and professional soloists, I decided I wanted to do similar performances in Edinburgh. Consequently, I formed a chamber choir of good singers who provided the chorus, with or without the Cathedral choir and established annual performances of Handel's *Messiah* or Bach's *Christmas Oratorio* at the appropriate season, and in alternate years, Bach's *St John Passion* and *St Matthew Passion* on Good Friday evening. The Passions were performed in their entirety and in German. A translation was provided for the congregation/audience. These attracted very large numbers of people. At this time it was customary for the performers and the audience to leave in silence and a note requesting them to do so was included in the programme. On one occasion a row of American visitors began to applaud and on realising that no one else was doing so, stopped. One of them turned round to the people in the row behind, which included my wife, and she told him that it was not usual for people to applaud. He replied, "Gee lady, I reckon that if the good Lord was down here, he would want to applaud!" Customs have changed over the years and spontaneous applause breaks out at the end of all performances nowadays. I also introduced extra-liturgical performances of passion settings by Heinrich Schütz and the liturgical setting of the Gospel by Victoria on Palm Sunday.

The first three months in Edinburgh were something of a baptism of fire, as a torrent of special events crowded one after another in addition to the daily routine of a new job. As Cathedral Organist, I also held the appointment as Lecturer in Music at Edinburgh Theological College. This was a euphemistic title as I was not required to give any lectures. My duties were to take the weekly choir practice and teach the ordinands to sing the priest's part in the services. The College (Coates Hall) was residential and stood in its own grounds at the convergence of the two Crescents facing the west front of the Cathedral. The view of the Cathedral from the upper floors of the College across the Crescent garden is very attractive. My first meeting with the ordinands took place on the Saturday morning of my first week in office. The music for the College services was chosen by the staff and students, and at this time included a good deal of plainsong. I greatly enjoyed this link with the staff and future clergy. It gave me the opportunity of getting to know them as individuals and hopefully to impress upon them the importance and value of music in worship. It was also an opportunity to persuade them that professional church musicians could and should be fellow workers in proclaiming the Gospel. There was a tradition that at the end of an ordinand's course he should be tested in his ability to sing the priest's part in the various services. If successful, a certificate of competence was awarded, signed by the Principal and the Lecturer in Music. Inevitably, some were incapable of coping with the requirements at all, and had to be told, whilst others seemed capable at the time and were granted the certificate. Many years later, some of these decisions came home to roost! I was asked to give the opening recital on the restored organ in Christ Church, Lochgilphead, Argyll. After the recital, the Rector, The Revd Roy Flatt addressed the congregation to thank me and said that he had always wanted to get his own back and "give me the bird" for telling him at Theological College that he was a failure as a singer.

RSCM Course, Edinburgh (1964)

Photo by A G Ingram of Edinburgh

74

He then presented me with a box containing a beautifully crafted porcelain oyster catcher and on two further occasions he gave me similar presents.

As so often happens people from the past turn up unexpectedly. At the reception, after the first recital in Lochgilphead, a member of the audience walked up to me, carrying a large parcel under his arm. It was an enlarged framed photograph of Lincoln School First Eleven soccer team in which I featured together with George Campbell, a contemporary at school. George was farming in the area at Tarbert, unable to get to the recital and had asked a friend to show me the photograph and to pass on his good wishes. The bearer of the message was the son of Canon Caulton, Vicar of Burton, near Lincoln, where I had played the village organ for a short period. He was also a former pupil of Lincoln School. I had not seen nor heard of either since schooldays. Alas, the next time I visited Lochgilphead, I was told that George Campbell had died. In 1998, I attended the Federation of Cathedral Old Choristers' Associations' Festival at Chester and met the Bishop, The Rt Revd Peter Forster, who greeted me with the words, " I was one of your failures at Theological College." He did not seem in any way resentful and I felt glad that I had always tried to be polite to the ordinands! Many of them achieved eminent positions in the Church. Of those who were students during my time in office, at least four have subsequently become Bishops, George Pattison is currently Dean of King's College, Cambridge and Graham Forbes was appointed Provost of St Mary's Cathedral, Edinburgh, in 1990, a year before I retired.

The Principal of the College in 1961 was Richard Knyvet Wimbush. He also held the title of Pantonian Professor of Divinity. This was derived from a legacy given in 1810 by Miss Kathrein Panton of Fraserburgh to erect and endow "A Seminary of Learning or Theological Institute for the education of young men desirous to serve in the sacred ministry of the Scottish Episcopal Communion." She also provided an additional endowment to pay the salary of the Professor. At the end of 1962, Richard Wimbush was elected Bishop of Argyll and the Isles and was consecrated in St Mary's Cathedral, Edinburgh, in January 1963. Only just over a year earlier, on 20 December 1961, Kenneth Carey was consecrated and enthroned in the Cathedral as Bishop of Edinburgh, and I was consequently responsible for the music of two major events soon after taking up the new appointment. Kenneth Carey succeeded Kenneth Warner who had retired earlier in 1961. Warner had been Archdeacon of Lincoln and was one of a number of connections between the Lincoln and Edinburgh Dioceses. Colin Dunlop, Provost (1940-1944) subsequently became Dean of Lincoln and Reginald Woodward, a former Lincoln Cathedral chorister was Precentor of St Mary's and head teacher of the Choir School from 1948 to 1953. Soon after Kenneth Carey's arrival he told me that he did not have much time for cathedrals and cathedral music but he did recognise that there were some people who did!

Kenneth Woollcombe succeeded Richard Wimbush as Principal in 1963. He had been trained for the ministry at Westcott House, Cambridge during Kenneth Carey's period as Principal of the College. He was ordained in Lincoln Cathedral and served two years as a curate at Grimsby Parish Church, thus providing yet another link between Edinburgh and Lincoln Dioceses. He had a lively and extrovert personality and made many changes both to the training of the ordinands and to the accommodation at Coates Hall. In 1969, a new house was built for the Principal in the College grounds and an extension at the rear of the College buildings was made for a new dining hall. His appointment coincided with the beginnings of a period of considerable ferment and turmoil within the universal church. These included the replacement of Latin for the vernacular in the Roman Catholic Church, liturgical revision in the Anglican Church, the introduction of free-standing altars and westward position of celebrating the Eucharist, greater congregational participation in the services, the beginning of the charismatic movement and the more general replacement of Mattins by the Eucharist as the main Sunday service.

There were inevitably musical repercussions which permeated the choral and congregational repertoire. Responsorial psalms devised by Father Gelineau, a French Roman Catholic priest, Music from Taizé, simple congregational settings for the new words of the Anglican Liturgy, hymn tunes in a more secular and light musical idiom by composers such a Geoffrey Beaumont and Patrick Appleford, were all introduced into services up and down the country.

In 1971, Kenneth Woollcombe was appointed Bishop of Oxford and was succeeded as Principal of Coates Hall by Alastair Haggart. He came from the strict Calvinist tradition of the Free Church of Scotland but seemed to relish the liturgy and music of the Anglican Church. I first met him in Dundee where he was Provost of St Paul's Cathedral. He asked me to be his musical adviser for the appointment of a new organist and choirmaster. He had a "pawky" sense of humour and was a remarkably versatile man. He was a former student of Coates Hall and knew the building intimately. He seemed to be equally at ease with mending fuses or sorting out the problems of the College's plumbing as with preparing and delivering erudite sermons. Among the changes during his term of office was the admission of a number of married students to the College and the introduction and training of non-stipendiary clergy. Another development was the link with the University of Edinburgh Department of Theology at New College. In 1975, Haggart was elected Bishop of Edinburgh and in 1977 he became Primus of the Episcopal Church in Scotland.

Frank Weston followed in 1976, together with his wife "Poppy" and family. Their son Simon had a good treble voice and sang in the Cathedral choir for a couple of years until voice-change caused him to leave. His sister, Victoria, was a gifted 'cellist. More changes took place during Weston's six years as Principal. As well as ordinands for the Congregational Church who had moved into the College during Alastair Haggart's time, a number of lodgers (non-theological students) resided in the building. A non-resident Deaconess became the first woman to train full-time for the Ministry (non-stipendiary) at the College. Alternative accommodation for married students was provided outwith the College. Frank Weston left in 1982 to take up the appointment of Archdeacon of Oxford and subsequently became Bishop of Knaresborough.

The Revd John Armson served as Principal for seven years from 1982 to 1989, before leaving to take up an appointment as a Residentiary Canon of Rochester Cathedral. During his time in charge of the College, the first woman member of staff was introduced in 1983 and in 1985 the first woman ordination candidate took up residence in Coates Hall. In 1986, the first women were ordained as Deacons. The future of the College and the training of ordinands had been an increasing issue of concern and matters came to a head during the period of Kenneth Mason's term as Principal from 1989. A decision was taken to rename the Theological College as Theological Institute and to move from Coates

Hall to alternative accommodation at St Colm's College, which was run by The Church of Scotland. In 1994, Coates Hall and its grounds were sold to St Mary's Music School. This left Coates House in the Cathedral Precincts empty until, by a strange reversal of roles, the Theological Institute took it over in 1998.[8]

The opportunities for teaching the students to sing the priest's parts in the services or of passing on any information concerning the place of music in worship gradually passed out of my hands altogether. When I retired from my position as Organist and Master of the Choristers in 1991 my successor was not given any place on the staff of the Institute. In my opinion, this was a loss to all concerned.

Before leaving the subject of the Theological College, two minor events involving the students deserve mention. The first was participation in a series of programmes on the subject of European Revolutions for German television. I was asked to record a metrical psalm purportedly sung by Cromwell's soldiers as they marched into battle at Naseby against the Royalist Army, and decided that the corporate voices of the ordinands would produce the required effect! The psalm was recorded in the open air on the College tennis court. For the same programme, the choristers recorded a two-part motet by Richard Deering (c.1572-1650) in the Resurrection Chapel of the Cathedral, which I accompanied on the chamber organ. Deering, a Catholic who spent much of his life on the Continent, was a favourite composer of Cromwell. It is interesting that despite his antipathy to the formal services and music of the Church of England, Cromwell nevertheless employed singers from disbanded cathedral choirs to sing Latin church music during and after meals in his private residence.

The second event involving the theological students was prompted by a request from a Mr Andrew Rose for me to record music for a series of church services on cassette. He owned a large property at Port Sonachan on the shores of Loch Awe, near Dalmally in Argyllshire, which had been converted into holiday flats. It is overlooked by the imposing mountain, Ben Cruachan, and the scenery of the whole area is consummately beautiful. The small Episcopalian church was only open during holiday periods and had no organist. To give a lead to the congregation, I used the students as a choir in the responses, psalms, canticles and hymns for Mattins and Evensong. In order to make the effect more realistic and suitable, we recorded the music in the Cathedral Song School and I accompanied the singers on the small two-manual and pedal organ and also recorded some organ pieces as voluntaries before and after the services. Andrew installed good recording equipment in the church in Argyll and he was delighted with the result. In lieu of payment, he invited me and Mabel to a week's free holiday at Sonachan House. We elected to go after Easter and were fortunate in having good weather and saw the area at its best. Andrew had a large collection of recordings and superb equipment for playing them. He invited us for an evening meal in his house and, after dining and wining sumptuously, we sat in his drawing room gazing at the sunset over Loch Awe to the accompaniment of Bruckner's Seventh Symphony. It was an experience of sheer magic and bliss that comes but rarely. During the week, I found a spare half hour or so to write a free organ accompaniment to the tune *Leoni* for the hymn *The God of Abraham Praise*. It was a contribution to a

8. Ref. A Seminary of Learning (1994), Edward Luscombe.

collection of *Accompaniments for Unison Hymn Singing* compiled by Gerald Knight and published by the RSCM. The other contributors were all well-known figures in the world of church music in this country.

Chapter 7 - Some Personalities

"Mostly Clergy"

Cathedrals have always attracted outstanding clergy and St Mary's is no exception. Colin Dunlop (1940-1944), has been mentioned previously in another context. He was a renowned liturgical scholar and became Bishop of Jarrow before his appointment as Dean of Lincoln. His successor in Edinburgh was Ivor Ramsay (1944 - 1949) who left to become Dean of King's College, Cambridge. At the consecration of the Cathedral in 1879 there were six stipendiary clergy headed by the Dean, James Montgomery, but this arrangement did not last for long. In the early 1900s, I imagine for financial reasons, the number of clergy was reduced and the Cathedral was administered by a Provost with the assistance of a Vice-Provost, Precentor and Chaplain. This was the position when I took up my appointment in 1961. The Very Revd Dr Reginald Foskett (1957-1967) was Provost at the time. He was small in stature and rather shy and retiring but very supportive. Indeed, all the clergy whom I was privileged to work with in Edinburgh gave wholehearted support and encouragement to the work of the Choir and its music, for which I was immensely grateful. Dr Foskett's wife, Daphne, was a tall and well built lady and on first meeting, somewhat formidable but thawed on longer acquaintance. She was an expert of international reputation on miniature paintings.

The Vice-Provost, Samuel Getty (1954-1965) was a "character" with a couthy sense of humour. He had a powerful voice and distinctive Scottish vowels. I can still recall his recitation of the Creed and the phrase, "I believe in the Hooly Ghoost, the Hooly Catholic Church" resounding round the building. On one occasion, the choir were lined up in the Choir Aisle ready to enter for a wedding service. Sam turned to me and said, "You know, the bridegroom is a former chorister and the young blighter has gone and put her (the bride) in the bag!" The Revd J E F Styles was the Precentor and assistant master in the Choir School. He was an able singer but had clear favourites among the choristers and could be unfairly hard on the others. Patrick Rodger succeeded Sam Getty as Vice-Provost in 1965 and then became Provost (1967-1970) when Reginald Foskett was appointed Bishop of Penrith. Pat Rodger was Scottish by birth and served a curacy at St John's Church, Princes Street, Edinburgh. He returned to Edinburgh from Geneva where he had been serving on the administrative staff of the World Council of Churches. He had trained for the ministry at Westcott House, Cambridge, when Kenneth Carey was Principal. Fundamental changes in the pattern of the Cathedral services took place during his time as Provost. The number of services was drastically reduced to 8am, said Communion, 10.30am, Choral Eucharist, 3.30pm, Choral Evensong and the 6.30pm, Nave Evensong replaced by experimental non-liturgical services. Thus Choral Mattins was abandoned and I greatly regretted the loss of opportunity to perform the splendid corpus of settings of the Te Deum, Benedictus Dominus, Jubilate Deo and the morning psalms. However, the advantages and benefits of one main Sunday morning service have resulted in a steady increase in the number of people regularly attending the Cathedral and a substantial increase in income. Lacking large endowments, the Cathedral is heavily dependent upon the financial support of those who come to the services and other events, and on this ground alone, the changes have been vindicated. Perhaps more importantly the Cathedral attracts and ministers to an ever larger congregation of very diverse age groups including many families and children. Happily, this is done without any diminution of the quality or quantity of music and the regular daily choral services maintain the distinctive features and traditions of cathedral worship.

Philip Crosfield joined the Cathedral clergy as Vice-Provost in 1968 and when Pat Rodger left to become Bishop of Manchester in 1970, succeeded him as Provost and served for twenty years until 1990. Philip Crosfield came to St Mary's from Gordonstoun School on the Moray Firth Coast of Scotland where he was Chaplain. He had the distinction of preparing HRH Charles, Prince of Wales for confirmation at the school. Crosfield was a man of great imagination, enthusiasm and vision and it was fortunate that he remained at the Cathedral long enough to initiate some far-reaching ventures that have ensured its future witness. More of that anon.

Seated One Day at the Organ   Cartoon by Clare Beber

Pat Rodger kindly invited me to take part in his Consecration at York Minster and in the Service of Installation at Manchester Cathedral. At both services I played organ voluntaries, but what I found most memorable was to walk side by side with Francis Jackson, in York, during the Litany Procession. Pat was subsequently translated to the See of Oxford and on reaching retirement age returned to Edinburgh where he is now a highly respected and valued Assistant Bishop in the Diocese.

Norman Wickham, David Jowitt, Geoffrey Connor and Ian Paton have been a worthy succession of Vice-Provosts following Philip Crosfield. Norman Wickham was particularly musical and had a euphonious singing voice as well as an admirably clear speaking voice. Geoffrey Connor had been Chaplain at St Chad's College, Durham University, when Philip Crosfield's son, Paul was a student there, which may have been a factor in his move to Edinburgh. Ian Paton had been Chaplain to Pat Rodger in Oxford and is now Rector of Old St Paul's Church, Edinburgh.

There have been but seven organists of St. Mary's Cathedral since it was built. Dr Thomas H Collinson (1878-1928) was appointed at the age of twenty-one after serving his apprenticeship under Dr Philip Armes at Durham Cathedral. His son, Francis, also a distinguished musician and conductor, published his father's diary recording his training as an articled pupil. It is a fascinating account of the time honoured preparation for a career in cathedral music. It is believed that Philip Armes intended to recommend Collinson for the post of organist at St Paul's Cathedral, London, but fortunately for St Mary's the Edinburgh appointment came first. Dr Robert Head (1929-1957) had been a chorister at St Paul's Cathedral. He was both feared and revered by his choristers and lay clerks and there are many stories told of his sometimes unpredictable and eccentric behaviour. He was highly regarded as both an Organist and Choirmaster but had a love-hate relationship with the clergy.

In 1897, the Organ console was re-sited in line with the choir stalls at the High Altar end on Cantoris side, giving a clear view of Decani choristers and lay clerks and also clergy, seated on that side. Apparently, on one occasion, Head placed piles of books on the console so that he was unable to see or to be seen. A friend sitting beside him during the service asked him why he had done this. Bending round the side of the console, he whispered, "See that parson over there? I can't stand the sight of him!"

At a Diocesan Choirs' Festival, a small boy from a visiting choir standing just in front of Dr Head came in at the wrong moment. Head stopped the rehearsal and told the boy that when he wanted a solo from him he would ask for it. The boy vowed never to darken the doors of the Cathedral again but did, when many years later he was appointed Vice-Provost and then Provost. Fortunately, by that time Robert Head was no longer the Cathedral Organist!

Eric Parsons (1957-1961) moved to Edinburgh from York where he had been assistant organist to Dr Francis Jackson. I do not know why his tenure was so short but was told that after his resignation, he took up a career in school music. Timothy Byram-Wigfield succeeded me in August 1991. He had been a chorister at King's College, Cambridge, Organ Scholar at Christ Church Cathedral, Oxford and Assistant Organist at Winchester Cathedral. In common with many other cathedral organists at the present time, he held the title of Master of the Music. As far as I am aware, there are no great changes in role or duties but happily their salary and conditions are better! Tim is a very talented musician and it was great to see and hear such a high standard of music and performance being consistently maintained. In August 1999, he left to take up the appointment of Director of College Music, Jesus College, Cambridge, and was succeeded by Matthew Owens from Manchester Cathedral.

Before my time at St Mary's the assistant organists had often been former choristers at the Cathedral or local pupils of the Organist. Kenneth Mackintosh was a Cambridge graduate and came from outwith Scotland. He held the fort during the interregnum before my arrival, and remained assistant for six months until he was appointed organist at St Mary's Cathedral in Glasgow. I decided to advertise the post in the national church press and was fortunate in attracting Donald Cullington to Edinburgh. He had been teaching Classics at Watford Grammar School in north London and wished to pursue a career in church music. There was very little money for the assistant and no other work immediately available to supplement his income. However, the Cathedral did have accommodation and I approached the City Director of Education for employment for him in local authority schools. As a result, Donald was given some music teaching in both primary and secondary schools. This solved his immediate financial problems but he found great difficulty in coping with the secondary pupils and after about three months, he told me he felt he would have to give up and leave. I persuaded him to stick it out in the belief that better opportunities would arise. This proved correct, and it was not long before he obtained a job as an assistant music master at Edinburgh Academy, one of the leading independent schools in the city. He was an extremely able and hard-working man and during his relatively short time in Edinburgh, he obtained the Degree of B Mus and the Diplomas of FRCO and LRAM. Eventually, he also gained a musical doctorate. He even found time to marry, and after a variety of appointments in England, Northern Ireland and New Zealand, he and his wife, Stella (a medical GP), settled in Carrickfergus, near Belfast, where Donald became Head of Music at the University of Ulster. Some years after leaving Edinburgh, he gave me a copy of *the Keyboard Music of Thomas Weelkes* (c 1572-1623) and wrote in the inside cover, "From Donald, with happy memories of the excellent start you gave me." The gift and comment were greatly appreciated.

Two young organ pupils at this time became competent to give valuable assistance. James Crowe was and still is, an enthusiastic supporter of church music and a staunch churchman. He pursued a successful career in the railway industry for which he received the MBE and after early retirement became Administrator of The Conference Centre at Hengrave Hall, in Suffolk. He and his family live in Ipswich and for the past few years he has arranged for me to give recitals in the Parish Church of St Mary-le-Tower, and other fine churches in the county of Suffolk.

George Hay was an academic high-flyer and eventually graduated with a BSc Degree. He also obtained a number of musical qualifications and could have pursued a professional career in music but chose to go into computer technology. He joined the international firm of IBM and spent many years in Stockholm and Bangkok. I lost contact with him until four or five years ago when he turned up unexpectedly at a recital I gave in Winchester Cathedral. He had left IBM and set up as an independent consultant at Basingstoke where he was organist and choirmaster at the parish church. I received a charming letter from him after the recital in which he said he found himself instinctively recalling what I would say and do at choir practices, and following the same line. Considering his tendency as a young man to go his own way, his letter was a gratifying volte-face!

Richard Galloway was assistant organist for only a short period as he obtained a school appointment in Dunfermline and could not fit in Cathedral duties as well. He had been an organ pupil whilst he was studying for a BMus degree at Edinburgh University and gained a prize in the FRCO Diploma paperwork examinations. He was a very able musician and had a highly successful career in music education becoming a County Music Adviser. He was also Organist and Choirmaster at the historic Church of The Holy Rude in Stirling.

After Richard Galloway's all too short spell, the connection with Edinburgh Academy was resumed with the appointment of Keith Griffiths, Assistant Music Master at the school. It was made clear to me by the Headmaster that Keith's school duties must have priority, but happily few problems ever arose. Keith was an excellent assistant and a very congenial colleague. I was sorry to lose him when he was appointed Head of Music at Ipswich School. He subsequently became Director of Music at Merchant Taylor's School in London and an Associated Board Examiner. He was succeeded by Richard Walker at Edinburgh Academy, and it was fortunate that he too agreed to accept the assistant's job at the Cathedral. Richard was also a fine musician with a lively, extrovert personality. His wife, Gay, was a professional musician with a University Degree and a good singer. They were both a great asset to the musical life of the Cathedral, although I thought that Gay felt a certain amount of frustration at not being able to take part in the statutory choral services. Richard eventually moved to another Edinburgh independent school as Head of Music at Stewart's Melville and this created a potentially tricky problem of relationships. The Head of Department at Edinburgh Academy was Brian Head, a former choral scholar at King's College, Cambridge, and thus Richard's superior. By a strange quirk of fate, Brian was appointed Headmaster of Stewart's Melville Junior School but Richard had overall responsibility for the music in both the Senior and the Junior School! As far as I know, friction between them was avoided. When Richard was offered the post of organist at St John's Church in Princes Street, he decided that it would give him greater scope and he accepted. It also provided the opportunity for Gay to sing regularly in the mixed choir at St John's. It was not surprising that Richard should move further afield still. After a spell as Director of Music at The Leys School in Cambridge, he is now occupying a similar position at Harrow.

This time I decided to advertise nationally as there was some teaching work available in the newly re-organised Choir School. From an encouraging field of candidates, John Taylor was appointed and joined us in the summer of 1972. He was a cheerful and efficient assistant for five years until he moved to Loughborough as Organist and Choirmaster of the Parish Church and Head of Music at a school in the town. Meanwhile, in 1973, Peter Backhouse, a former chorister at York Minster, came to Edinburgh to read Music at the University. He joined the Cathedral choir as a bass lay clerk, singing for four years until he graduated with B Mus (Hons). He was also a very talented organist and won the coveted Tovey Memorial Prize for his playing. On completion of his degree in 1977, he was planning to return to York to take a course in teacher training. Luckily, I was able to persuade him to remain in Edinburgh and arranged for him to do his teacher training at Moray House College in the city. Peter was duly appointed Assistant Organist in 1977 and remained in the post until the end of 1997. He was not only a fine player but also a superb service accompanist who prepared his work meticulously. As an added bonus, he was a loyal and conscientious colleague and he and his wife, Anne (also an Edinburgh music graduate) became our good friends. He related well to both choristers and lay clerks and was known as "Fingers" Backhouse to the latter, no doubt because of his unusually long digits. It was a pity that the increasing demands of his work on the music staff of Edinburgh Academy caused him to retire as Assistant Organist after twenty years' outstanding service to the Cathedral. His two successors were appointed after my retirement in 1991. Stuart Nicholson was a temporary replacement for nine months until Simon Nieminski took up the post in the autumn of 1998.

Chapter 8 - The Song School and Cathedral Instruments

"O all ye works of the Lord"

Just as the first Dean and Chapter recognised the need for a Choir School they also recognised the necessity of providing a suitable rehearsal room for the choir. Consequently the Song School was built in the Cathedral precincts. It was designed by John Oldrid Scott (son of Sir Gilbert Scott, Architect of the Cathedral) and completed and opened in November 1885. It stands parallel to the Cathedral, with the manor house of Easter Coates in between them. It is an unpretentious stone building harmonising in style with Coates House and cost £1,895 7s.6d. The exterior has crow-stepped gables, lancet windows and a slated flèche, whilst the simple open interior has a blue-painted wooden vaulted roof, decorated with gold motifs. It is unique among such buildings as the walls are covered by paintings executed by the artist Phoebe Anne Traquair between 1888 and 1892. Now a highly regarded artist of the period she carried out the work without fee, asking only for the cost of scaffolding and materials amounting to £10 0s. 0d. The subject of the murals is the morning canticle, Benedicite omnia opera (O all ye works of the Lord) illustrating all created things. The panels also portray many notable Victorians such as Tennyson, Browning, Dante Gabriel Rossetti, Holman Hunt, Stanley (the African explorer), General Gordon and Cardinal Newman. There are also portraits of the first clergy, choir and organist on the East Walls. They are obviously good likenesses for as late as 1974, Fred Belford, a chorister in 1889, could identify each individual boy![9]

When I arrived in Edinburgh in 1961, the paintwork had become dingy and was crumbling in places. The windows were not airtight and the building quickly became very dusty. The lighting was inadequate and overhead heaters plus storage heaters round the room were unsightly. Wooden cupboards had been installed to house the choir music library and the floor space was filled with heavy wooden bench seats. Whilst the murals, and indeed the whole building, were in need of restoration it was not until the researches by Dr Elizabeth Cumming highlighted the importance of the paintings that funding was sought to tackle the project.

Happily with generous support from Historic Scotland and other bodies and individuals, the restoration was begun in 1996. It was completed in 1998 and HRH The Princess Royal officially re-opened the building. It now looks splendid and the vivid colours of Phoebe Traquair's murals make a stunning impression. New heating and lighting, appropriate for the period of the building, have been installed and the choir music library transferred to new cupboards in the adjoining passage.

The Cathedral possesses three organs, two grand pianos, a harpsichord and three hand-tuned timpani. The Great Organ stands in the north transept of the Cathedral and was built in 1879 by "Father" Henry Willis, the leading British organ builder in the second half of the 19th century. The instrument is regarded as one of the finest of its kind and is especially appropriate for the choral tradition maintained by the Cathedral. The original

9.   Ref. Some Notes on the Mural Paintings in the Song School of St Mary's Cathedral (1995), Margaret G Campbell.

specification was drawn up by Sir Herbert Oakeley, Reid Professor of Music in the University of Edinburgh (1865-1891). It cost £2,500. The case was designed by John Oldrid Scott and made by Farmer & Brindley of London at a further cost of £970. It was the first of "Father" Willis's organs to have a sixteen foot Contra Oboe stop. Restoration work and additions have been undertaken periodically, mainly by the firm of Harrison & Harrison of Durham. In 1931, the reeds were revoiced, the Choir division enclosed, new electro-pneumatic action provided and a detached draw-stop console placed to the east of the north choir stalls. The present specification of the instrument (1999) is given below, and additions to the original stops indicated by the dates of their inclusion.

GREAT ORGAN

Double Geigen	16
Large Open Diapason	8
Small Open Diapason	8
Stopped Diapason	8
Claribel Flute	8
Octave	4
Principal	4 (1979)
Harmonic Flute	4
Octave Quint	2 2/3
Super Octave	2
Spitzflute	2 (1979)
Sesquialtera II	(1979)
Mixture V	
Double Trumpet	16*
Trumpet	8*
Clarion	4*

(*enclosed in Solo box in 1959, when the Double Trumpet was added)

SWELL ORGAN

Open Diapason	8
Lieblich Gedeckt	8
Salicional	8
Vox Angelica	8
Principal	4
Lieblich Flute	4
Fifteenth	2
Mixture III	
Contra Oboe	16
Oboe	8
Vox Humana	8
Tremulant	

Double Trumpet	16 (1931)
Trumpet	8
Clarion	4
Octave	

SOLO ORGAN (ENCLOSED)

Viole d'Orchestre	8
Viole Celeste	8 (1995)
Harmonic Flute	8
Concert Flute	4
Concert Piccolo	2
Corno di Bassetto	16 and 8
Orchestral Hautboy	8
Tremulant	
Tuba	8
Octave	
Sub Octave	
Unison Off	

CHOIR ORGAN (ENCLOSED)

Open Diapason	8
Gamba	8
Claribel Flute	8
Gemshorn	4
Flauto Traverso	4
Nazard	22/3 (1959)
Fifteenth	2
Tierce I	3/5 (1959)
Octavin I	(1959)

PEDAL ORGAN

Double Open Wood	32
Open Wood	16
Violone	16
Sub Bass	16
Dulciana	16 (1931)
Violoncello	8
Flute	8
Mixture III	
Ophicleide	16
Corno di Bassetto	16
(made available	
from the Solo in 1931)	
Posaune	8

COUPLERS

Solo to Great
Swell to Great
Choir to Great

Solo to Choir
Swell to Choir

Solo to Pedal
Swell to Pedal
Great to Pedal
Choir to Pedal

Great reeds on Solo
Great reeds on Choir
Great reeds on Pedal

Great and Pedal combinations coupler
Generals on Swell toe pistons

8 pistons to Great, Swell and Pedal
6 pistons to Choir and Solo
12 general pistons; 8 memory channels
(1995)

Setter piston
General Cancel

In 1979, work on the instrument coincided with the centenary of the Cathedral's consecration and of the organ's installation. It had always irked me that there were three stops provided for but which had never been put in, presumably for lack of funds. I suggested that the Centenary would be a particularly appropriate time to complete the specification, but was told firmly that it would be difficult to raise the money for essential work and that no extra "fancy frills" could be considered! However, I got my way, for I received a letter from relatives of the late Lord Glentanar saying they had read of the impending restoration of the Cathedral organ. They had been waiting for some opportunity to establish some memorial to Lord Glentanar and knowing of his love of St Mary's Cathedral and its organ, wondered if they could pay for the addition of the new pipes. And so the specification of the Great Organ was completed by the revoicing of the Harmonic Flute and addition of a new Principal, Spitzflute and Sesquialtera. A plaque was attached to the organ console marking the gift. Baron Glentanar had established the successful cotton thread business of Thomas Coats, in Paisley, and bought an estate in Aboyne in Aberdeenshire. He was especially interested in organ and church music and in 1927 had a four manuals and pedal organ built by Harrison & Harrison for the ballroom of his castle in Aboyne, and engaged Ian Whyte, a distinguished Scottish musician as his private organist. Whyte subsequently became the conductor of the BBC Scottish Symphony Orchestra and first Director of the BBC in Scotland. Glentanar was a member of the Middle Temple and on his visits to London he attended the services in the Temple Church which he greatly admired. The organ in the Temple Church was destroyed by bombs

Dennis Townhill at the Song School organ (1999)

Photo by Peter Backhouse

The interior of the Song School (1999)

Photo by Peter Backhouse

during an air raid in the second world war. After the war ended, Glentanar gifted his instrument from Aboyne to the church. It was dismantled and transported from Scotland to the Temple where it was placed in a new organ chamber in 1953 and dedicated by the Archbishop of Canterbury, Dr Geoffrey Fisher, on 23 March 1954 at a special service marking the re-opening of the Quire of the church.

Lord Glentanar had been in the habit of breaking his journey in Edinburgh on his periodic visits to the Inns of the Temple in London, and he was allowed to sing with the choir of St Mary's at the Sunday services. These facts were unknown to me, when, on a Sunday morning soon after my arrival in Edinburgh, the Choir Warden, Jack Scotland, came to the organ console before the morning service and whispered in my ear in reverential tones "Lord Glentanar is here." I was irritated at being interrupted whilst I was playing and told him I could not speak to anyone at the moment. "But it's Lord Glentanar and he wants to know if he can sing with the choir. No, certainly not! I don't know him and he has not attended any practices but I shall be pleased to meet him after the service." He did come to speak to me after the service and apologised profusely for not making himself known in advance, and said he quite understood my reasons for not allowing him to sing. He explained his connection with the choir and asked if I would allow him to sing the next time he was in Edinburgh, if he gave me due warning and attended the required rehearsals. I agreed, subject to a successful audition, and after that he always telephoned in advance to let me know he was in Edinburgh and enquired if he might sing and asked the times of the necessary rehearsals. He was a charming and delightful man and we became good friends. He took a close interest in the work of the choir and gave me a number of useful gifts including a record player for use in the Song School for the particular benefit of the choristers. Together with the equipment he gave me a number of LP recordings of church music performed by the choir of the Temple Church. Another gift, which I greatly treasure, was a copy of "A Spiritual Song" which is the story of the Temple Choir and "A History of Divine Service in the Temple Church, London." It is inscribed in the fly leaf, "Feb 4th 1963. To Mr Dennis Townhill from Glentanar with best wishes" on his headed notepaper, Glen Tanar, Aboyne, Aberdeenshire.

In 1887, a two-manual-and-pedal organ was built by "Father" Henry Willis for the Song School at a cost of £195. It stands against the west wall of the building. In 1942 it was cleaned and restored by Rushworth and Dreaper of Liverpool, who also added pipe-work for two stops originally prepared for. When I arrived in 1961, the instrument was unplayable. Consequently it was restored in 1963 by Harrison & Harrison, retaining the original voicing and tracker action. On the restoration of the Song School in 1996-1998 the opportunity was taken to clean and overhaul the organ again. This time the work was carried out by A F "Sandy" Edmonstone of Perth who also provided a new pedal board. The specification is given below.

Pedal Organ

Bourdon   16

Great Organ

Open Diapason   8

Dulciana   8

Principal   4

Fifteenth   2

Swell Organ

Open Diapason   8

                           (12 from Gedact)

Lieblich Gedact   8

Lieblich Flute   4

Couplers

Great to Pedal

Swell to Pedal

Swell to Great

Catch Swell pedal and two combination pedals

Electric blower

The third organ is a chamber instrument, presented to the Cathedral in 1970 by Sir Ronald Johnson, who obtained it from Miss Edith Robertson of Edinburgh. It was restored by Ronald L Smith of Edinburgh.

Stop Diapason	8	23 pipes
Diapason Treble	8	12 pipes
Principal	4	55 pipes
Flute	4	32 pipes
Fifteenth (new)	2	32 pipes

The Fifteenth replaced the original Dulciana.

The compass is CC to G, 55 notes (CC sharp has neither pipes nor mechanism).
The organ is now on wheels and has an electric blower.

The large grand piano in the Song School used for choir rehearsals was old and really past its usefulness. It had an ashtray on the side of its music desk which encouraged me to smoke cigarettes in the building - not during rehearsals though! In 1962 a medical report was published which linked smoking with lung cancer and this prompted me to stop the habit. Ash Wednesday and the discipline of Lent provided an excuse to give up for a period of six weeks at least. With the aid of chewing gum and sweets as substitutes I managed to conquer the addiction and have never smoked since. I have to confess that I was motivated more by self preservation than religious observance. In 1975 I bought a Bluthner grand piano for private domestic use and was able to offer our larger Ibach instrument to replace the "clapped-out" piano in the Song School. The other Cathedral piano was a Bechstein grand which was kept in the Chapter House but has now been permanently installed in the Cathedral. It has been placed on a wheeled frame which facilitates its movement around the building.

In 1974 the family of the late Sir George Younger offered to pay for a harpsichord for the Cathedral in his memory. The Provost told the family it would cost about £400. When I told him that the cost would be more likely in the region of £2,400 he was horrified and chastened. However, he suggested I write to the family and apologise for the Provost's miscalculation, and ask if they would be prepared to meet the true cost - and they did! On the advice of Professor Peter Williams of Edinburgh University, we commissioned Robert Davies of Levens, Westmoreland, to make a two-manual instrument based on late 17th-century French harpsichords. It was dedicated on 20 October 1974 at Evensong, and I gave a public concert on it that evening with the Scottish Baroque Ensemble and played Bach's *Concerto in D minor*. Subsequently I broadcast a programme on it for the BBC including Bach's *Partita No 1 in B flat* and *The Italian Concerto*. In order to achieve greater clarity the recording was made in the old choir vestry off the ambulatory leading to the Chapter House - now replaced by toilets!

I had no idea when, or from where the three timpani were obtained but they are splendid instruments and a valuable and useful asset. I was told recently that Dr Robert Head acquired them, and had them played at the annual performances of the Requiem on Remembrance Sunday.

"I think I shall play Mendelssohn's Violin Concerto"

For some years the Choir School had been a matter of concern on both financial and academic grounds, and there had been a number of attempts to tackle the problem. Suggestions were made to close the school and to arrange for choristers to be educated at one or more of the many independent schools in the city. Fortunately, in my opinion, this plan was resisted and future developments proved a better and more satisfactory solution. It was obvious in my early years at St Mary's that the school had problems. These were reflected in difficulty of recruitment of choristers and periodic withdrawals. Typical were the remarks of a parent who said that she would have to take her son away from the choir and school as "he needs to get his eddication!" Matters came to a head early in 1970 with the publication of the Scottish Arts Council's McKenzie Report which highlighted the shortage of first-class string players and the lack of adequate training provision at an early age. This report came to the notice of Philip Crosfield, Provost of St Mary's at the time, who discussed its contents with me. We shared the vision of our choir school becoming a specialist music school for children showing exceptional musical gifts, especially in string-playing, alongside the choristers.

There followed two years of wide consultation and innumerable meetings with people involved in music and academic education throughout Scotland and elsewhere. Our plans met with a mixture of disbelief, incredulity and opposition from many quarters, but we persevered. Philip Crosfield gathered together a number of influential people in the general public life of Scotland, whilst I obtained the enthusiastic support and expertise of a number of musical colleagues. Chief among these were Joan Dickson, the distinguished Edinburgh 'cellist and teacher, and Roger Raphael, Head of the Junior Department at The Royal Scottish Academy of Drama and Music in Glasgow. Joan was one of a remarkable trio of sisters who were the children of an eminent Edinburgh lawyer and his wife. Joan was unmarried but the other two were married. Hester, also a professional musician and an accomplished pianist, was married to Canon George Martineau, Rector of St Columba's Church in Edinburgh and Dean of the Diocese. Their son, Malcolm is now one of the leading piano accompanists in the world. The third sister, Elizabeth (Betty), was married to Sydney Newman, Reid Professor of Music in the University of Edinburgh.

Joan Dickson had visited the USSR and had first-hand knowledge of specialist music schools there and of their training methods. Roger Raphael had been a violin pupil of Yehudi Menuhin and he was able to obtain his interest and advice. Menuhin had established his own school in Stoke d'Abernon, some years earlier, and this provided a model, in many ways, for St Mary's. Happily, Lord Menuhin subsequently agreed to become Patron of the School and referred to it as his younger sister-school in Scotland.

The first instrumental pupils were admitted in August 1972 but not without a great deal of anxiety. The intention was for them to continue being taught by staff at the Junior

Department of the RSAMD and this required the agreement of the Principal. A week before the school was due to open, confirmation had not been received. In desperation, I telephoned him and told him that the young people had been enrolled with the consent of their parents and that we could not go back on that commitment. Fortunately, he agreed and the first four instrumentalists entered the school. They were John Doig, Rosalind Ferguson, James Robertson, all violinists from the west of Scotland and Sharon Nye, 'cellist from the north of the country.

Sharon's parents moved to live in Edinburgh, but the other three were boarded in private homes as there was no boarding house attached to the school at this time. John Doig and Rosalind Ferguson stayed with us and Colin Harrison (from Durham) and Michael Nolan (from Gargunnock, near Stirling) subsequently joined John Doig in our home.

Roger Raphael and Joan Dickson were the principal string teachers initially and they had oversight of the music timetable of the instrumental pupils. In addition to my Cathedral duties and other professional work, I acted as voluntary, unpaid Director of Music for the first four years until the number of pupils grew to the point where it became necessary to appoint a full-time, paid Director.

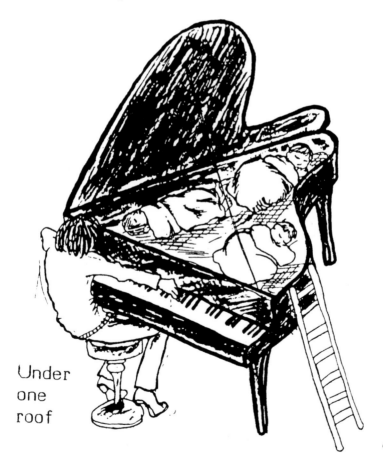

Under
one
roof

Cartoon by Clare Beber

The Revd J F Styles, Precentor of the Cathedral, served as Headmaster in the first year of transition to the now independent St Mary's Music School. On his retirement, Reynold Elder was appointed Headmaster in 1973 and guided the school through its early growth to 1976. His father was the Governor of Saughton Prison in Edinburgh and this proved a useful link. He was able to arrange for the inmates of the prison to make a number of music stands for use in the Song School in place of the heavy wooden bench seats with attached wooden music desks which more or less filled the building. This released much-needed space for the room to be used by instrumentalists for practice as well as for the daily choir rehearsals. Various buildings had to be used for teaching and practice, but the academic work continued in Old Coates House. With the extended age range of the pupils, and a wider curriculum, extra teaching staff were recruited to join Ishbel Gray who had faithfully taught in the school since 1969 and who served for twenty-three years in total.

The Cathedral Chapter House and rooms in a nearby building were also used for instrumental lessons and practice. These were clearly insufficient as numbers grew, and part of a large house in nearby Eglinton Crescent was acquired. The basement and ground floor had previously been used as a ballet school with a warren of rooms, numerous mirrors, corridors and connecting doors. As one former pupil said, "It tempted us all to explore when we should have been practising!" In due course, practice supervisors were employed and they ensured pupils were getting on with their work! The owner of the upper floors of the house was a Mrs Traill. She was so impressed by the young people she saw and heard that when she moved house, she generously bequeathed the property to the school.

In 1976, it was decided to appoint a head of the school who would have oversight of both music and academic work. Dr Carolyn Coxon was selected and took over from Reynold Elder. She was an Edinburgh University music graduate, and a professional singer resident in the city, who had sung solo parts for me on a number of occasions. She was, and still is, a lively and enthusiastic musician who made a great contribution to the life and development of the school, not least in providing two outstanding pupils and establishing a highly successful Saturday Music School for children in the community at large. Her two sons, John and Edmund, entered as choristers. Edmund was a gifted violinist and is now pursuing a successful career as a performer, while John went on to study biology at St Andrews University but since then has been involved in producing recordings of "pop" music. In 1977, Philip Allison joined the staff as Deputy Head and then Headmaster from 1979 until 1995. In his own words he described the school as a very, very new world to him. He had been teaching in a smart prep. school educating small boys where music had been a charming lady giving piano lessons and weekly bagpipe instruction. When he arrived at the school he found the Head was in hospital, himself in a very different world, apparently in a state of primeval chaos, and no timetable prepared for the new school year!

About this time, by a stroke of good fortune for the school, arising out of misfortune for him, I was able to recruit Nigel Murray on to the staff. He had been a member of the Menuhin Orchestra in London but had developed muscular problems which caused him to abandon his career as a violinist. He returned to Scotland and after a period of study at Edinburgh University, he joined St Mary's, first as a practice supervisor, then violin teacher and in 1980 he was appointed full-time Director of Music. He served in this capacity until 1996 with great distinction and developed the music of the school through a period of growth and stability. His father, David, was Organist and Choirmaster at St Machar's Cathedral in Aberdeen and Head of Music at an independent girls' school in the city. He was not a professionally qualified musician but he was intensely musical and a very successful teacher and church musician. He and his wife Jean, a professional teacher of the piano, were among the first to welcome us on our arrival in Scotland and we became good friends. I believe that David was one of the first to introduce me to the taste of scotch whisky although I have never taken to drinking it regularly. It was this personal connection which made me aware of Nigel Murray's availability.

Funding of such a venture as we entered into was obviously vitally necessary and a constant and increasing problem. Whilst the Cathedral provided buildings and some funding, it was necessary to raise considerable sums of money from other sources. Philip Crosfield persuaded Lady Jean Polwarth to act as Convener of fund-raising and as Chairman of the Board of Management. Her infectious enthusiasm and enormous skill were invaluable. During the initial discussions as to how we might change the Choir School into a specialist Music School, we heard that Yehudi Menuhin was to play in a concert in the Usher Hall. Jean Polwarth agreed to go to the concert and ask to see

French Horn

Cartoon by Clare Beber

Menuhin and get his advice. In her own words she said that in fear and trepidation she barged into the "green room" after the concert and met the great man. She asked him what he would think if a music school was started in Scotland. With a smile he exclaimed, "What a marvellous idea!" When she explained it was to be developed from the Cathedral Choir School, he said, "You will have the added advantage of the great tradition of church music. I wish I could have had that for my school. You must start straight away - borrow your first pupils if necessary!"

Yehudi Menuhin generously arranged for Jean Polwarth to visit his school in Stoke d'Abernon and showed her around himself. His remarks on the importance of the choral tradition were repeated when he paid his first visit to St Mary's to hear our four instrumental pupils play. When I told him that we had not arranged for him to hear the choristers, he said, "But singing is so important for all musicians and you are so lucky to have the choristers in your school."

This brief outline of the early years of the Music School would not be complete without mention of the selfless and important contribution of my wife, Mabel. Not only did she look after some of the first instrumentalists in our home, she later spent six months caring for twelve pupils in a boarding house set up in Lynedoch Place. In 1975 we moved from Claremont Park to a double upper flat in Grosvenor Crescent, only a few yards from the Cathedral. By this time, the number of boarders had grown to over twenty instrumentalists who were housed in a former Officers' Nursing Home in Belgrave Crescent. This was a splendid building at the end of a row of elegant Georgian style houses overlooking a large private park. Problems had arisen with the house-parents and Mabel was asked if she would look after the boarding house for a term, to allow things to settle down and to give time for the school to find a successor. She agreed, and we both moved into the house and remained not for three months but for three years! Meanwhile, greatly daring, we let our flat to two of the cathedral lay clerks. Fortunately, they were a responsible pair of lads and looked after the property carefully. Although running the boarding house was a completely new experience, Mabel coped with all its demands superbly well. The twenty-two young people were great fun and delightful to live with, and we treated them as an extended family. Many of "our babies" as we called them, have returned to see us in later years, often trundling their "babies" with them.

The rest, as they say, is history but it is a source of immense pride and pleasure to see the seed which was sown, grow and develop so successfully. It would take a long and separate book to chronicle the story of the school in detail, but I cannot leave the subject without mention of some of the personalities involved. Gifted pupils need gifted teachers and the school has been fortunate in attracting a succession of dedicated and skilful teachers, both for music and academic subjects. Roger Raphael and Joan Dickson and the links with the RSAMD in Glasgow and the Music Department of Edinburgh University were invaluable and crucial, especially in the early years. Happily, some of the instrumental teachers such as Warren Jacobs (violin), Richard Beauchamp (piano) and his wife, Ruth ('cello) and Audrey Innes (piano) are still on the school staff. An added bonus was Nigel Murray's wife, a professional flautist, who also became a valued teacher.

The pianists, Dr Colin Kingsley and Francesca Uhlenbroek and Malcolm Layfield, (strings) were among the first batch of teachers. Geoffrey King was recruited to teach

Yehudi Menuhin and instrumental pupils (1973)

Photo by Scotsman Publications Ltd

composition and theory. I had hoped he would be able to relieve me of some of the administrative burden but this did not work out. He was a gifted composer and wrote an anthem for the Feast of St Andrew for the Cathedral choir and a Toccata for organ for me. Both are technically very difficult but broadcast performances were given of both pieces. It did not help that Geoffrey had not checked the range of the manuals and pedals on the Cathedral organ before writing the Toccata and adjustments had to be made! He was a demanding teacher as Rupert Jeffcoat, a former chorister found. He said that Geoffrey insisted on his tackling tedious exercises and all he wanted to do at the age of eleven was to write the Rite of Spring. He said that, of course, he now knows Geoffrey was right! From the same article he wrote for the booklet commemorating the first twenty-five years of the school, Rupert said that I vainly tried to teach him the organ! Someone subsequently must have been more successful for he is now a very accomplished organist and the first of my former choristers to gain a cathedral appointment - as Director of Music at Coventry Cathedral.

He was the second of five brothers, all of whom served as choristers in St Mary's Cathedral. The eldest, Richard, is also a professional musician and is on the staff of the RSAMD in Glasgow. When their father first enquired about places in the choir for the boys, he described himself as a "failed" dance-band musician! On the other hand, his

98

wife was a highly successful accountant who became Cathedral Treasurer whilst he was house-husband. The chemistry produced splendid choristers as did that between Bill and Carol Wood, whose six boys were all also in the Cathedral choir concurrently with the Jeffcoats. Is this a record of some kind?

Like the Jeffcoats, the Wood brothers were very musical. Martin, the eldest, chose a medical career, Stuart is a teacher, whilst William and Mark are singing students at the Guildhall and RCM in London respectively. Steven won a musical scholarship to Shrewsbury and is a promising organist. Michael has just finished as a chorister as I write. I once asked Carol if she would like a girl rather than a succession of boys and she replied that she only produced choristers!

Although the teachers of non-musical subjects did not impinge upon my consciousness as much as the instrumental staff, they played an important part in the life of the school. Among the early imports were Alison Howard who taught modern languages and Alex Gaudin, mathematics. Alison and her husband, John, are devoted members of the Cathedral congregation and Alex was a retired headmaster of a school in Ireland before coming to St Mary's. The annual exhibitions of drawings and paintings by the school pupils are always of an astonishingly high standard. They are not only a tribute to the skill and inspiration of teachers such as Mrs Grant and Kirsty Laird, but also a reflection of the natural talent of gifted young musicians for a "sister" art.

All the pupils in the school were and are equally remembered and special to me, whether instrumentalists or choristers, especially the best and the worst! Inevitably, a few stand out by virtue of particular personal qualities or circumstances. Carol Gould was one of the most naturally talented of all the pupils. She entered the school at the age of eight as a first-study violinist, and I clearly recall showing her to a practice room. Trying to be helpful, I asked her if she would like me to put up the music stand for her. "Certainly not," she replied, "I can put up my own stand." On asking if she would like me to tune her violin for her, she equally firmly assured me that she could tune it herself - and did! I enquired what she was going to practice and she said, "Mendelssohn's Violin Concerto." I supposed that she would be attempting the leisurely melody of the slow movement, but she brightly told me that she would be playing the lively Finale - and she did! As with many gifted children, she felt isolated in her previous school and was regarded by her peers as an oddity. Consequently she tended to react by throwing tantrums and indulging in anti-social behaviour. St Mary's provided a more congenial environment for her and she thrived on the companionship of children with similar talents and interests. Immensely gifted as she was, she nevertheless had a ready appreciation of other people's abilities. One day she burst into the Song School whilst I was auditioning a potential chorister. "Who's that?" she said. When I told her that the boy had come for a vocal audition, she replied, "Well, can he sing?" I got the little lad to sing his set piece for Carol and with great solemnity she said, " My word, he sings beautifully. I wish I could sing like that."

I was always puzzled that, talented as she was, she did not produce an expressive sound on her instrument. Eventually, she changed to the viola as it transpired she disliked the high-pitched sounds of the violin and much preferred the more mellow sounds of the lower instrument.

Music School pupils and staff (1974)

When she was in her 'teens she learnt to play the double-bass and became a valuable asset to the school orchestra. On one occasion, at a public concert given by the school, I watched in amazement as she played the bass part of a demanding programme from memory - her part remaining unopened from beginning to end! But it was the piano that Carol loved best of all and she would stroke the top of her favourite Bosendorfer grand as if it were a pet animal. After she left St Mary's she went to music college in London where I believe she learnt to play one or more woodwind instruments. The last time I had news of her she had acquired a pilot's licence to fly!

Kari and Louise Jones came to St Mary's from Machynlleth in north west Wales. They were both violinists and two of our boarding house babes who have kept in touch with us since leaving school.

Kari married a medical GP and lived in Port Stanley on the Falkland Islands for a time, where she taught violin and piano and played the organ for the services in the Cathedral. She showed no particular interest in the organ or church music while she was at school, but since returning to the UK she has entered one of her children for a place in the choir at Hereford Cathedral near where she now lives. Her younger sister moved from St Mary's to Chethams School in Manchester, and is making a name for herself as a solo violinist. She has called to see us a number of times and presented us with some of her recordings in which she is accompanied by Dr Malcolm Miller, pianist, critic and musicologist. They play beautifully and their recording of the complete works of Frederick Delius for violin and piano is especially memorable. Inevitably, former instrumental pupils have been successful in various musical competitions, both national and international. They include:-

Paul Galbraith (guitar) who won the Strings Section of the BBC Young Musician of the Year.
1985 Andrea Jacobs (violin) - Winner of Scottish International Education Trust Scholarship to study at The Peabody Centre for the Arts, Baltimore, USA.
1988 Steven Osborne (piano) - Winner Scottish Final of BBC Young Musician of the Year. 1989 Brighton Philharmonic Society Piano Competition. 1991 Clara Haskil International Piano Competition.
1988 David Horne (piano) - Winner London Final of the BBC Young Musician of the Year and in 1989 - Scholarship to The Curtis Institute, Philadelphia.
1989 Helen Fairer (piano) - Winner Southport Mozart Competition.
1989 Claire Docherty (violin) - First Scottish Trades Union Council Scholarship to study in Moscow.
1991 Esther Geldard (viola) - Prize Winner Tertis International Viola Competition. 1997 Rafal Zambrzycki-Payne (violin) - Winner London Final of the BBC Young Musician of the Year.

Many former instrumentalists are now making their way in the music profession. These include John McCrae ('cello) teaching and performing in Italy. Claire Docherty (violin) Scottish Chamber Orchestra; Jackie McCreadie (violin) Royal Scottish National Orchestra; Sarah-Jo Izzett (violin), BBC Welsh Orchestra; David Horne (composer); Steven

Osborne (solo pianist).

Neil Ertz (violin) is developing an instrument making business in Cambridge. His parents emigrated from Hungary to the UK and lived on a small island off the north-west coast of Scotland which could only be reached by rowing boat!

Gillian Haggerty and Robin Mason distinguished themselves for non-musical reasons. Gillian known to her school friends as "Hagblogs"(!) married the conductor Nicholas Braithwaite and emigrated to Australia where he holds an appointment. His father, Warwick Braithwaite, was also a conductor. Robin, a 'cellist, imprinted himself on our memories in the boarding house for seeming to eat nothing but marmite sandwiches! There are, of course, many more who could be mentioned and no doubt some of their names will appear later.

Further developments in the life of the school have been the acquisition of more suitable and convenient buildings. In 1985, the Trustees bought a large property on the corner of Palmerston Place and Chester Street, just across the road from the Cathedral grounds. It was officially opened by Yehudi Menuhin, and was large enough to accommodate the boarders and to provide sufficient space for music teaching, library and practice rooms. Old Coates House continued to be used for the academic classes and school administration. In 1995 the school moved, lock, stock and barrel to Coates Hall which had been vacated by the Theological College. This fine, Category B listed building of 1850 was designed by David Bryce and later extended by Sir Robert Lorimer. It stands in an acre of grounds and contains boarding accommodation, classrooms, practice rooms and offices which have all been refurbished and modernised. A new science laboratory has been created and there are junior and senior common rooms, a well-stocked library and spacious dining-room. Now the pupils can work, play, eat, sleep, practice and rehearse, take music and academic lessons, relax and enjoy outdoor activities, all on their own quiet campus in the heart of the city. Behind the scenes, successive, distinguished directors of management have guided the school's progress. These include Morrison Dunbar of the RSAMD, Lord Clyde, Professors Kenneth Leighton, Michael Tilmouth and David Kimbell of Edinburgh University Music Department, Sir David Lumsden, formerly Principal of RSAMD and RAM in London, Sir Philip Ledger, Principal RSAMD, Professor Gordon Kirk, Principal of Moray House Institute of Teacher Training, Professor W D Munro, Dr Marjorie Rycroft, Senior Lecturer (Music), Glasgow University, Richard Chester, National Youth Orchestra of Scotland, Lady Marion Fraser and Dr Nicholas Phillipson, Reader in History, Edinburgh University. Honorary Vice-Presidents include Sir Peter Maxwell Davies, Joan Dickson (deceased), Sir Alexander Gibson (deceased), Evelyn Glennie, Steven Isserlis and Jerzy Maksymiuk. The present Head Teacher, Jennifer Rimer and Director of Music, John Grundy are successfully taking the school into this new millennium. During the struggle and problems of the early years, Jean Polwarth said that the pioneers get the callouses and their successors get the rewards. How right she was, but it is thrilling to see our vision come to fulfilment.[10]

---

10. Ref. St Mary's Music School - 25 Years (1998), compiled and edited by Sally Wyllie.

Chapter 10 - Some Special Services and Extra-Liturgical Events

"Please Sir! Go and ask her to come and speak to us!"

The main function of a cathedral choir is to share and enhance the daily offerings of worship. Even in the depths of winter, with perhaps no one else visibly present except for the members of the clergy and the choir, there is something special about a service prepared and performed with as much care as for the great occasions when the cathedral is filled to overflowing. Nevertheless there inevitably are many times when services and events take place which have a particular purpose and impact. Reference has recently been made to the Consecration and Enthronement (nowadays called Installation) of various Bishops. The last, for which I was responsible, took place in June 1986 when Richard Holloway succeeded Alastair Haggart as Bishop of Edinburgh. Earlier in his ministry he had been Rector of the historic church of Old St Paul's in Edinburgh, where he trained a succession of outstanding curates. These included Tony Whatmough, now Vicar of St Mary's, Redcliffe, Bristol, Alan Moses, Vicar of All Saints, Margaret Street, London, Graham Forbes, the present Provost of St Mary's Cathedral, Edinburgh and Martin Shaw, Precentor of St Edmundsbury Cathedral. Martin trained as a professional singer before becoming ordained and has a fine baritone voice. It was no surprise when the Bishop requested that Martin should sing the solo part in Vaughan Williams' *Rise, heart; Thy Lord is risen*, at his Consecration. Richard Holloway is an outstanding preacher and a theologian with liberal views which he is not afraid to express publicly. Consequently he attracts a good deal of media attention, much of it distorted and unfairly selective. In my opinion, he is a warm-hearted man and a caring pastor and now has an even higher profile as Primus of the Episcopal Church in Scotland.

Among the weddings for which I have directed the music have been a number which I can only describe as "Royal Occasions". The first took place on 1 June 1974 in St Mary's Cathedral, when Donald, eldest son of Sir Donald Cameron of Lochiel, Lord Lieutenant of Inverness-shire married Lady Cecil Kerr, daughter of the Marquis and Marchioness of Lothian. The service was conducted by The Most Reverend Richard Wimbush, Bishop of Argyll and the Isles, assisted by Cardinal Gordon Gray, Roman Catholic Archbishop of St Andrews and Edinburgh, Dom Fabian Cowper, OSB, a cousin of the bride and The Very Reverend Philip Crosfield, Provost of St Mary's. The Very Reverend Ronald Selby Wright, Minister of the Canongate Kirk in Edinburgh and former Moderator of the General Assembly of The Church of Scotland was among clergy of other denominations present.

The bridegroom was an Episcopalian and the bride a Roman Catholic, hence the ecumenical character of the service. The bride was a friend of Prince Charles and Princess Anne, both of whom attended the service together with Princess Anne's husband, Captain Mark Philips, Lady Helen Windsor, Princess Margaret, the Duke and Duchess of Kent, Princess Michael of Kent and Lord Nicholas Windsor was one of the pages.

103

The second was the marriage of Lady Elizabeth Kerr, youngest daughter of the Marquis and Marchioness of Lothian, to the Earl of Dalkeith, heir to the Duke of Buccleuch, a cousin of the Queen. This took place on 31 October 1981 in St Mary's Chapel, Dalkeith, on one of the Duke's estates. The service was conducted by the Primus, The Most Reverend Alastair Haggart, assisted by Dom Fabian Cowper, OSB. Again, many members of the Royal Family attended including Princess Anne and her husband, the Duke and Duchess of Gloucester, Princess Alice, Dowager Duchess of Gloucester and Prince and Princess Michael of Kent. Among the 1,600 guests were many notable public figures and politicians (who were conveyed by buses to the reception) including the well-known politician, Quintin Hogg. He walked with the aid of two sticks and seeing his difficulty in alighting from the bus, I offered my help. This was brusquely refused with the assurance that he was perfectly capable of getting off the bus by himself! Further embarrassment was to follow. Our table at the reception was placed near to the main protagonists with a clear view of the wedding cake. Before the meal began the choristers spotted Princess Anne standing with her husband and chatting to another guest. "Please Sir! go and ask the Princess to come and speak to us," they said. On replying that I could do no such thing, they said, "Well, if you won't, we will." Faced with that prospect, I plucked up courage and walked across towards the Princess. Her husband spotted me and asked what I wanted. I explained, and he asked me to wait until Her Royal Highness had finished her conversation and then he would put my request to her. This he did, and after a pause she walked up to me and asked who the group were and what special services or concerts we had in the offing. She then walked over to the choristers' table and chatted informally to them all. They thought this was magic and my stock rose considerably in their estimation.

Among other weddings of special interest was that of Susan Landale and Marc Rouit. Susan was from Duns in the Borders where her parents were farmers. She was educated at Lansdowne House School in Edinburgh and then read music at Edinburgh University, obtaining the Bachelor of Music Degree. During this time she received her first organ lessons from Dr Robert Head at St Mary's Cathedral. After completing her degree, she was awarded a scholarship to study for four years with the eminent blind French organist, Maître André Marchal at the Church of St Eustache, Paris. She won the first prize at the first International Organ Competition at St Alban's Abbey in England, and has since become one of the world's leading concert organists and teachers.

The Cathedral was full for the wedding service and attended by a great many distinguished musicians. Her husband is a French architect and his family chartered a plane to bring their guests from Paris. André Marchal played before, during and after the service, and I directed the music sung by the Cathedral choir. It was thrilling and instructive to watch and hear Marchal play. I especially remember his stylish, classical performance of Bach's *Prelude and Fugue in C*, (S 547) and the expressive shaping of César Franck's *Choral No 3 in A minor*.

Sir James Miller was a fellow-member of the Rotary Club of Edinburgh in my early years in the city. He had possibly the unique distinction of holding the offices of Lord Mayor of London and Lord Provost of Edinburgh - not simultaneously, I hasten to add! On his death, the management of the family firm of building and construction contractors was inherited by his son James. James and his wife, Iris became good friends and firm supporters of the Cathedral choir. They have three daughters and the choir was invited to provide the music for each of their wedding services in the Church of Scotland Parish Church at Murrayfield, which the family attended. I was responsible for the music for the first two and my successor for the third. A special link arose between us through the Society of the Friends of the Royal Scottish Academy of Art which has its galleries standing at the foot of The Mound in Princes Street. Iris Miller succeeded Lady Marion Fraser as President of the Friends and continued her invitation for the Cathedral choir to sing at a Christmas carol service in one of the galleries. This was a splendid annual occasion for not only were the setting and acoustics attractive but we were given a sumptuous meal afterwards. An unexpected consequence was a request by a distinguished Edinburgh sculptress and artist to paint my portrait! Edith Simon was a member of the RSA and attended the annual service of carols. It was pure coincidence that she lived a few houses from us in the same Crescent. She asked me to wear my doctoral robes for the preliminary sketches. The finished portrait shows a front view superimposed upon one of my back, with arms raised as if conducting. As she said, it was the colour of the robes and academic hood which really attracted her and she much preferred the back view! The painting was put on exhibition at the RSA and the original was bought by James and Iris Miller, whilst we bought a more modest photographic reproduction.

A year or two after our arrival in Edinburgh, I was asked by Alex Thain, Conductor of the Gorgie Salvation Army Band, if I would be willing to resume the link between the band and the choir. He explained that the association had begun in 1949 when the choir joined the band in the city Christmas carol service at the Usher Hall, and had regularly held annual gatherings in the Cathedral since then, but which had lapsed in recent years. I agreed and the band filled the Cathedral for its Spring Festival in 1964, and for many years until Alex's death. Leading Salvation Army conductors and composers such as Eric Ball and Dean Goffin, were invited to conduct. The choir took part and I also played the organ with the band or as soloist. The Band played to a high standard and it was an added bonus to be invited to conduct it from time to time. The tradition of singing at the carol service in the Usher Hall on Christmas Eve was also resumed. It made for a very heavy schedule, for the appearance in the Usher Hall followed rehearsals, Evensong and our own carol service in the Cathedral! Alex Thain and his wife were lovely people and I developed a great affection for them and unbounded admiration for the work of the Salvation Army in general. He worked in the Entertainments Department and was in charge of the ticket office for the famous Military Tattoo held annually during the Edinburgh International Festival. We received complimentary tickets two or three times and once they were for seats in the Royal Box from where the Salute was taken at the conclusion of each performance. It provided a wonderful view of the Castle Esplanade and of the archway from which the performers emerged.

On two occasions, I was asked to conduct the music for celebrations of the Russian Orthodox Liturgy in St Mary's. The first was in 1964 and the celebrant was Archbishop Anthony Bloom, whose father was of Scots descent but whose mother was Russian. Both services proved to be different, interesting but also unpredictable. I was given a copy of the order of service in English and the music for unaccompanied voices arranged by Sir Ronald Johnson, choirmaster of the Church of St Columba's-by-the-Castle, who had an interest in the Orthodox Liturgy. I met the Archbishop at the Theological College the previous evening in order to be briefed as to where and how the music fitted into the service. This proved to be largely a waste of time as he would not commit himself, nor could I find out the pitch at which he was likely to sing the Priest's part which preceded a good deal of the choral music. The service turned out to be something of a nightmare as the Archbishop never intoned his part at the same pitch twice and without warning he would thunderously interject the phrase, "O Wisdom" on a low G! However, the result of our labours must have been acceptable as the press report commented on the fine singing of the Cathedral choir, who had obviously rehearsed the liturgy beforehand!

Conductor

Cartoon by Clare Beber

In 1960, an annual festival was established between the Border Cathedral Choirs of Carlisle, Newcastle and Edinburgh. It was held in each city in turn and took the form of a service or concert. Distances between the three cities limited rehearsal time on the day, but it was nevertheless always an enjoyable and friendly occasion. I found myself in charge, for the first time, in June 1962 when the Festival was held in Edinburgh. Choral Evensong was sung and recorded for subsequent broadcast by the BBC. In view of future developments, it is interesting to recall the music sung on that occasion as being representative and adventurous. The 16th and early 17th centuries were represented by the Introit *O come ye servants of the Lord* Tye *Responses* Smith, and anthem *Laudibus in sanctis* Byrd. The 20th-century setting of the *Canticles in E* was by Herbert Murrill and Sydney Campbell's *Te Deum in B flat*, written for the Enthronement of The Archbishop of Canterbury in 1961, rounded off the service. The programme for the next Festival to be held in Edinburgh in 1965 was even more ambitious and severely taxed the abilities of the choirs. I had decided to feature music by contemporary composers, with Scottish connections. I asked Professor Frederick Rimmer of Glasgow University to write chants for two of the psalms and I also composed a couple. Greatly daring, I asked Professor Kenneth Leighton of Edinburgh University if he would compose a set of Preces and Responses for the occasion. To my delight, he readily agreed and they have become the most widely and frequently sung setting by a 20th century composer since publication by Novello, and our first performance. Kenneth Leighton's *Magnificat and Nunc Dimittis in G*, written for Bernard Rose and the choir of Magdalen College, Oxford, and his *Te Deum for the Festival of St Cecilia* at St Sepulchre's, Holborn, in 1964, completed the choral music for the service. It began with Robin Orr's Introit *They that put their trust in the Lord*. He was born in Brechin, Angus, and had a distinguished career as Organist of St John's College, Cambridge, Professor of Music at Glasgow University and then of Cambridge University. Organ preludes on Scottish Psalm Tunes by Frederick Rimmer preceded the service and Robin Orr's *Toccata alla marcia* provided the postlude. They were played by Colin Ross and Andrew Seivewright, the organists of Newcastle and Carlisle Cathedrals respectively. Despite complimentary reviews in the press for both services, I felt that the restricted timetable on the day, and inadequate preparation before the day militated against a really high standard being achieved. I suggested that the Festival should be extended over a weekend but clergy and organists would not agree to this. It was not until after I retired that a new and more flexible group of clergy and organists were willing to agree to their choirs leaving their own Cathedrals for a weekend two years out of three. This certainly made for a more relaxed Festival and more generous rehearsal time.

It also increased the scope of music that could be performed, although it did not always lead to a high standard. I did manage to persuade the other two choirs to come a day early in 1965 when we were invited to make an LP recording of hymns, entitled "Songs of Praise". We rehearsed on the Friday evening, recorded the hymns on the Saturday morning and then rehearsed for Choral Evensong after lunch! My colleagues, Andrew Seivewright and Colin Ross played the organ accompaniments and I directed the choirs.

Many years later, an annual joint Evensong with the choir of Durham Cathedral was established, taking place in each city in turn. This has proved a very happy connection and musically, very rewarding . On the first occasion that the service was held in Durham, the Bishop of Durham, The Right Reverend David Jenkins and Diocesan clergy were present. After the service, the Bishop said that he had noticed the choir was twice as large and that half of them (the Edinburgh contingent) wore red cassocks. He thought that must be a deliberate attempt to reflect his political views!

In 1986, the choirs from the seven Scottish Episcopal Cathedrals of Aberdeen, Dundee, Glasgow, Inverness, Oban, Perth and Edinburgh joined together to sing Evensong in St Mary's to mark the twenty-fifth anniversary of my appointment as organist and they gathered again in 1991 to mark my retirement. Andrew Morrison, Robert Lightband, Bernard Porter, Russell Grant, Richard Finch and Alastair Pow all worked very hard to maintain their choirs under very difficult circumstances.

In May 1975, the Cathedral choir was invited to join the choirs of Llandaff, St Patrick's Armagh and St Paul's at the three hundred and twenty-first Festival of the Sons of the Clergy in the London Cathedral. The report in the Church Times stated that this innovation had drawn the largest crowd in post-war years and filled the Cathedral to hear the music - and of course, the Archbishop of Canterbury who preached. Since then, similar invitations have been extended to other cathedral choirs. We had the unique privilege of singing for a second time at a subsequent festival when the Bishop of Edinburgh, Alastair Haggart, was invited to preach. Christopher Dearnley conducted the choirs on the first occasion and Barry Rose, on the second.

On 6 October 1987 a special service was held in Westminster Abbey to mark the four hundredth anniversary of the death of Mary, Queen of Scots. The seven Scottish Bishops took part in the service and I was invited to play organ music before and after. It was a great thrill to play on such a splendid instrument in the atmosphere of that great building. By one of those freak coincidences, that occasionally happen, I met our friends John and Mary Freeman and their son, Stephen, from Lincoln, coming out of the Abbey as I walked in!

1979 was a momentous year which began sadly with the death, at the age of eighty-two of Gordon Slater, my former choirmaster and teacher. At the funeral service held in Lincoln Cathedral on 31 January, I was invited to play some of his organ music before and after the service.

The rest of the year was largely celebratory as the centenary of the dedication of St Mary's Cathedral fell on 30 October, and a special series of events was arranged. They began with a short service to mark the completion of the nave on 25 January 1879. On 4 June, a detachment of The Royal Scots fired ten volleys from the base of the Spire, repeating the exercise of one hundred years previously on its completion. A group of choristers stood with outstretched hands on the ground below hoping to catch the spent cartridges! However, the main celebrations were concentrated during the week of 28 October to 4 November. A number of new pieces were commissioned. These were a *Te Deum* by Francis Jackson, an anthem by Kenneth Leighton, *Fanfares for Brass* by Frank Spedding and an Introit and Choral Responses by myself.

The first service of the week took the form of a Diocesan Eucharist of Thanksgiving at which the preacher was the Primus, The Most Reverend Alastair Haggart, Bishop of

Edinburgh. The music included the Fanfares by Dr Frank Spedding, Head of Academic Studies at The Royal Scottish Academy of Music and Drama, my Choral Responses, the setting *Missa in Tempore Belli* by Haydn, with soloists and orchestra from the RSAMD, Peter Backhouse, assistant organist, conducted by Dr David Lumsden, Principal of the RSAMD (now Sir David Lumsden). Disaster ensued during the first movement of the Handel *Organ Concerto in F (The Cuckoo and The Nightingale)* in which I played the solo part on the Cathedral chamber organ. A cipher developed on one of the notes which resisted all frantic attempts to correct it. Fortunately, the harpsichord was available at the side of the organ and the performance was completed without further mishap. Twenty-four choirs from the Diocese combined to provide the chorus and in order to accommodate them and the orchestra, they were placed at the west end of the Cathedral.

On 30 October, the date of the anniversary of the Consecration of the Cathedral, a congregation of some 1,500 attended the special Festal Evensong, including the Duke of Buccleuch, Lord Home of The Hirsel, Trustees of The Episcopal Church. The Archbishop of York preached the sermon, the Lord Provost, Kenneth Borthwick read a lesson, whilst Magistrates, members of the City Council and representatives of other churches were also present. The anthem was Kenneth Leighton's *Awake my Glory* for choir and organ, conducted by the composer. It is a splendid setting of words by Christopher Smart (1722-1771) taken from his long, rambling poem *On the Eternity of the Supreme Being*. Benjamin Britten used extracts from the same poem for his memorable cantata-anthem *Rejoice in the Lamb*.

The words contain flashes of brilliant poetic imagery which the composer wonderfully illuminates in musical terms. The young choristers never failed to be excited by the phrase, "Soon as the stately night-exploding bird, In lively lay, sings welcome to the dawn." My short unaccompanied setting of *Lo, God is here! Let us adore and own how dreadful is this place!* was also sung. The words are a translation by John Wesley (1703-1791) of a poem by the German, G Tersteegen (1697-1769). Both reflect the impeccable and imaginative literary taste of The Very Reverend G P C Crosfield, Provost of St Mary's, who chose the words. The psalm chant was by Dr Robert Head and final Amen after the Blessing by Dr T H Collinson, former Cathedral organists.

The services on Sunday, 4 November, were of a more domestic nature for the regular members of the Cathedral congregation and church people of the city. The preacher at the morning Eucharist was The Right Reverend Patrick Rodger, Bishop of Oxford, and former Provost of St Mary's Cathedral. The setting was *The Little Organ Mass* by Haydn and the specially-composed *Te Deum in D* by Francis Jackson was sung at the conclusion of the service. The Te Deum is a most effective and well-written setting, worthy of many more performances than it is likely to get in these days when Mattins is so rarely sung in our Cathedrals. In the evening, a Service of Thanksgiving at the close of the centenary week took the form of a Songs of Praise. The singing was led by the combined choirs of St Mary's Cathedral, St Giles' Cathedral (High Kirk of the Church of Scotland), the Roman Catholic Cathedral and the choirs of St Cuthbert's, St George's West, Palmerston Place and St John's, whose congregations belong to the ecumenical Council of West End Churches in Edinburgh.

Brass introductions to the hymns were specially composed by Frank Spedding and played by an ensemble of the Royal Scottish Academy of Music and Drama who also played music before and after the service. My Introit anthem, *Lo, God is here* was sung at the beginning of the service at the request of the Provost. The organ accompaniments for the hymns were shared by Herrick Bunney, CVO, organist of St Giles, and Peter Backhouse, and I conducted. Passages of scripture and poetry were read by representatives of each of the five congregations of the Council of West End Churches.

Other events during the week included a Service of Thanksgiving in the Ringing Chamber on 29 October to celebrate the centenary of the Dedication of the bells on that date in 1879. A quarter peal was rung to mark the occasion and on the same evening a party was held for the Cathedral congregation in the Walpole Hall. A flower festival was mounted in the building and performances of what was described as a dramatic journey in words and music entitled, *To be a Pilgrim* was produced by Terry Mobbs, father of two of the Cathedral choristers. The four readers were from the Cathedral congregation and the music was provided by pupils of St Mary's Music School. Finally, an organ recital was given on 3 November by Francis Jackson. The week was padded out with rehearsals for the various services in addition to normal routine activities such as teaching of private pupils, visits to RSAMD in Glasgow and meetings of one kind or another!

From my diary for 1979, it seems that the following week was no less typically hectic. It included an overnight train journey to London on Tuesday 6 November to attend the Cathedral Organists' Conference in Canterbury the next day; then on to Grimsby to conduct a special concert in memory of Alec Redshaw in the Parish Church on Saturday 10 November. Intensive rehearsals with the Grimsby Philharmonic Choir and Manchester Mozart Orchestra took place during the two days prior to the concert leading to what the press report described as an outstanding and excellent concert. The young husband-and-wife team, Michael George and Julie Kennard, were the soloists in Brahms' *Requiem and Song of Destiny* and the *Five Mystical Songs* of Vaughan Williams. I stayed with Norman and Pat Finch in Goxhill and returned home on Monday 12 November to resume activities in Edinburgh!

A leaflet was produced outlining some of the special services and events during the centenary year. Some of them have already been mentioned and others included regular annuals such as the Commemoration of King Charles I on the Thursday nearest to his beheading on 30 January. The Scottish liturgy of 1637 is always used for this service and the sermon given by a special preacher is reprinted in the magazine of the Royal Martyr Church Union. The now established performance of Bach's *St John Passion* (in German) was given on Good Friday by the Scottish Cantata Singers, Cathedral choir and orchestra including pupils and staff from St Mary's Music School. The soloists on this occasion were Martyn Hill (Evangelist), Graham Titus (Christus), Colin Fox, a former chorister and lay clerk (Pilate), Carolyn Coxon (soprano), Katrine Townhill, our son's wife (mezzo-soprano) and Duncan Robertson, of Scottish Opera (tenor).

From 30 April to 21 May, a series of exhibitions and lectures on the work of Sir George Gilbert Scott were mounted in the Chapter House, with particular reference to the building of the Cathedral under the heading "Victorian Heritage 1979." As part of this theme, the Cathedral choir and the choir of Paisley Abbey gave a concert of unaccompanied Victorian church music on 4 May. The programme included works by Mendelssohn,

Samuel Wesley, S S Wesley and Parry. The choristers attending the RSCM Scottish residential course sang the daily and Sunday services from 30 July to 6 August. The Incorporated Association of Organists chose to hold their Annual Congress in Edinburgh during the week beginning 13 August. This happily coincided with the completion of the restoration of the Cathedral organ and the delegates were able to attend the re-opening recital which I gave on 16 August. The programme was recorded by the BBC for subsequent broadcast on Radio 3 on 27 August. It included Liszt, *Fantasia and Fugue on B-A-C-H*; Bach Chorale Preludes, *Liebster Jesu, wir sind hier* (S 731) and *Wir glauben all an eine Gott* (S 680); Gordon Slater Preludes on *St Botolph* and *Lasst uns erfreuen* and Kenneth Leighton, *Prelude, Scherzo and Passacaglia*, Op. 41. As in 1963, when the IAO Congress was previously held in Edinburgh, the closing service was held in St Mary's. Partly to allow the organ to be more widely heard and to help raise money towards the cost of the restoration, I arranged a weekly series of recitals running from the re-opening to the next July. This proved to be over-ambitious and whilst many of the recitals attracted good audiences, some were disappointingly small. However, we got off to a good start during the Edinburgh International Festival period when the guest organists were Allan Wicks from Canterbury Cathedral, Daniel Hathaway from Trinity Cathedral, Cleveland USA, and my colleague Herrick Bunney from St Giles, Edinburgh.

Two major choral works were certainly high spots for me during the year. We performed both the Monteverdi *Vespers of 1610* and J S Bach *Mass in B minor* during the Edinburgh Festival. I was lucky to have the distinguished violinist, Jürgen Hess to lead the orchestra in both works and play the various solo obbligati parts. Jürgen's daughter, Rachel, was a pupil at our Music School and it was lovely to hear father and daughter play the "echo" violin solos in the Vespers. We managed to assemble first-rate soloists and the chorus for both was made up of the Scottish Cantata Singers, the Cathedral choristers and a gathered orchestra of mostly professional players. The vocal soloists for the Vespers were Linda Stuart and Carolyn Coxon (sopranos), Gordon Stuart and Alastair Thomson (tenors) with Nigel Waugh and Colin Fox, two of the Cathedral lay clerks (baritones). Those for the Mass were Kathleen Livingstone, Cynthia Buchan, Neil Mackie and Alan Oke.

From 14 to 16 September, the Federation of Cathedral Old Choristers' Associations held their annual Festival in Edinburgh. We arranged for the Border Cathedral choirs to hold their festival at the same time and invited some members of the choirs of Durham Cathedral and York Minster also to join us. This was a major operation as those attending the Federation Festival were housed at the Heriot-Watt University campus, a few miles from the Cathedral and had to be "bussed" in and out of the city for the various events. We were greatly indebted to members of the St Mary's Old Choristers' Association, especially the Secretary, Tony Cormack, who masterminded the arrangements and Dr Francis Thomas, Chairman. The extra choral resources enabled us to provide an adventurous range of music at the services. Leighton *Responses,* Byrd *Great Service* and Vaughan Williams' *Let all the world in every corner sing* were performed at the Friday Choral Evensong. On the Saturday, the responses were by William Smith of Durham, the canticles, Stanford in A, Brahms *How Lovely are Thy dwellings* and Herbert Howells Te Deum *Collegium Regale* were all accompanied by orchestra. It was the first time that the Federation Festival had been held north of the border and the distinctive features of tartan dress, bagpipes, haggis, neeps and tatties were greatly enjoyed and appreciated.

The centenary celebrations were completed by a Son et Lumiere production and two peals rung on the Cathedral Bells. One on 27 October by the Cathedral Ringers and the other by a band drawn from the Central Council of Bell-ringers arranged and conducted by John Freeman. The annual Remembrance Day performance of Brahms' *Requiem* was conducted by Peter Backhouse in my absence in Grimsby, and Handel's *Messiah* in December completed the oratorio performances. Two other events deserve mention. On 25 August, Evensong sung in Gaelic was broadcast on Radio Scotland and Yehudi Menuhin paid one of his periodic visits to the Music School. A truly memorable year.

There are many other performances during my career which are specially memorable for me. In 1966 and in 1982, I organised and conducted performances of Benjamin Britten's *Noye's Fludde* during the Edinburgh Festival. The response from the public was astonishing and long queues formed outside the Cathedral before each nightly performance, during the period of a week in each case. Of course, with a cast of over two hundred schoolchildren, the potential support from their families was guaranteed. Indeed, in 1966, we had to add an extra matinée on the Saturday afternoon for parents and relatives only, as so many had been unable to obtain tickets. In 1966 I sought and obtained wonderfully enthusiastic support from Dr George Reid, Director of Education for the City of Edinburgh and members of his staff. The children's chorus of animals was drawn from Local Authority Primary and Secondary Schools and the members of the Edinburgh Secondary Schools Orchestra provided the players (trained by their conductor, Eric Roberts). The Edinburgh Society of Recorder Players took part and adults (some instrumental instructors for the LEA) played the professional solo parts. Alasdair Mitchell, the 'cellist in the string quintet has since developed a successful career as a conductor. Alastair Hair, a pupil, played the organ and William (Bill) Stevenson subsequently married Lorna Murray, his piano duet partner! Bill is now Organist and Director of Chapel Music at St Andrews University. The splendid set, props, costumes and animals' heads were all designed and made by the staff and pupils of a designated LEA secondary school, and they were all superbly done. I was very fortunate to obtain the services of John McColl to produce the show. He was teacher of English at Leith Academy Secondary School at the time and also a well-known amateur actor in the city. We established a good rapport between us and he was a most dedicated and professional colleague.

Gordon Clinton, a well-known and experienced professional singer took the part of Mr Noye and Marjorie McMichael, a young Edinburgh singer starting out on her career, took the part of Mrs Noye. They made a good team and Gordon endeared himself to the small "animals", especially as they entered the Ark by asking them whether they had fish and chips or beans-on-toast for their tea! We had a double cast for the Sons of Noye and their Wives. Four of the boys were Cathedral choristers including Eric Ibler, who has since become a successful solo counter-tenor and singing teacher. Of the girls, Enid Bannatyne became a professional singer as did Cynthia Buchan. The latter is now on the teaching staff of RSAMD. The programme had an attractive cover with a wide selection of heads of animals photographed in Edinburgh Zoo. Press reports were complimentary and I had a charming letter from Dame Flora Robson, the celebrated actress, accepting my invitation to attend one of the performances. She was in Edinburgh to take part in a Festival production.

The 1982 production was equally memorable but inevitably different in many respects. It had been my intention, as before, to involve as wide a cross-section of the community as possible, but this time I was unable to obtain the same degree of co-operation from the region Education Authority and turned to the Independent schools. My approach was received with great enthusiasm, especially by Brian Head of Stewart's Melville College. The 1982 production was part of the official programme of the Edinburgh International Festival and consequently benefited from its world-wide publicity. The result was that all of the performances were sold out long before the opening dates, save for a few limited visibility seats!

The principal parts of Mr and Mrs Noye were sung by the well-known Scottish singers, William McCue and Linda Ormiston, both soloists with Scottish Opera. "Bill" McCue began his working life as a miner and did not take up professional singing until he was in his thirties. He had a fine voice and great ability for dramatic characterisation. However, his musical knowledge and background were limited and his singing could be unpredictable. At the final rehearsals, he told me he relied on me to keep him right and that I should get the blame if anything went wrong! I have to say that whilst his interpretation of Noye was superb, no two performances were exactly the same! However, these problems were minimal compared to the difficulties I had with God! This spoken part has to be declaimed rhythmically to accompanying music and the actor playing the part seemed incapable of doing this. After many frustrating attempts to teach him, in the end I placed him immediately in front of the conductor's desk and mouthed the words for him. Even then, he was not always rhythmic! Among the cast of over three hundred performers were a good number of pupils from St Mary's Music School and choristers of the Cathedral choir. The "professional" string quintet and piano duet parts were played by Music School pupils and choristers sang the solo parts of the Sons of Noye and their Wives. As in the previous production, a number of the young people have subsequently entered the music profession, notably, Rupert Jeffcoat and Susan Hamilton, making a name as a solo soprano. Other choristers singing solo parts were Alexander Armstrong, Lindsay Allan, Richard Lewis, David Henderson, Celia Birkinshaw (now a professional bassoonist) and Eva Patterson. The players in the solo string quintet were Claire Docherty and Edmund Coxon (violins), Judith Busbridge (viola), Alison Brown and Catherine Smith ('cellos) and Elizabeth Bradley (double-bass). All of them have entered the music profession. The piano duettists were Kevin Cockburn and Christopher Hobkirk. Christopher was a former chorister, lay clerk and is now making a career as a solo tenor as well as singing in the choir at Salisbury Cathedral. Simon Archer was the timpanist and he is also now a professional. Our able producer was Patricia Tulloch and the performances were widely praised in the press. An extra performance was recorded by Scottish Television and shown nation-wide throughout the UK in the following January. For this I was offered a fee which was considerably less than that being paid to the principal soloists. I thought I should check this with the ISM. (Incorporated Society of Musicians) and was told that my fee should be no less than the soloists. This was received with some surprise by the TV company but the amount was agreed. It was the largest fee I had ever received up to that time.

Both productions required months of preparation, planning and organisation but they were among the most rewarding and satisfying ventures. They were also great fun!

In 1975 the choristers were invited to provide the children's chorus in Andrew Lloyd Webber's musical *Joseph and the Amazing Technicolor Dreamcoat* in the King's Theatre and in 1989, four of the choristers, Simon Roulston, Matthew Pritchard and brothers, William and Mark Wood, took part in an Edinburgh Festival production of *Boris Godunov* presented by the Moscow State Theatre Company in Leith Town Hall. Their principal function was to sing The Lord's Prayer in Russian! I received a charming letter of thanks from the Russian repetiteur, Jahnova Tania and also an invitation to visit Moscow with the choir. Alas, we were never able to take this up, but pupils and staff from our Music School have exchanged visits with the Gnessin Music School in Moscow.

The visit of the Hungarian State Ballet Company from Budapest in 1983, to perform a "Rock" Ballet in the Playhouse Theatre at the Edinburgh Festival, provided an unlikely, surprising and unexpected invitation for me to conduct the music. The title of the Ballet was *Proba* (meaning both rehearsal and trial) in which the central part was the portrayal of a rehearsal of a work concerning the Passion of Christ. The opening section, during which the dancers are seen limbering up, is accompanied by electronically produced "Rock" music, whilst the music for the main part of the Ballet is recorded extracts from Bach's *St John Passion, B minor Mass* and *The Toccata and Fugue in D minor* (S 565), for organ. A problem arose because the Musicians Union insisted that the Bach should be performed by "live" musicians. I was asked by the Director of the Festival, John Drummond, to gather together a group of singers and a tenor soloist with less than a month's notice. As an orchestra was considered too expensive to engage for a whole week, I was asked to use the Theatre's Wurlitzer organ for the accompaniments and the solo Toccata and Fugue. I selected sixteen singers of my Scottish Cantata Singers, John Robertson from Scottish Opera to sing the solo aria and Michael Chibbett, an Edinburgh organist, to play the accompaniments and I played the solo organ piece. The Playhouse had previously been a cinema and in common with many cinemas throughout the UK in the 1920s and 1930s had a theatre organ and resident organist to entertain the audience during the intermission breaks. In boyhood days in Lincoln, I had been fascinated by the sight and sound of the organ in the Savoy Cinema, rising from below the stage with colourful lights and played by Arthur Barraclough, the resident organist. Now, I thought my youthful ambitions to play such an instrument were to be realised, but because the stage area was required by the dancers, the organ and the singers had to remain in the pit, unseen, and so my vision of rising into view with flashing lights was thwarted!

Closed circuit television cameras enabled me to see the dancers and to judge when to start and stop each musical extract and recordings of the music were given me in advance so that I could absorb the tempi at which the company were accustomed to perform. All went well until the matinee performance on the final Saturday, when without warning, the A above middle C failed to sound at the beginning of the organ Fugue! Since the note is an essential and frequently recurring part of the fugal subject, it was a major problem and was temporarily solved by quickly transferring to another manual. The dancers were in full flow so that the continuity of the music had to be maintained. The company were a delight to work with and presented us with bottles of Hungarian wine, after the final performance, as a token of their appreciation. We played to capacity audiences in what is a very large auditorium and the press reports referred to the production as "a major popular success which would prove the year's biggest crowd-puller."

The performance of contemporary music has always been a special interest and particularly by composers living and working in Scotland. Hans Gál, David Dorward, and Frank Spedding have been previously mentioned, whilst John McLeod, Ronald Stevenson and Kenneth Leighton provided some very special opportunities. In 1980, the first performance of John McLeod's *Hebridean Prayers* was given in St Cuthbert's Church by the Scottish Chamber Choir and the Cathedral choristers, conducted by Colin Tipple. The press report described the opening and closing "Ave Maria" as most beautifully sung by the choristers of St Mary's Cathedral. A further performance of the work was given on BBC television in 1983 from Merchiston Castle School in Edinburgh, where John McLeod, at that time, was Director of Music, in a programme of hymns and readings entitled "Rejoice and Sing". The School choir and orchestra, the Scottish Chamber Choir, Scots Brass and Sancha Pielou (harpist) were also involved.

In March 1986, John McLeod conducted the world premiere of his *Stabat Mater* in the Usher Hall. This large-scale work had been commissioned by Edinburgh Royal Choral Union and was scored for adult choir, orchestra, soloists and children's choir. The Latin text of the *Stabat Mater* was interspersed with five poems ranging from 7th-century Arabian to 20th-century Russian. The ERCU were joined by the Scottish Chamber Orchestra, distinguished soloists Jane Manning (soprano) and Benjamin Luxon (baritone), a children's choir drawn from St. Mary's Music School and the Edinburgh Academy, and off-stage boys' choir and treble soloist from the choristers of the Cathedral. I was asked to train the children's choir and to prepare the choristers and the solo treble. It was a memorable event and the press especially praised the soloists for their skill. "The Scotsman" referred to "a remarkable treble soloist, Richard Townhill, a small boy attacking confidently a very difficult part and the off-stage boys' chorus sounding angelic at the end of the piece." Since Richard was our eldest grandson, the comments were particularly pleasing. He was an outstanding chorister who sang a great many solos during services, broadcasts and recordings. He was the treble soloist in the Scottish performances of Andrew Lloyd Webber's *Requiem* and was invited by the composer to sing the "Pie Jesu" with the distinguished Scottish soprano, Judith Lovat, in a commercial recording of Lloyd Webber's music.

In 1985 the BBC commissioned Ronald Stevenson to compose settings of poems from the volume by Robert Louis Stevenson, entitled *A Child's Garden of Verses* to mark the centenary of the first publication. Ronald's grandson, Daniel, was a chorister in the Cathedral choir at the time and this led to the composer's interest in its music and to our friendship. He set the poems for tenor and two children's voices, with piano accompaniment, and the work was given its first broadcast performance on BBC Radio Scotland on 29 November 1988. The soloists were Neil Mackie (tenor), Richard Townhill and Susan Hamilton, both Cathedral choristers, rehearsed and accompanied by the composer.

In 1985 the London Festival Orchestra established a Summer Festival of Music in selected cathedrals throughout the UK. The founder of the orchestra and its Director, Ross Pople, had given up his position as principal 'cellist of the BBC Symphony Orchestra to gather together some of the finest professional instrumentalists in the country. The mixed programmes of choral and orchestral music featured the cathedral choirs conducted by their choirmasters and distinguished international vocal and instrumental soloists. St Mary's was one of the first venues to be chosen and the choir and the orchestra established an immediate rapport which led Ross Pople to book us annually, in advance, for as long as the series continued. The choral repertoire included Mass settings by Mozart, Haydn and Schubert, Fauré *Requiem* and Holst *Psalms* all performed before capacity audiences.

The second-half of the 1980s and the beginning of the 1990s contained a number of notable anniversaries and milestones which were marked by musical celebrations of one kind or another. 1986 was the twenty-fifth anniversary of my appointment at St Mary's and we were very moved by all the kind and generous things that were said and written, and the gifts we received. There were two principal musical events to mark the anniversary weekend: (1) Festal Evensong sung by the combined choirs of the seven Scottish Episcopal Cathedrals of Aberdeen, Dundee, Glasgow, Inverness, Oban, Perth and St Mary's Edinburgh on 4 October and (2) the first performance of an anthem commissioned by the Provost, composed and conducted by Kenneth Leighton during the Choral Eucharist on Sunday morning, 5 October. I had no idea that this was to happen, and never cease to marvel how the choir had secretly rehearsed and learnt the music with Peter Backhouse without my knowledge! It is a beautiful setting for unaccompanied voices of memorable words by Edward Taylor (c. 1642-1729) *What love is this of thine, that cannot be in thine infinity, O Lord, confined?* After the service, the composer presented me with an inscribed copy of his original manuscript, flung his arms round me and kissed me! It was a very memorable occasion.

Earlier in the year, I had organised two concerts of church and organ music by Francis Jackson and Kenneth Leighton, both close friends and associates of long standing. In the first concert, Kenneth Leighton conducted the choir in a number of his canticles and anthems including the *Te Deum in D* (1964), *The Second Service* (1972) and *Awake, my glory* (1979) and I played a selection of the organ pieces. For the second concert, Francis Jackson played some of his organ music, whilst I conducted the choir in the choral pieces which included *The Benedicite, Evening Canticles and Communion Service in G*, the first performance of the anthem *Eternal Power* and the *Te Deum in D* (written for our choir). The organ accompaniments on both occasions were, as always, impeccably played by Peter Backhouse. In addition the Cathedral Music Society decided that it would arrange a special concert to mark my Jubilee and invited me to choose a work that I would like to perform and conduct. *The Creation* by Haydn had long been a favourite work and one that I had only once previously conducted, probably because of the large orchestra required and expense involved. The Music Society obtained financial support from the Scottish Arts Council through, the National Federation of Music Societies and private sponsorship which enabled them to engage Sarah Leonard, Andrew Murgatroyd and Richard Suart as soloists. They had all sung for me previously which ensured relaxed rehearsal and total commitment. Our daughter-in-law, Katrine, joined them in the solo quartet in the third part of the oratorio. The Scottish Cantata Singers provided the chorus, the orchestra of mostly professional players included the strings of the Meadows Chamber Orchestra, and Kenneth Leighton played the harpsichord part. The Society invited a number of special guests to the performance including as many personal friends as I wished. Philip Crosfield wrote an appreciation and Peter Backhouse the notes on the music for a special souvenir programme and a gala performance of the happy work was given on 16 November to a capacity audience. In addition, the BBC invited me to introduce and play some of my favourite organ pieces for broadcast in the series entitled, "The Musician in Scotland". The programme consisted of Bach, *Prelude and Fugue in G minor* (S 535); Chorale Prelude *Nun freut euch* (S 734) Thomas Arne, *A Maggot*; Vaughan Williams, *Prelude on Rhosymedre*; Gordon Slater, *Prelude on St Botolph*; Howells, *Master Tallis's Testament*; Leighton, *Fantasy on St Columba* and Vierne, *Postlude in B minor*.

In 1987 the Royal School of Church Music celebrated its diamond jubilee with a number of special events. The centrepiece was a Festival Service in the Royal Albert Hall, London, on 25 June in the presence of Her Majesty the Queen. A choir of eight hundred and fifty singers was selected from the affiliated choirs throughout the world. Our choir provided three choristers and three lay clerks plus myself for the service which was televised and recorded. The anniversary was also marked in Scotland with a special service, organised by the Scottish Committee of the RSCM and held in St Cuthbert's Parish Church, Lothian Road, Edinburgh, on 30 May. Our choir took part together with over seven hundred singers from affiliated choirs of all denominations in Scotland. The order of service and music was the same as that devised for the service in the Royal Albert Hall. On both occasions, the choirs were rehearsed and conducted by Dr Lionel Dakers CBE, Director of the RSCM, and I played the organ accompaniments for the Scottish service. A professional brass and percussion group added extra brilliance and splendour to some of the accompaniments.

Mention of brass reminds me that later that year I was invited by the Edinburgh Festival Society, to give a concert in St Mary's Cathedral with Michael Laird and William Houghton, two of Britain's leading trumpet players. Organ and brass sound well in the acoustics of a cathedral and pieces by John Stanley, Vivaldi, Aaron Copland and Malcolm Arnold made a splendid effect. An arrangement of Copland's *Quiet City* for trumpet and flugelhorn was quite magical, and organ pieces by Hollins, Bach, César Franck and Kenneth Leighton were well received.

The second-half of 1988 was marked by a number of significant events. The first brought us great sadness, for on Wednesday, 24 August, the composer, Kenneth Leighton died at the age of 58. It so happened on that date, I was giving one of my regular organ recitals during the Edinburgh Festival period and found myself thinking of him with a sense of foreboding. He had been diagnosed as having inoperable cancer of the oesophagus earlier in the year, and although he remained remarkably cheerful and positive, he eventually succumbed. We spent a happy afternoon at his home in June, when he told me that he had ideas in his mind for a fourth symphony and we discussed plans for me to record his complete organ works to mark his sixtieth birthday in 1989. Alas, it was the last time I saw him.

The private funeral service attended by members of the family, was held on 27 August. I played his Fantasies on *Lumetto* and *St Columba* on the small electronic organ in the Crematorium Chapel and two of his favourite hymns, "The King of Love", to the tune *St Columba* and "Shall we gather by the river" to the American tune, Boston, were sung. It all seemed incongruous but very moving in its stark reality.

A public Service of Thanksgiving for the life and work of Kenneth Leighton was held in St Mary's on 27 October, at which the choir was joined by that from St Giles' Cathedral, representatives from Wakefield Cathedral choir, in which Leighton had sung as a boy, and the Waverley Singers of Edinburgh. All the music in the service, except for the hymn tunes, was by the composer. The address and tribute was given by the Provost of St Mary's , the lesson by the Provost of Wakefield and the prayers led by the Revd. Gilleasbuig Macmillan, Minister of St Giles. Before the service, John Scott, a former Wakefield chorister and at this time sub-organist and Assistant Director of Music, St Paul's Cathedral, London played *Veni Redemptor - A Celebration* (for organ) Opus 93. The piece was commissioned by the North Wales Music Festival in 1985, dedicated to John Scott, who gave the first performance in St Asaph Cathedral. After the service I played *Paean*. Herrick Bunney, Master of the Music at St Giles conducted St Giles' choir in the Kyrie, Credo and Agnus Dei from The Mass Opus 44, written for him and the Edinburgh University Singers in 1964. The Service began with The Finale from *Sequence for All Saints* Opus 75 sung by the combined Cathedral choirs with the congregation joining in the hymn, "Give me the wings of faith." The work had been commissioned by the West Riding Cathedrals' Festival, and first performed in Wakefield Cathedral by the choirs of Wakefield, Bradford and Sheffield, conducted by Jonathan Bielby. The other anthem, *What love is this of thine?* was sung by St Mary's choir which I conducted as well as the finale from the Sequence. Three of the *Six Elizabethan Lyrics*, Opus 65 for childrens' voices were sung by the Waverley Singers conducted by Pamela Duncan. Their more secular idiom made a refreshing contrast and seemed entirely apt and appropriate. The hymns, "The King of Love" (Tune St Columba) and "All my hope on God is founded" (Tune Michael by Herbert Howells) completed the musical part of the service. The organ accompaniments were played by Peter Backhouse and Morley Whitehead, assistant organists at St Mary's and St Giles respectively.

In September, a two day conference for church musicians was held at Carberry, near Edinburgh. It was a new venture arranged by the Church of Scotland Panel on Worship Committee and attracted about one hundred organists, choirmasters and Ministers from all parts of Scotland. It was symptomatic of the increasingly friendly relationship and co-operation between the different church denominations that I had been co-opted on to the Church of Scotland Music Committee, and invited to rehearse and conduct the choral music for the conference and take workshops in organ playing. Others involved were The Revd Andrew Scobie, convener of the Panel on Worship, Alan Tait, an Edinburgh organist and Convener of the Music Committee, Jock Stein, Warden of Carberry, The Revd Fred Muir, Chairman of the RSCM Scottish Committee and The Revd John Bell. John Bell has emerged as a significant figure in church music throughout the UK, especially in the promotion of worship songs and the use of traditional melodies. The conference revealed the increasing use of more popular styles of music in worship and the greater variety of instruments for accompaniment. It was a trend begun in the 1960s with the advent of new liturgies and language which affected all denominations for good or ill!

In 1985 the Cathedral architect reported that urgent restoration work was needed on the fabric of the building. In response to this the Provost gathered a group of people together to discuss the problem and it was eventually decided to establish the Cathedral's own team of stonemasons. This imaginative scheme was launched in January 1986 and on 23 October 1988, the Cathedral Workshop buildings were formally opened by HRH Prince Edward. After the unveiling of a plaque, the Prince attended Festal Evensong in the Cathedral, together with the Lord Provost of the City (Mrs Eleanor McLaughlin), the Bishop of Edinburgh, the Chairman of the Workshop Project and other dignitaries. The music of the service included my Introit Anthem, *Lo, God is here*, Byrd *Responses*, Canticles *Murrill in E* and the anthem, *Come, Holy Ghost, The Maker* by the Scottish composer Cedric Thorpe Davie. After the service, a number of people, including myself, were presented to His Royal Highness in the Chapter House. He congratulated me on the singing of the choir but said that he found the anthem of Cedric Thorpe Davie rather lugubrious!

In the 1980s the issue of girls singing in cathedral choirs attracted a great deal of attention in the media and became a matter of contentious debate which continues to rumble on, rather like the issue of women priests in the church. As I was very much involved, and feel it cannot be dismissed in a few sentences, I intend closing this account of some special services and events and devote a separate chapter to the subject.

Chapter 11 - Girls in Cathedral Choirs - A Contentious Issue

"Are girls different? Not really but they sometimes have longer hair"

In 1978 the first girl chorister was admitted into the Cathedral choir alongside the boys. It was an issue that had come under increasing scrutiny since the admission of girls into St Mary's Music School in 1972. The decision to take this step was finally made in response to an application from a neighbouring local authority on behalf of a musical girl whom the authority felt would benefit from the opportunities and environment of our school. Eva Patterson, the girl in question, was auditioned on the piano, oboe and singing. Whilst her playing showed some promise, it was not of sufficiently high a standard, at that time, to justify the school offering her an instrumental place. However, she possessed a good voice and clearly loved singing. Aural tests also revealed that she had a keen musical ear. The Head Teacher, Dr Carolyn Coxon, suggested that Eva could be admitted into the school as a chorister if I would agree. After consultation with distinguished musical colleagues and a good deal of heart-searching and initial reluctance, I did agree. I have never regarded myself as a revolutionary of any kind, musical or otherwise, and I certainly did not wish to see the disintegration of the unique boys-only tradition, but in our context the experiment has proved successful.

Whilst girls had previously sung in the choirs of St David's Cathedral in Wales and St Edmundsbury Cathedral in Suffolk we were the first British Cathedral to establish a treble line of boys and girls of the same age. Our decision attracted a good deal of interest and curiosity, not least among my fellow Cathedral organists and their clergy. In 1987, I was asked by Lionel Dakers, Director of the RSCM and Honorary Secretary of the Cathedral Organists' Association, to give a talk on the subject at the COA Conference in Coventry. Significantly, the vote of thanks was given by Richard Seal, Organist and Master of the Choristers at Salisbury Cathedral, who wrote to me three years later to tell me that he was interested in starting a girls' choir there. In 1990, the COA was invited to hold its two-day residential conference in Edinburgh which was also open to wives. Stephen Cleobury, Director of Music at King's College, Cambridge, and President that year, asked me to produce a discussion paper.

In addition to hearing the choir sing at the daily services Stephen said that the delegates wished to attend a choir practice and see how I trained the boys and the girls together. Richard Seal's letter and my Paper are probably as good a way as any for the issue to be set out.

Letter from Richard Seal, Organist and Master of the Choristers, Salisbury Cathedral.

Salisbury, 14 June ,1990.

Dear Dennis,

As you can imagine, ever since the news broke about Salisbury being interested in starting a girls' choir, being run parallel to that of the boys, I had hoped that I would be hearing from you at some stage. For you are the one person in the country who has had experience and skill at developing girls' voices. In fact, when the whole idea occurred to me last autumn of this particular venture I had it in mind to pay you a visit and pick your brains. But alas, this never came about. So in a sense I'm going into the whole business with my eyes closed - into the unknown without knowing really what I am going to find. Nevertheless, there is still plenty of time before this scheme gets under way and I really would value your expertise on this subject, besides which it would be nice to pay you a visit in Edinburgh and see you on home ground.

As you may imagine, ever since the Sunday Independent got hold of our plans about a month ago (which was a little bit before we were prepared for it) I have had all sorts of reactions from all kinds of people. On the whole, reactions have been favourable, but always with the proviso that the boys' choir tradition will continue and will be not be dented to any degree. All along this view has been my intention because I do value the male choir tradition, which is unique in this country, very highly.

I remember your talk to the COA in Coventry a few years back when you spoke about working with boys and girls together and you played us all a very remarkable tape of your choir. If I remember rightly one of the items was a Te Deum in D by Francis Jackson which I did not know and which impressed me. I was also impressed by the standard of singing and the fact, that to all intents and purpose's it sounded just like a boys' choir. I am most grateful to you for letting me have a copy of your paper as requested by Stephen Cleobury, for it contains so much useful and practical information. I reckon I have already learnt a lot simply by reading this.

Of course, before the scheme gets under way here in Salisbury there's a lot of work to do, not least the raising of a considerable sum of money which will endow the music scholarships for the girls. We are in the process at the moment of gathering together a small group of Trustees who will, hopefully, look after the finances. If my optimism is rewarded then in January of next year it could be that we will be auditioning our first girls with a view to starting the choir in September 1991. It all seems a bit of a pipe dream I must say, but I'm optimistic and enthusiastic and sometimes where there's a will there's a way.

In conclusion, I do hope that you and I can have a few minutes together perhaps later this year. I would value it greatly.

With very best wishes from all in Salisbury.

Yours sincerely,
Richard Seal

BOYS AND GIRLS IN CATHEDRAL CHOIRS

Do they mix and can they mix?

This article is written in response to a request from The President of the Cathedral Organists' Association, Stephen Cleobury, that I should produce something on the question of boys and girls singing together in the choirs. He said that this is an area which is going to move into the centre of our concern in coming years and he thought it might be stimulating to have a paper to start off our discussions.

I claim no special knowledge of this subject, only some experience of running the choir at St Mary's Cathedral, Edinburgh, in which the treble line is sung by a combination of boys and girls. Of course, such a combination is nothing new. For centuries, boys and girls have sung together in school and church choirs and still do so. But it is a fairly recent phenomenon for both to sing together in a normal Anglican Cathedral Choir and very rare.

It is not the intention of this article or its author to proselytise or persuade the reader to adopt the practice, as in Edinburgh, but rather to give a factual account of how it came about and how it works. The reader can then make up his or her own mind.

Perhaps the best way to begin is to pose some of the statements that were made, and the questions that were asked, when we were considering taking girls into the choir and try and give some answers and comments.

1) Has not the treble line in Cathedral Choirs always been sung by boys? Yes, but you could ask why this has been so and find that it has not been entirely, or even primarily, for musical reasons. It is arguable whether the music would have been very much different if the top line had been girls and/or boys.

2) Are not girls different from boys? Yes, in some respects, but not all that different before puberty. Length and style of hair can be the most obvious and visible sign, but even that is no guarantee of identification.

3) Boys' voices are different from girls'. I believe that, generally speaking, boys' voices have a different timbre from those of girls before puberty. During the last year of a boy's treble voice, there is a special power and quality that is distinctive. Generally speaking, girls' voices are not so strong before puberty and tend to develop resonance at a later age than boys. It is my experience that boys' and girls' voices do not differ all that much between the ages of seven and thirteen years and that girls can be trained to make much the same sound as boys. I have also known many boys whose voices one could only describe as "girlish" and many girls whose voices one could only describe as "boyish". Girls' voices tend to be thinner and lighter in quality than boys but that is a generalisation. Both are capable of coping with a vocal line of two octaves upwards from middle C. It is of primary importance that both boys and girls have potential voices of good quality, freely produced and a keen musical ear. That is surely more important than their gender.

4) There would be social and discipline problems if girls were mixed with boys in the choir. It is true that boys do not particularly like girls at chorister age but they will tolerate them. It is true that you cannot treat girls in the same way as boys and they respond to discipline in different ways. In general, boys forget reprimands very quickly and will accept discipline with surprising tolerance. Girls are much more likely to harbour a grudge after reprimand and to recover much more slowly from criticism. Boys and girls tend to keep to their own kind at play and in making friends, but this is true in a school context as well.

Up to the year 1972, the Choir and Choir School attached to St Mary's Cathedral had consisted entirely of boy trebles. In that year, the school was reorganised into a specialist music school for children showing outstanding gifts on an instrument, mainly strings. Places were guaranteed within the school for boys who sang in the Cathedral Choir. Their admission was on the grounds of vocal potential and suitability as choristers, not because they showed special musical aptitude as instrumentalists. It is a small school of between forty and fifty pupils ranging from the age of seven to eighteen years. At the same time, girls were admitted to the school as instrumentalists. Boys and girls, therefore, worked together in small groups for both academic and musical activities. It was not long before girls were asking to sing in the choir. Many of the instrumental teachers were opposed to instrumental pupils doing so. In response to my argument that the Cathedral choral training was musically valuable to all children, they asked why girls were denied the opportunity. We therefore had to face the question and come up with a convincing answer. We sought advice from many sources such as the RSCM, Sir David Lumsden, Professor Kenneth Leighton and Professor Michael Tilmouth. The three latter distinguished musicians were all members of the school Management Committee at the time. The result was that we decided to grasp the nettle and take girls into the Cathedral Choir alongside the boys. Whatever the result musically, the decision has led to a greater integration of choral and musical instrumental pupils. It has led to a more harmonious relationship between members of choir and school music staff. It has led to greater appreciation and respect for the choir by both instrumental pupils and instrumental teachers.

How does the system work?

The boys and girls enter and leave the choir at the same age, i.e. they enter at seven or eight years old and leave between the ages of thirteen and fourteen years. They attend all practices and services together and receive the same vocal training alongside one another. Statistically, the girls have always been in the minority, approximately one girl per three or four boys. This is not by design but simply how it has worked out. It may well be asked whether this has a bearing on the sound of the treble line and on its social success. I do not know the answer.

Some of the positive benefits I have noticed are the following:-

The commitment and loyalty of the girls is as great as the boys'. The girls' voices are, in general, the equal of the boys. Some of the girls have developed into good solo singers as do the boys. There have been some outstanding girl choristers who have maintained as good an example and upheld discipline as well as any boy. The girls, in general, seem to have as much stamina as the boys. There have been few problems of blending the timbre of boys' and girls' voices into an acceptable musical sound. I have

124

only had one girl with such a distinctive vocal sound that blend proved a problem. The same problem could well arise with a boy's voice.

Are there any disadvantages?

Appearance and hairstyle are sometimes a problem. Girls tend to grow bigger sooner than boys and become self-conscious around the age of thirteen. Girls tend to become interested in the younger choral scholars and lay clerks at that age too. None of these things creates insuperable problems nor do they outweigh all the positive benefits that have accrued for us in our context and circumstances.

Dennis Townhill
Organist and Master of the Choristers
St Mary's Episcopal Cathedral, Edinburgh, 1990.

The conference was duly held in May 1990 and some thirty-one organists and their wives sat in the Song School whilst the choristers went through their daily routine of vocal exercises and rehearsal of service music. I was also asked to allow them to hear the boys and the girls together and separately so that the difference, if any, of the voices could be noted.

The group included organists of many of the most important establishments in the country such as King's and St John's Colleges, Cambridge, Westminster Abbey, the Cathedrals of Durham, Norwich, Peterborough, Gloucester, Wells and York so that we were acutely aware of being placed under intense critical scrutiny.

The reaction of the choristers was, "What a cheek!" The two head choristers, both of whom were girls, suggested that after we had finished our routine, a screen should be placed in front of the listeners and then their ability to distinguish between the girls and the boys tested. We gave each a sheet of paper, asking them to put their names on it and then we arranged for the choristers to sing in ten different permutations of voices and age groups. The papers were collected, marked and revealed a surprising degree of inaccuracy. Interestingly, the highest marks were scored by two of the wives! The choristers suggested the results should be sent to the press, but I refused to submit colleagues to such potential embarrassment. The whole exercise was received with good-humoured appreciation.

Dr Harry Bramma, Director of the RSCM, who also attended the conference wrote a thoughtful and well-reasoned article for the October issue of the RSCM quarterly magazine. In it he states, "Having, I hope, made out a strong case for the retention of the all-male choir in our churches, I will now try to demonstrate why I believe an equally strong case can be made out for the introduction of choirs of girls. I am fully aware of the brilliant work Dr Dennis Townhill has done in recent years in St Mary's Cathedral, Edinburgh, training a choir in which girls sing alongside the boys. I don't believe this should become normal practice - particularly as I suspect success in this area is only achieved by a very remarkable choir trainer."

Whilst it was flattering to receive such generous praise, I believe there are many other choir trainers capable of achieving equally good if not better results. However, the next stage in the development of girls' choirs was taken by Richard Seal who was invited to produce a discussion paper for a meeting of the Working Party of Deans, Provosts, Cathedral Organists and Choir Schools in January 1991. This outlined his plan to begin a separate girls' choir in Salisbury in September of that year. It is interesting to note that he proposed that the girls should be drawn from the same age group as the boys i.e. 8 to13 years. Since then, many cathedrals have formed girls' choirs, all separate groups, as at Salisbury, except for Manchester, where the top line is mixed as in Edinburgh. There are obvious financial implications in running two separate groups, especially where the choristers are educated in fee-paying schools and also extra rehearsal time involved. As far as I know, the introduction of girls' choirs has not led to the disappearance of the boys' tradition, but rather extended the range of musical opportunities.

Chapter 12 - Overseas Tours (1962-1990)

"The whole thing's a surprise!"

Living and working in a city such as Edinburgh provided many opportunities for making contacts with music and musicians from other countries. After the war, nations acquired civic and cultural links with one another through a system of "twinning", with comparable cities. Edinburgh has a number of prominent "sister" cities such as Nice (France), Munich (Germany), Florence (Italy), San Diego (USA), Ziang (China) and Kiev (Ukraine). Soon after our arrival in 1961, the Lord Provost received a letter from the Chaplain of Holy Trinity Anglican Church, Nice, asking him to provide a contact with Edinburgh's Anglican Cathedral. 1962 was the anniversary of the centenary of Holy Trinity Church and the Chaplain, Canon Harry Hearsey, wished to invite the Cathedral choir to sing at the Sunday services during July. To mark the centenary the Church had sold some of its land and built a hall with the proceeds. An upper floor could be used as a dormitory and enabled the Chaplain to invite groups of young people .

The Côte d'Azur has been a favourite winter resort for wealthy British people since Victorian times and many settled in the small towns along the Mediterranean coast. One of the main thoroughfares in Nice is named Avenue des Anglais and Anglican churches in places such as Beaulieu, Menton, Vence, Monte Carlo and Cannes reflect the connection. The resident congregations were now predominantly elderly and a choir of young people was an obvious attraction. Our party of fourteen choristers, the Provost and his wife, the Precentor and myself set off by plane on 4 July for a fortnight's visit. I had never travelled outwith the UK before, nor by plane, so that it was a very new experience. I was certainly unprepared for the warm, humid atmosphere which enveloped us when we arrived in Nice, and for the first sight of palm trees at the airport. The next morning the choristers appeared for breakfast smartly dressed in school uniform , ties, grey woollen jumpers, woollen socks and black shoes. Canon Hearsey looked at them in astonishment and told them to change immediately into their lighter leisure clothes! The brilliant sunshine was already producing temperatures in the high 70s F at 8am. We were advised to keep out of the sun during the middle of the day, and restrict periods of sunbathing. Despite this, there was plenty of opportunity for swimming in the warm Mediterranean sea, and we all returned to Edinburgh with well-tanned bodies.

Our main meal was provided out of doors from a Kosher restaurant abutting the church garden. The restaurant was owned by a Polish refugee Jewish family and the food prepared by the owner's amply-built wife, Madame Lache. The meals were wonderful and we were treated to many unfamiliar dishes such as "Coq au Vin", mushroom omelettes, plain yoghurt and other French-style recipes. Unfortunately this type of menu was not to the liking of the choristers, and a disheartened Madame Lache was perplexed by their refusal to eat what she provided. I had to explain to her that whilst the adults greatly enjoyed and appreciated her efforts the choristers were more used to such things as fish and chips, meat pies and chips and beans on toast. Towards the end of our stay the menu changed drastically and we received "pommes frites" with everything!

We sang for the Sunday services as required and also sang either an Evensong or concert in the churches along the coast to large and appreciative audiences and congregations. We were given a civic reception by the Mayor of Nice at the Town Hall and another highlight was a visit to Prince Rainier's Palace at Monaco. Our visit coincided with the celebration of France's national holiday on 14 July during an annual folk-lore festival held in Nice. Singers, bands and dancers in their national costumes from many European countries, process down the Avenue Victoire to the Place Messena, watched by huge, cheering crowds. After the défilé of about a mile, each group's national flag is raised, their national anthem sung and then all join hands and dance a farandole to music by Bizet. The tempo of the music grows faster and faster, and the dance more and more vigorous so that by the end everyone is in a state of exhaustion. Evening concerts of national songs and dances are given in the open air Théâtre de Verdure, and a spectacular, late-night fireworks display is given on Bastille Day, 14 July, which we watched from the beach. We were invited to take part in this festival and sang Scots songs in the Théâtre de Verdure, wearing our scarlet cassocks. The organisers of the festival asked us to wear national costume on any subsequent visit. We made six tours to Nice in successive years and wore tartan kilts for the festival and civic receptions, including myself! Another regular feature was a day's outing by bus to the ski resort of Colmiaine, in the Alpes Maritimes. The three hour journey wound its way like a corkscrew up the mountain road. There was no ski-ing, of course, at this time of the year but the ski-lifts were operating. We were all given food in plastic bags and taken to the top of the mountain for a picnic. Afterwards, I noticed the choristers filling their empty bags with insects which resembled large "daddy-long-legs". Asking them what they were, they replied, "dinnakens". In my ignorance of insects, I accepted their word. Some time later when I became more familiar with Scottish expressions, I realised they were fooling me and what they really meant was they "dinna ken" (did not know) what they were! Worse was to follow, as on our descent from the mountain in the ski-lifts, they proceeded to empty their (dinnakens) on to the heads of those walking down. The Master of the Choristers "wiz nae pleased!"

Our last visit to the Côte d'Azur was in 1967 when we were able to take a group of lay clerks as well as the choristers. This was an extended tour as we spent five days in Paris at the invitation of Susan Landale before travelling down to Nice. Susan arranged for us to sing Sunday morning service at St George's Anglican Church where she was organist, a weekday Capitular High Mass in Notre Dame Cathedral and at the Sunday evening Mass in St Séverin Church in the Latin quarter of the city. Coincidentally, an organ recital before the service at St Séverin was given by Martin Neary, subsequently organist of Winchester Cathedral and Westminster Abbey. The choristers were housed in the Choir School at Notre Dame and were most impressed by the toilets which were simply holes in the floor and the fact that they were allowed some wine with their meals!

Through a recommendation from Susan, I was invited to record a programme of organ music in the Concert Hall of the ORTF. This proved to be an interesting experience. The hall was empty when I arrived for a practice in the morning with a couple of lay clerks to assist, but the console was open and there were no problems. After having a break for a snack, we turned up at the allotted time for the recording session. Again the hall was empty and there was no sign of a producer or engineers or indeed, anyone.

128

Eventually, wires appeared from the ceiling with microphones dangling from them, and a voice called out, "Quand vous voulez." I took this to mean that I was to begin and duly played through the first piece. Fully expecting someone to come and comment on the performance over questions of balance or other problems as in Britain, it was surprising when no one came. After a short period of silence, the disembodied voice called out again, "Quand vous voulez", and so the second piece was played. By this time we had discovered that the recording engineers were operating from a control room at the back of the concert hall as we could see heads through narrow windows at the top of the wall! The next unexpected event was the appearance of a lady with a clip-board who announced, "Je suis le speaker" and asked for information on the pieces and composers. After that, someone else appeared, handed me a cheque in payment, for which I signed a contract and receipt. Then the recording continued as before without any repetition or critical comment. When we had completed the programme, the voice called out, "Au revoir, merci bien" and that was that! Susan wrote some time later to tell me she had heard the subsequent broadcast and that all was satisfactory and it had been well received.

Another opportunity for overseas tours was provided by the Ecumenical Festival of Choirs in Worship, held in different European cities every three or four years. These gatherings were begun by Harald Wolff, Cantor of Unser Lieben Frauen, Bremen, and Evert Westra, Cantor of Nieuwe Kerk, Groningen. Their intention was to foster better international relations between the different European countries through church music after the conflict of the second world war. Choirs took part from Germany, France, Holland, Denmark, Italy, Norway, Sweden and Great Britain, representing different traditions - Lutheran, Anglican, Roman Catholic and Dutch and French Reformed. Our choir was invited to attend the third Festival in Rotterdam in April 1961, but my first experience of the event was in September 1965 when it was held in Bremen over a period of five days. Some four hundred singers, young people and adults, from ten choirs took part ranging from Trondheim, Kristiansand (Norway), Uppsala (Sweden), Herning (Denmark), Groningen (Holland), Paris, Marseilles (France), Naples (Italy), the hosts, Bremen (Germany) and ourselves from Great Britain. We took fourteen choristers, seven lay clerks, the Provost and Precentor and were hosted by families from the choir and congregation of Bremen Cathedral. Joint services in different churches in the city, a folksong concert, sight-seeing and a civic reception by the Mayor soon filled the five days of the Festival. We were also invited to give a special concert in the cathedral by the organist, Hans Heintze. The 11th-century building was filled by a very large audience and I found it thrilling to conduct the choir in the west-end Gallery where Brahms' Ein Deutsche Requiem was given its first performance. Our programme included 16th and 17th-century motets and anthems by Tallis, Tye, Redford, Byrd, John Mundy, Henry Purcell and William Blitheman, with 20th-century anthems by John Joubert and Frederick Rimmer. The organ accompaniments were played by Hans Heintze whilst I contributed organ solos by John Stanley and Samuel Wesley on a chamber organ, and Kenneth Leighton's *Prelude, Scherzo and Passacaglia* Op. 41 on the large Walcker instrument in the gallery.

The press reports were complimentary, commenting on "the sweet tone of the boys, clear intonation and precision throughout, giving evidence of excellent choral training, blending with clear-toned, sonorous men's voices producing an enchanting sound picture of perfect clarity!" The playing of Leighton's Opus 41 was described as "a magnificent performance of an impressive piece, calling for outstanding virtuoso technique."

The festivals led to the various choirs visiting one another's countries in the years between the gatherings, and we hosted several in Edinburgh. The adult choir from Groningen came in 1962, Unser Lieben Frauen from Bremen in 1963, Groningen Youth Choir in 1967, and in 1972 we hosted the festival in Edinburgh. The two main services were recorded for broadcast by the BBC - the first, a Choral Eucharist in St Mary's in which the combined choirs sang the *Nelson* Mass by Haydn, accompanied by an orchestra led by Leonard Friedman, and the other, of hymns, motets and readings in St Giles High Kirk, for which the organ accompaniments were played by Herrick Bunney. The soprano soloist for the Mass setting was Margaret Marshall, a former student at the RSAMD. We were lucky to engage such a gifted singer before she launched on her successful international career. The BBC producer for the service in St Giles found the overuse of powerful pedal stops in the organ accompaniments created problems of balance and asked me to do something about it. I told Herrick Bunney of the request and for the remainder of the rehearsal he avoided them but when it came to the recording he reverted to his original registration!

The previous International Festival of Choirs was held in Herning, Denmark in 1969. A number of features of the festival, some non-musical, have remained in my mind. We were met on arrival by a group of young people from a school which was hosting us. In contrast to our choristers who were tidily dressed in school uniform, the Danish children wore a variety of casual clothes. Most surprising of all, ten-and eleven-year old Danish boys were openly smoking on the bus. Apparently it was not illegal in Denmark. Four hundred and fifty singers from ten choirs took part in the Lutheran High Mass in Herning Kirk, where the first part of the service was sung in English by our choir, the lessons were read in Danish and our Vice-Provost, Philip Crosfield, preached a sermon in Danish!

A concert was given on the Saturday evening in the Town Hall before an audience of two thousand people. Each of the choirs contributed their own individual items. As there was no organ in the hall, accompaniments were played on the piano. The choir of Hampstead Parish Church were seated just in front of us, and after they had performed *My beloved spake* by Patrick Hadley, I complimented their conductor, Martindale Sidwell, adding that I was surprised to hear the anthem sung with piano accompaniment. "The whole thing's a *****y surprise!" he replied. His accompanist was a young, former organ scholar of King's College, Cambridge, called Andrew Davis, now Sir Andrew Davis, Conductor of the BBC Symphony Orchestra. On our way back we visited Copenhagen and sang Evensong in the English-speaking church. Among the congregation of about five hundred were the Danish Foreign Minister and the British Ambassador who very kindly provided our entire group with lunch the following day at the British Embassy.

Our connection with Bremen led to a visit to Edinburgh during the International Festival in 1964 of the Bremer Domchor to perform Bach's *Mass in B minor* with the Hamburg Chamber Orchestra in St Mary's. It was conducted by Hans Heintze, with German soloists and I had the privilege of playing the harpsichord continuo. A long queue formed outside the Cathedral for the performance on the opening night of the Festival and extra

Hans Heintze and B Minor Mass soloists (1964)

chairs had to be brought in and placed in every available corner of the building. It was a magnificent performance, as was the choir concert the following Tuesday when they sang motets by Brahms, Reger, Bruckner and the contemporary composer, Ernst Pepping, and I played some organ solos. Heintze and his wife became very good friends, and our musical connection grew ever closer over the years. He is a great musician, still alive and active despite increasing old age. He was a pupil of the renowned Karl Straube, Cantor of Thomaskirche, Leipzig. By a strange quirk of fate, I had heard him play in Lincoln Cathedral in 1954 and still remember his performance of Bach's *Fantasia and Fugue in C minor* (S 537) and the *Fourth Trio Sonata in E minor*. What struck me most forcibly was the completely different registration and articulation from that which I had been taught, with no use of the expression pedal and no frequent changes of stops such as were common in the symphonic view of Bach's organ works by the majority of British organists. On mentioning this to Gordon Slater, he dismissed my comments by saying, "Oh, they do things differently on the Continent, you know." It was a reflection of the fact that at that time, few British organists had either heard the sound of continental organs or seen and played them. Recordings and overseas travel were far less common than they were shortly to become. Heintze was the first German organist to play in Britain after the war, and on the occasion of his visit to Lincoln he also gave recitals in Westminster Abbey and King's College, Cambridge. His father had been a Lutheran pastor and although Hans was forcibly conscripted into the army, he was not in sympathy with the regime and after the war he did all he could to foster better relationships with other countries through his music.

Performances of the music of the Jewish composer, Mendelssohn, were banned in Germany during the Nazi regime and unknown to many musicians. I remember Heintze telling me how excited he had been in discovering and performing the Oratorio *Elijah*.

Whilst the programme mounted in the Cathedral during the Edinburgh International Festival in 1964 was typical of our attempts to use the building as a centre for artistic performances, there were some very special events. I had begun to include regular series of organ recitals, and in this year played the complete organ works of Buxtehude and César Franck in twelve programmes spread over the three weeks of the Festival. In addition, we invited Dr Marilyn Mason, the distinguished American organist to give a recital. In 1960 she was the first woman organist from the USA to play in Westminster Abbey. To add to the international flavour, there were performances by the Elgar Choir of British Columbia and the combined Cathedral choirs of Carlisle, Newcastle and St Mary's. But perhaps the most adventurous programme was given by the six combined choirs of St Giles Cathedral, St Columba's Singers, Sine Nomine Singers, Royal High School, St Mary's Roman Catholic Cathedral and our own Anglican Cathedral. I had gathered them together to perform Tallis's 40-part motet *Spem in alium nunquam habui*. Performances of this superb work were rare and so the ten-minute piece was sung twice - at the beginning and end of the concert. Each choir contributed its own items and they again joined forces in the middle of the programme for the Magnificat for three choirs by Andrea Gabrieli. The concert was repeated in its entirety in St Giles the following week, and in October in the University McEwan Hall. On each occasion, the venues were packed and I was deeply moved by the music and the co-operation of the different church traditions, possibly the first time since the Reformation that Presbyterian, Roman Catholic and Anglicans had joined together.

The Cathedral events were extensively reported and reviewed in both the UK national press as well as Scottish newspapers. The following extracts from those on the Tallis 40-part motet concert reveal the high level of interest it created. They are taken from a review of the October concert which happened unintentionally on the same day as a general election!

"Listening to Tallis's 40-part motet is as splendid a way as any of passing election night. The performance deserves a small place in Edinburgh history since it was surely the first time that six choirs of different denominations had ever joined together in the echoing vastness of the McEwan Hall. It was an impressive performance both aurally and visually - aurally, because the choirs, obviously deeply moved to be singing together gave the music its due sense of grandeur and occasion; visually, because the sight of six choirs, all differently costumed, all singing from music that looked about a yard deep, could hardly fail to be impressive. The performance was presided over by Dennis Townhill and was remarkably well sung. It was given a shape and coherence which, in the circumstances, was quite outstanding. A combined account of a Gabrieli Magnificat was put over with striking stereophonic effect by placing singers at both sides of the highest galleries (also on ground level). It is seldom that music sounds good in the McEwan but this time it did."

As if all this were not enough, The Lambeth Players staged T S Eliot's *Murder in the Cathedral* every night of the final week for which I directed the music, and an exhibition

Lay Clerks

Cartoon by Clare Beber

of pictures taken in South Africa was presented by the SPCK. The daily and Sunday choral services continued as usual, of course, with the necessary rehearsals!

In September 1966, we made the first of our choir trips to Norway, singing in the Cathedrals of Kristiansand, Stavanger and Bergen as well as in Norway's oldest church at Oldernes. We took eighteen boys, six lay clerks, the Provost, the Precentor, Chaplain and George Hay, assistant organist. The welcome and reception we received throughout the visit was quite overwhelming. Apart from historic ties between the two countries there was evidence from older people that we met, that memories of war-time occupation by German troops and the liberation by the British were still clear in their minds. Many Norwegians made the perilous journey across the North Sea in what was known as "The Shetland Bus" to serve alongside British troops. After taking part in the Lutheran Hoymesse in Kristiansand, we were entertained to a Civic luncheon which provided us with our first experience of reindeer meat! We were favoured with lovely sunny weather and greatly enjoyed the journey north by train to Stavanger the following day through spectacular scenery. The recital in Stavanger Cathedral was scheduled for the same evening which barely left time for a rehearsal of the choir. The organ duet by Samuel Wesley, included in the programme, had to be performed without prior rehearsal or sight of the instrument which was in a high gallery at the west end of the building. At the appropriate time I followed George Hay to the organ loft where I found him occupying the larger part of the organ bench designed for one player only and I had to perch uncomfortably on what was left!

From Stavanger we travelled to Bergen by hydrofoil - a boat which raises itself on stilts and travels at considerable speed. It was a comfortable mode of travel within the sheltered waters of the fjords but rocked alarmingly in the open sea. The approach to the lovely city of Bergen through the spacious harbour was unforgettable.

Two years later I received an invitation to serve on the panel of adjudicators at the seventeenth International Festival of Organ Music in Nuremburg. The medieval, walled city had been remarkably and faithfully rebuilt after suffering considerable damage from Allied bombing during the war. One could only admire the vision and skill in carrying out such a project whilst the modern industrial part of the city, which had grown alongside it, appeared incongruous and to my mind, ugly in comparison. The other members of the jury for the competitions were Professor Körner of Nuremburg, founder of the Festival, Hans Heintze (Bremen), Rune Engsö (Stockholm) and Herr Johannes Knabel of West German Radio (Cologne). The organ competitions in performance and improvisation took place in Egidienkirche and out of a large number of competitors the first prizes were awarded to Martha Schuster (Germany) and Guy Bovet (Switzerland). Visiting members of the jury were each required to give two public recitals and Luigi Tagliavini (Italy) was an additional visiting player. I was allotted Sebalduskirche in the old part of Nuremberg and Schwabach, a nearby town. Competitors and students were allowed to attend rehearsals by recitalists and to watch their preparations at close quarters - a somewhat nerve-wracking experience. For my concert in Sebalduskirche, I was joined by the distinguished Nuremburg trumpeter, Werner Fink, with whom I played pieces by Purcell, Stanley, Jeremiah Clarke and a Canzona on *Christ ist erstanden* by the contemporary German composer, Hans Ludwig Schilling, who was present. My solo organ pieces included Buxtehude *Prelude and Fugue in D*, J S Bach *Dorian Toccata and Fugue* (S 538) and *Pastorale and Toccata* by Frederick Rimmer, Professor of Music at Glasgow University.

From Nuremburg I travelled to Bergen to give the opening recital in an international series of organ recitals at Johanneskirke and to give a radio broadcast. The latter included Buxtehude *Prelude and Fugue in D*, and pieces by Tallis, Purcell and Stanley. The organist of the church, and also a music critic, was Thorlief Aamodt. He was a member of the Royal College of Organists in London and known in Bergen as the "English" organist because of his interest and enthusiasm for our music and choral tradition. He told me that many people in Norway listened to BBC radio programmes and that he regularly heard the weekly Choral Evensong and organ broadcasts including those from our Cathedral. It was a very busy few weeks, for the day after I returned to Edinburgh I set off for Liverpool to do a week's examining for the Associated Board, then home, only to travel south again for a short holiday. The next week I took charge of the annual RSCM Choristers' Course in Dundee before resuming the daily routine at St Mary's and preparing for concerts in the Cathedral during the Edinburgh Festival. Notably among these in 1968 were the performance by The English Opera Group of the three church operas *Curlew River*, *The Burning Fiery Furnace* and *The Prodigal Son* by Benjamin Britten, directed by the composer with principal solo parts sung by Peter Pears. Philip Ledger, later to become Principal of the RSAMD, played the chamber organ in the instrumental ensemble.

In 1969 I visited Bergen again and Stockholm for the first time. A new Bach-Orgel by Vulpen with mechanical action had been installed in Bremen Cathedral in 1965 and I was invited to give one of the recitals in the winter series. The programme consisted of five preludes from the *Orgelbüchlein* and the *Prelude and Fugue in C* (S 547) by Bach and a second half of pieces by British composers including two Psalm-tune adaptations by John Black (16th century), Purcell, Samuel Wesley and three Preludes on Scottish Psalm Tunes by Robin Orr.

The press reports were complimentary and described the playing of Bach as "a spiritual interpretation inspired by a fluency that lies far beyond all academic pedantry whilst the British compositions were lovingly played with a breadth of poetry and gave the organist an opportunity to demonstrate his splendid capabilities." A note from Hans Heintze with the one word "Congratulations" was even more appreciated. The invitation to play in Johanneskyrka in Stockholm came from Rune Engsö whom I had met at the Organ Festival in Nuremburg. He was a large man in every way whilst his German-born wife, Hildegard, was a very attractive blond. They were a very friendly pair and we established an instant rapport.

This burgeoning international recital activity came to a temporary halt, and I did not travel outside the UK for another four years. Pre-occupation with the development of the Choir School into a specialist music school, and efforts to lay the foundation for the continuity of the Cathedral choral tradition left no time. However, I received an invitation from Samuel Nygren, of the Swedish Cultural Department, to give eleven recitals in Sweden in the Spring of 1973. The invitation simply asked me to travel to Gothenburg on 15 March without any information as to where I should be playing, staying, or what I should be paid! It all sounded too vague and risky and I was inclined to refuse, but decided to telephone Nicholas Danby whom I knew had fairly recently toured Sweden. He told me that he had had a similar experience but reassured me that all would be well, that I would be met on arrival, and that the arrangements would be satisfactory. Encouraged, I accepted the invitation, submitted a list of pieces for the programmes and flew to Gothenburg on 15 March. On arrival at the airport, and after passing through Customs, I stood in the arrivals hall waiting for someone to greet me. All the other passengers disappeared and I was left alone feeling very anxious. Eventually, a tall man approached me and introduced himself as Nils Hammarberg, organ builder, whose firm was sponsoring many of the recitals. From that moment, as Nicholas Danby had predicted, everything clicked into place, although I was not told of the next venue until after the previous recital! My first recital duly took place in the Cristinekyrka in Gothenburg - a city not unlike Edinburgh with its spacious streets and squares. I was hosted by the verger and his wife, and it was interesting to see a biography of Brahms by Hans Gál in their bookcase.

On my previous visit to Stockholm I had seen nothing of the rest of the country and as this time I should be travelling by train daily from one place to another, I was keenly looking forward to seeing more of the countryside. The winter had been unusually mild and I had a fortnight of gloriously sunny spring weather which made most of my carefully packed warm clothes redundant. The countryside was flat, somewhat monotonous, and covered with "Christmas" trees and lakes unlike the spectacular scenery I had seen in Norway. There was little snow to be seen except in Falun which was the northernmost town I visited. The big trains were fast, smooth and punctual and I found it slightly strange and almost magical when they glided silently out of the station apparently without warning, as no whistles were blown! The coaches were warm, wide, with luggage compartments and wardrobes with padded coat-hangers. I was told it was virtually unknown for anything to be stolen from the trains. Hotels were comfortable, but very expensive, and I was warned not to buy anything on the trains as that was also prohibitive. I cannot help thinking that the present buffet services on British trains have caught up in price, if not surpassed, the Swedish ones!

The principal towns, Stockholm, Gothenburg and Malmö, were spacious and clean and there was no litter in the streets. The Lutheran church is maintained by taxation and because of this seems to have no financial problems. The church buildings were well-kept, well furnished and so warm that I played in shirt-sleeves where possible. The organs were mostly very good, new or re-built with mechanical action, many by Hammarberg. Many churches had two organs - the larger in the gallery and the other at the east end. There was great interest in British organ music, although the recitals were not always particularly well attended, often they included a short religious service and Malmö gave me my first experience of seeing and hearing a robed woman priest. On the first Sunday it was possible to attend morning service, the general structure of which was similar to ours but without Communion.

Travelling was not difficult - most people understood English and the young people spoke the language well. Many of our television programmes were shown in English and a British football match was shown every Saturday afternoon. On one journey, I sat next to a fellow passenger who was filling in a football pools coupon and who asked me what I thought the result would be in a forthcoming match between Chelsea and Aston Villa! People were friendly, hospitable and keenly interested in Britain and especially in Scotland. There were, of course, some who had visited Edinburgh and St Mary's, and it was gratifying to learn how impressed they had been by the building and the beauty of the services and the music.

As well as recitals in the larger towns, arrangements were made for me to play in smaller places and on small instruments. I was asked to give the opening recital on a new 8-stop organ by Hammarberg in Skepperstad church where Samuel Nygren was cantor. The concert was organised by the Sävsjö Rotary Club and was preceded by its weekly meeting which I attended and at which I was given the Club pennant to take back for our club in Edinburgh. The press report commented that "the happy occasion that Samuel Nygren had brought about, had its climax at the end, when in the Scottish tradition and under the direction of the famous Scottish guest (sic!), all joined hands and sang Should auld acquaintance be forgot (Auld Lang Syne)".

As Sävsjö was not on a main railway line I had to travel on a small cross-country train and was told that I would be met at the station and taken to Sävsjö by car. The "station" turned out to be merely a drop-off point in the middle of nowhere and with no sign of any habitation or car! Eventually, a small vehicle appeared and a cheerful lady got out and beckoned me to get in. Since she spoke no English and I spoke no Swedish, communication was difficult to say the least. However, we laughed a good deal as we tried to express ourselves with hand gestures! The concert was well received by the large audience which filled the church, although the start was delayed for about half-an-hour whilst the one reed stop was tuned! After the recital, I was introduced to a Baron Augustin

Mannerheim who told me he would be taking me to my next venue in Linköping.

He drove me, somewhat erratically, in his British-made Standard car, informing me that he always bought this make and model. He also told me that he had a two-manual-and-pedals pipe organ in his library, which he wished me to play after we had had a meal. After travelling some distance, he turned into spacious grounds and to my surprise stopped outside a castle. He said that he would have a hot meal ready in a few minutes. To my astonishment this is precisely what he did! It was only later that I discovered that he had "hotted-up" a pre-prepared meal in a microwave oven. At that time, I did not know that such cooking aids existed - they were not introduced into Britain until some years later. As requested, I played a selection of pieces on the delightful instrument in the library, including the Chorale Partita *Christus der ist mein leben* by Pachelbel. After I had finished he told me Anton Heiller had also played the Pachelbel Variations to him and Heiller considered a common pulse should be maintained throughout such pieces. The Baron did not consider my version so successful or effective!

Experiences in Växjö and Stockholm taught me two salutary lessons! In Växjö I played in the delightful Cathedral and stayed in the home of one of the clergy. He was a Canon of the Cathedral and a keen follower of sport, especially football. I noticed that his bookshelves contained a great many magazines with photographs of numerous football teams. He had a full-size table-tennis table in a games room and two teenage sons who were keen players. Since I also enjoyed playing, I challenged one of the boys to a game between supper and the recital. We each won a game and I suggested we should play a third to decide the rubber. I cannot remember who was the victor but I do remember that I got very hot and was not in a sufficiently relaxed and controlled state so close to the beginning of the concert. In Stockholm, I had an even more chastening experience.

The previous venue was some distance away and I had to catch a very early train and had time only for a light breakfast. I was due to play in Johanneskyrka again, and Rune Engsö had written to tell me that the church would be open and access to the two organs would be available. On arrival, I decided to do my practice first, have a meal, and then have a rest in my hotel before the concert which was due to begin at 7 pm. I spent three to four hours practising and then went to a nearby restaurant and enjoyed a substantial meal as by that time I was very hungry. I had a sherry as an aperitif and a bottle of Carlsberg Special Brew with the meal. I am not sure why I decided on the Carlsberg, as I rarely drink beer, and had not reckoned on its lethal effect. After the meal, I went to my hotel room, undressed, drew the curtains, got into bed and fell into a deep sleep. Stupidly, I had not asked to have a wake-up call and to my horror it was nearly seven o'clock when I opened my eyes! Dressing as quickly as I could, I ran to the church which stood on a green not far away but which was reached by a flight of stone steps. By the time I got to the church I was puffing and panting and in a state of panic. Hildegard Engsö was at the church door anxiously waiting for me, whilst Rune had gone home to pick up some music to play in case I failed to turn up! Hildegard tried to calm me down by saying, "Do not vorry, Dennis, the people are all here and they can vait until you are ready!"

Fortunately, the first half of the programme was to be played on the small, classical organ at the east end of the church, beginning with Bach's *Allabreve in D*. Its stately opening helped me recover my poise and control over shaking hands and all was well.

I learnt my lesson and since then have maintained a strict rule never to drink any alcohol or indulge in vigorous exercise before a recital.

On 3 July 1973 accompanied by Mabel and our daughter Barbara, we left Edinburgh by car for three-and-a-half weeks' tour in Germany, covering a total of three thousand miles and ten concerts. The tour was arranged for me by Werner Jacob, the distinguished organist of Sebalduskirche in Nuremburg. We had become acquainted during the Organ Festival in 1968, and he and his wife, with their small son Andreas, stayed with us on his visit to Edinburgh in 1972 to give recitals. We crossed the North Sea from Harwich to Hamburg and then drove to Bremen for my first recital in Unser Lieben Frauenkirche. Apart from some uncertainty and anxiety as we drove from the ferry on to the roads, especially at roundabouts, we were pleasantly surprised at the ease with which we adjusted to driving on the right.

From Bremen, we went on to Kiel for a recital in the church where Hans Gebhard was organist and whose relative, Ingrid, is married to Professor David Kimbell of Edinburgh University. Three recitals as part of the Schleswig-Holstein Organ Festival followed in Glucksburg, Kappeln and Burg. Whilst in this northern area of the country we visited Schleswig and its ancient and beautiful Cathedral, and I was able to try out the fine mechanical-action organ by Marcussen of Denmark. Meanwhile, Barbara travelled in advance of us by train to Nuremburg where she stayed as guest of Werner Jacob and his family. Our six hundred miles journey from Burg on the Isle of Fehman to Stuttgart was to prove eventful.

The weather was gloriously sunny and hot and I suggested we leave the autobahn and take a scenic route through quiet villages and countryside. This decision not only extended the journey but created problems in finding a toilet when I felt the need. This became ever more urgent so when we saw a signpost to Hameln (Hamelin) of "Pied Piper" fame, we drove into the town to the Hauptbahnhof (railway station) where we felt sure we should find toilets. Sure enough we did but, unfortunately, three of the four available were "out of order" and the fourth was occupied! By now, I was desperate and never have I felt so pleased to hear the sound of a toilet being flushed!

We eventually arrived in Stuttgart and I played in the splendid Stifftkirche the following evening. After Stuttgart we moved on to Kassel, checked in to our hotel and decided to have a walk round the town. On returning, we went to reception to get our room key. In my best German, I asked, "Die schloss, bitte" only to be greeted with a look of bewilderment from the girl behind the desk. I tried again, indicating with my hand the action of turning a key in a lock. With a smile, she gave me the key saying, "Der schlussel!" Apparently I had asked for the castle!

The next evening, a thunderstorm broke out just before the recital and we wondered whether the large number of people who crowded into the church had really come to hear the organ music or simply to shelter from the torrential rain! After a recital in Fürth, two days later, we linked up with Barbara in Nuremburg where we spent a happy time with Werner Jacob and his family, and I played in Sebalduskirche again. The visit was not without unexpected incident. We took the two Jacob children with us to an open-air swimming pool and on arrival asked for tickets for four swimmers and one spectator (myself). The attendant shook her head and tried to explain that admission was for swimmers only by saying, "You only come if you take your trousers off!"

Our last venue was at the Lutherkirche, in the beautiful old university town of Heidelberg, where Wolfgang Dallman was organist. He had stayed with us in 1970 when he came to give a recital in St Mary's. We arrived in the centre of Heidelberg during a thunderstorm and were at a loss as to how to find our way to Dallman's house, which was on the outskirts of the city on a modern estate. We decided to drive to the main railway station, hire a taxi to take Mabel and for me to follow. To our great relief, the plan worked successfully and we duly arrived at our destination. We were fortunate to be able to spend a few days exploring and enjoying the city and the surrounding countryside.

Two overseas tours were made in 1974 - the first in early August to Germany to give organ recitals in Oldenburg and Freiburg, and the second in September with the choir to Holland and Germany. In Oldenburg, I gave the final concert of the International Organ Conference and twenty-second meeting of The Society of Organ Friends on the Alfred-Führer Organ in Lambertinikirche, at the invitation of Dieter Weiss, organist of the church. The press report was complimentary and the English translation sent to me commented that "the Bach pieces: *Fantasie in G major*, Partita *O Gott, du frommer Gott* and *Prelude pro organo pleno* and *Fugue a 5 voci in E flat* were played with technical bravura in a style which was completely oriented by the composer's own instructions." The other half of the programme included pieces by Purcell and John Stanley, and Kenneth Leighton's *Prelude, Scherzo and Passacaglia* eliciting the comments that the "British organist had proved himself a virtuoso whose fluency and precision can hardly be exceeded."

The long journey from Oldenburg in the north to Freiburg in the Black Forest region was made by train and nearly ended in disaster. A change of train was involved at Stuttgart, and I had been informed that my train would leave from Platform 11 at a specified time. The train was standing in the platform ready to depart and I was just about to get on when I thought I had better just check it was the correct one. A large notice board on the platform listed the places through which the train was to pass and its ultimate destination, Istanbul, with no mention of Freiburg! After consulting the timetable I discovered that as I was travelling at a week-end, my train left from a different platform! With a huge sigh of relief, I caught the correct one and arrived safely at my destination. Freiburg Minster is a beautiful building standing in a spacious square in the centre of the city. The square seemed filled with brightly-coloured flowers and I stayed in a very comfortable old hotel with a lovely view of the Minster. The recital was one of the most memorable and enjoyable experiences of my playing career.

The regular Tuesday evening recitals during the summer attracted very large audiences, including many young people, and every part of the building was filled. It was lit by candle-light which gave a special atmosphere and magic to the concert. There are four instruments in the Minster and recitalists were expected to play on each in turn, finishing at the "Hauptspieltisch" (main console) which makes it possible to couple them all together! Access to the west-end organ was by a lift and the second was a two-manual mechanical action organ placed in the triforium of a side aisle. A precarious wooden walkway in the triforium led to the third, larger, three manual instrument.

Its console was suspended high above the nave at the east end with only a slender wooden board behind the player and I felt very apprehensive! The Hauptspieltisch was situated on ground level at the entrance to the choir area. The final piece in my programme was César Franck's *Choral No. 3 in A minor* and the last section was stunning in quadraphonic sound!

The return journey was somewhat tortuous, involving starting at about 6am by train to Appenweier on the German-French border, changing trains and travelling to Strasbourg, transferring to the airport for a flight to London, and then picking up a domestic flight to Edinburgh.

For the choir tour we hired our own coach and crossed the North Sea overnight by ferry from Hull to Rotterdam on the outward journey, and from Hamburg to Harwich on the return. We left Edinburgh for the fourteen-day trip on 9 September 1974 and broke the journey in Grimsby where we gave a concert in St James' Parish Church and received a very warm reception. The press reported that "The choir sang with a discipline, control and pure ringing tone which were a delight." Particular mention was made of the anthem, *Come, dearest Lord* by Peter Naylor, a colleague at the RSAMD who had recently written the piece for us.

We joined the ferry at Hull on 11 September. It was the first time I had taken the choir by boat and I was totally unprepared for the excitement which it created. After cabins had been allocated, the choristers set off to explore the ship and discovered they could buy canned drinks from slot machines, including beer and lager. The lay clerks noticed they were stocking up a supply of the latter in their cabins! These were duly confiscated and the boys were packed off for the night.

When we arrived in Rotterdam, we transferred to our bus which made such good progress that we got to Groningen too early. As our hosts were not due to meet us at the Nieuwe Kerk for a couple of hours, the choir were allowed to have a walk round the town. They were split into groups and given strict instructions to keep with their groups and return at the specified time. They all returned safely except for Duncan Hopkinson, a senior chorister, who was missing. We informed the police immediately and anxiously waited for him to be found. In the meantime, the rest of the group dispersed with their hosts. I was staying with Evert and Janni Westra and was greatly relieved when we received a telephone call at about 10pm to say that Duncan had been located and safely delivered to his hosts. He had become separated from his group because he had stayed gazing into a cycle shop window and the rest had moved on without him. He had the nous to go to a police station for help, but could not remember the name of the church! The police drove him around the city to see if he could recognise the place and eventually with the information we had given, he was taken to where he needed to be.

We gave a concert in the Nieuwe Kerk and sang during the service on the Sunday morning. We were also taken sightseeing, including a visit to a church which had a Carillon and where we were able to watch it being played from a keyboard by the Town Carilloneur. It was interesting to hear pieces of classical music played so expertly on the bells with the notes struck by the fists! From Groningen we drove to Bremen where we were guests of the choir of Unser Lieben Frauen. Cantor Harald Wolff arranged for us to give concerts in his church, and also in a very new modern church in Delmenhorst. Both concerts were very well attended and received. We sang Byrd's 4-part Mass, Purcell's *Rejoice in the*

Lord alway, and contemporary anthems by Britten, Cedric Thorpe Davie, Peter Naylor and Vaughan Williams. Our assistant organist, John Taylor, contributed a manuals-only Voluntary by William Boyce and Bach's *Prelude and Fugue in C* (S 547).

On the Friday, we left Bremen for Hamburg, and after the experiences on the previous ferry, I made a vow that the choristers would be kept together, in one place, on the ship for the return journey until bed-time. I need not have worried as the crossing was rough and they all felt sea-sick and were asking to be allowed to go to their cabins early! From Harwich, we made our way back to Grimsby and after singing at the morning service in St James' Church on the Sunday, travelled north to Edinburgh.

As well as all the preparations and hassle of the centenary celebrations, we managed to fit in a short tour to Holland with the choir, and an ensemble from the Music School, at the end of March, 1979. In addition to singing for a service and giving a concert on familiar ground in Nieuwe Kerk, Groningen, we also performed in two new venues at Martinikerk, Doesburg and Bethelkerk in Scheveningen, on the outskirts of The Hague. The press reports especially commended the solo singing of the two treble choristers, Douglas Butters and Alastair Mackie and lay clerks, Tim Barthorpe, Alistair Sutherland and Nigel Waugh. It is invidious for me to single this group out, for we had good soloists in the Choir in each generation. Our organist was Tom Oakshott, the organ scholar who was reading music at Edinburgh University and is now Head of Music at Aysgarth School and our Chaplain, The Revd Allan Maclean. In our free time, we were able to visit Madurodam with its fascinating miniature reconstruction of typical Dutch buildings, houses, canals and, of course, windmills.

After our Californian Tour in 1984 (recounted in another chapter) there was a six year gap before the next overseas trip, largely because of an abortive attempt to arrange a tour in Japan. The invitation came from Mr Shoici Watanabe who had been sent by the Japanese Government to spend a year studying (as he described) "British Gentlemanship" and elected to do this in Edinburgh. He had three musical children who gained entry to St Mary's Music School - Mako, a pianist, and her two brothers, Genichi, a 'cellist and Kiichi, a violinist. I was able to help the family over some housing problems and got to know them all quite well. I suppose this may have prompted him to suggest that I should take the choir to Japan. He told me that he was a Director of a British-Japanese Foundation, and that he would help obtain funding for us. I duly wrote to the Foundation and together with a substantial donation from the Japan-Scotland Society, I obtained promise of sufficient funds to meet travel, accommodation and subsistence but, alas, despite trying over two years, I was unable to find an agent to obtain engagements for us. It was a bitter disappointment and I had to write an apology to Mr Watanabe and accept the frustration and irony of defeat in such circumstances.

My last overseas tour with the choir took place in 1990 to Norway. We were invited to take part in the first International Choirs' Festival on the island of Stord, between Stavanger and Bergen. The organiser, Roald Sangolt, was Music School Principal for the area, and had spent some time in Edinburgh in 1986 to observe and study my choir training methods.

All the arrangements in Norway were made for us and after the preliminary organisation, I had the luxury of simply concentrating on rehearsing and conducting the choir. Robert Marshall, one of the lay clerks, acted as tour manager and three chorister mothers took responsibility for care of choir robes and ensuring that the choristers were tidily dressed and ready for all rehearsals and performances. They were also responsible for all pocket-money, medication and dispensation if necessary. Janie Beeston, Jane Kirk, Jan Harkin and my wife, Mabel were all wonderfully cheerful and efficient.

We were also fortunate that one of the lay clerks, Paul McBride, was a qualified doctor and another, Neil Watson, a qualified pharmacist. It was interesting that two of the lay clerks were committed Roman Catholics - Paul McBride has since taken vows and is now Brother Oswald in the Community at Ampleforth. I was greatly moved when he completed his time in Edinburgh and wrote thanking me for the happiest six years of his life in the choir. Tony Kehoe, the other Roman Catholic, has since qualified as a doctor and is serving in the Navy. But I am straying from the subject!

Nine choirs were invited to the Festival, all adult mixed voices except for Stord Ungdomschor, which was a youth choir of girls between the ages of 14 and 22. The others were the Choir of Plymouth Congregational Church from Des Moines, Iowa, USA; Trondheim Kammerchor, Norway; Kammerkoret Pax, a professional choir of twelve singers from Copenhagen; Balassa Balint Choir, Hungary who had won a first prize at Llangollen in 1986; Estonia Philharmonic Chamber, Tallin, a professional group of very high standard. Their conductor, Tonu Kaljuste was a young, handsome, charismatic personality who captivated everyone, including our chorister mothers! Minsk State Chamber Choir of professional singers, was directed by their founder and conductor, Igor Matjukov, a tall, burly man with an impressive black beard. He stood just behind me in a press photograph and the report referred to "big" Igor from Minsk and "little" Dennis from Edinburgh! His choir were superb and had basses who produced a rich sound down to C below the bass stave.

Bergen Domkantori was a choir of some fifty singers, most of them music students or teachers, founded by their conductor, Magnar Mangersnes, organist of Bergen Cathedral. We were the only choir of its kind with the traditional British composition of trebles, male altos, tenors and basses. We took sixteen choristers and twelve lay clerks, plus Peter Backhouse, our assistant organist. Although he had been assistant for over seventeen years, it was the first time that he had been on an overseas tour with the choir. I was delighted to have him with us and he certainly seemed to greatly enjoy it all!

The Festival featured the choral music of Knut Nysted, one of Norway's leading composers, and he was present throughout. Each choir was asked to learn, in advance, two of his pieces and to include them in their performances. In addition, Nysted composed a short, unaccompanied motet *Laudate Dominum* for the combined choirs to sing at the opening concert which he rehearsed and conducted. It is lively and attractive and we included it as an introit in a broadcast of choral Evensong from St Mary's the following year. At the Festival, each choir performed a selection from its own repertoire at two concerts - one in the Kulturhuset and the other in Stord Kyrka. In addition, all choirs attended the Lutheran Hoymesse on the Sunday morning and we were one of the three choirs invited to sing during the service and contributed Stanford *Beati quorum via* and Byrd *Agnus Dei* from the mass for four voices. Peter Backhouse played organ music before the service by S S Wesley and John Stanley.

It was not "all work and no play!" We were taken on a boat trip round the fjord, including lunch on board of fresh Norwegian prawns which were delicious. We became quite expert at peeling them! There were two official dinners at Stord Hotel and we were asked to visit the small island of Huglï and entertain the residents. The total population numbered one hundred and fifty and many of them assembled in the school hall for our informal concert. They provided a lovely light meal for us and it was a very happy and friendly event. We were taken round a pig farm (!) where some of our girl choristers enjoyed picking up and cuddling small piglets. We received the warmest of welcomes and appreciation throughout the Festival and, as the Rector of Tromsø University said in his speech of welcome (in English and Norwegian), "I am convinced that all of you will have unforgettable days on Stord." How right he was!

The press and radio coverage was extensive and commented on "The very high, professional standard" of our choir. I also received a charming letter from Knut Nysted.

July 5ᵗʰ 1990

Dear Dr. Townhill:

It was a great pleasure meeting you and having a good talk with you during the festival-dinner.

Thank you also for the fine performances you gave of my works during the Stord festival.

Enclosed you will find the score of two of my organ works, one conservative and one more modern in style.

The Resurrexit is recorded on the CD I gave you.

My best wishes for the summer to you and your wife from my wife and myself.

Knut Nysted

We had left Edinburgh on Wednesday 27 June and now at the conclusion of the Festival, we left Stord by flaggruten (fast boat!) for Bergen on 1 July. After a five-hour journey across a calm sea and beautiful scenery we were met by our hosts. This second-half of our tour was arranged for us by Jan Røshol, the young Director of Åsane Kirkes Kor in Ulset, fifteen minutes bus drive from Bergen. Mabel and I stayed with a doctor and his wife who had two small children, Irvine and Sigrid. We were allotted Irvine's bedroom and the little lad obviously did not approve of being turned out of his room, for he barricaded the entrance with as many obstacles as he could find and carry!

The next day, we travelled down the side of Hardanger Fjord, by train, to Voss, to give a concert in the 13ᵗʰ century church, built in early Gothic style. The wooden, octagonal steeple is unique in Norway. After the concert, we returned to Bergen, again by train. In the morning of Tuesday, 3 July, we had the chance to do some sightseeing in Bergen where we were booked to give an evening concert in the Domkirke (Cathedral).

We visited an old wooden church and the beautiful Mariakirken with its late medieval triptych behind the high altar and ornately decorated and canopied pulpit. For the concert in the Cathedral, we were able to use the small organ in the chancel to accompany Purcell's Verse Anthem *Thy word is a lantern* and perform other *a capella* pieces from that part of the building. The main organ was in the large west gallery. Peter Backhouse played some organ solos on it and accompanied Handel's *Zadok the Priest* which the choir sang from the gallery. The concert was reported by Thorlief Aamodt whom I had met in Bergen over twenty years previously. He had visibly aged but then I expect I had, too!

Our last full day in Norway was spent on a sightseeing tour by bus, arranged for us by Jan Røshol, which included a visit to Troldhaugen, Edvard Grieg's home. We gave an impromptu concert outside the house for the many tourists who were also visiting the place where Norway's most famous composer lived. In the evening, we gave our final concert in Fana Church and on 5 July left Bergen by bus at the ungodly hour of 6am for Flessland Airport, for a flight to Stavanger and then a transfer flight to Glasgow. After customs clearance and baggage claim, we boarded our bus and arrived home in Edinburgh sometime after 11 in the evening, tired after a long day's travelling.

It had been a busy but a most enjoyable and happy tour.

Chapter 13 - The American Connection 1784-1984

"Waal, ah declare, if yo all ain't jest cute!"

In the assembly hall of Louth Grammar School, there hangs a series of mural paintings depicting a number of people and scenes connected with the school at various times in the past. The first panel shows Captain John Smith, the leader of the first British settlement in Virginia being saved from death by the pleas of Pocahontas, an Indian Princess. The significance of this event, involving a former pupil of the school, meant little to me at the time I first saw it and I certainly never imagined that some twenty-seven years later I would visit the place where he and his companions landed in 1607. The invitation to take the Cathedral choir to the USA came from Jim Acosta, Director of Music of the American School in London. He had brought his choir to sing in St Mary's and told me that he was planning a short tour in the States with them during the Bicentennial celebrations of American Independence in 1976, and suggested that our choir should join them. This seemed too good an opportunity to miss and we accepted, immediately planning fund-raising events to meet the heavy expenses that would be involved. In the event, we had to go alone as Jim Acosta had to return to the USA unexpectedly. Some firm engagements had been arranged, notably at Washington Cathedral, Bruton Parish Church in Colonial Williamsburg and St Stephen's Church, Richmond, Virginia. These gave me a number of contacts and with their help and other connections, I was able to set up a three-

Waving the Flag   *Cartoon by Clare Beber*

145

weeks tour. Among the many historic and personal links between the USA and Scotland, there is a special bond between the Episcopal Churches in both countries. Samuel Seabury, the first Bishop of the Episcopal Church in America travelled from Connecticut to Scotland to be consecrated in Aberdeen on 14 November 1784 and this fact also helped to arouse special interest in our visit. In addition to the choir and some accompanying adults, we also took a group of instrumentalists from the Music School with us. This not only enabled us to present a wider and more varied programme of music, it also helped to integrate the choral and instrumental elements in the newly-formed specialist Music School.

And so a party of some fifty of us left Edinburgh at 8am on 28 June 1976 by plane for London, Heathrow, where we were scheduled to transfer to a British Airways Jumbo Jet for Dulles Airport, Washington. Unfortunately there was a strike of catering staff for the plane and instead of leaving at 11.30am we did not board until 5.45pm ! After a $7^1/_2$ hour flight across the "pond" a weary, bleary-eyed group arrived at Dulles Airport in the early hours. We were confronted by the unfamiliar sight of heavily-armed police at the Customs checkpoint. Two of the smaller choristers were given the job of carrying the double-bass, which was in a black rectangular box resembling a coffin! They were visibly startled when one of the policemen greeted them with the words, "Gee, you guys, whad ya got in there - tommy guns?" Having convinced the customs officers that we had neither firearms nor forbidden food, we boarded a bus for the thirty mile journey to Arlington where we were met by our hosts.

During our tour, we sang at church services and gave concerts in Arlington, Roanoke, Blackstone, Williamsburg, Richmond, Virginia Beach, all in Virginia; Chambersburg, Pennsylvania and the National Cathedral, Washington DC. We had time for sight-seeing, especially in Washington, visiting the Capitol, Smithsonian Museums and the White House. I had always sought the support of the city authorities, the Rotary Club and Scottish businesses and institutions for our tours, and I asked the Lord Provost of the city if he would write a message of greeting for the President of the United States, and also commend us to the mayors of the different communities we were to visit. He agreed and we also took a special souvenir book of the Cathedral as a gift. We were thrilled that the whole group were given a reception in the grounds of the White House and that the Provost and myself were invited into the President's office to present the letter and gift to one of his aides.

In Arlington, Mabel and I were hosted by Col John Sullivan and his wife Annette, and experienced our first taste of pecan pie and blueberries and the sight of the all-red cardinal bird. We sang for the two services in St Andrews Church on Sunday, 4 July, the anniversary of Independence Day, and in the evening were taken for a picnic and watched the fantastic fireworks display from a hill overlooking Washington. The display included a coloured laser beam which was something we had never seen before. It was hot and humid throughout the three weeks of our tour with temperatures between 90° and 110° Fahrenheit. We found the air-conditioning in the homes a great relief from outside temperatures, although shops and stores felt like refrigerators.

We were sponsored by the British Committee organising groups to mark the bicentenary from this country, and given official recognition by the Americans who presented us with a Bicentennial flag.

As well as a concert in Roanoke, we were featured on a live TV programme where we found the heat in the studio even more unbearable than outside. So much so that one of the choristers fainted and had to be carried off the platform! Fortunately, he was standing on the end of the row and it was possible to remove him without being noticed. I had to admire the *sang-froid* of the rest of the choristers who never batted an eyelid and continued to sing as if nothing had happened!

In Blackstone, six of us, including two of the choristers, stayed in a typical American colonial style house with a large covered front porch. Air-conditioning was provided by brass, rotating blades suspended from the ceilings of the rooms. Our hostess, Elizabeth Murray, was a most generous lady who went to endless trouble to provide food that the choristers would eat. When she saw the choir dressed in their robes for the concert, she exclaimed in a broad southern accent, "Waal, ah declare, if yo' all ain't jest cute!"

Williamsburg was very special, for the old colonial capital of the Commonwealth of Virginia had been faithfully restored and rebuilt as it was in the 17th century. Owners, assistants and workers in the shops and businesses were dressed in period costumes and no modern houses or buildings were allowed to be built in sight of the old town.

We performed a short concert in the Wren Chapel of the College of William and Mary, including a Purcell Voluntary on the 1760 organ, a recital by candlelight in Bruton Parish Church and sang at the Sunday morning service in the church at which our Provost preached the sermon. From Williamsburg, we were able to visit Jamestown where the first settlers landed in 1607, and I presented the colour print of Louth Parish Church from the Mayor to the Jamestown Foundation. In Richmond, we gave a lunch-time concert at a meeting of the three hundred members of the Rotary Club and a concert the same evening in St Stephen's Episcopal Church which was recorded.

Virginia Beach gave us the opportunity of sunbathing on the sand and swimming in the ocean, although we were warned to beware of sharks and jellyfish! A fun-park was an added attraction, and we were all invited to a dinner in a large and very expensive hotel.

John Taylor, our assistant organist, celebrated his thirtieth birthday at a midnight beach-party with the lay clerks! The invitation to give a concert in Chambersburg, Pennsylvania came from the Rector of the Episcopal Church there. He and his wife had spent their honeymoon in Edinburgh.

The visit also gave us the opportunity to visit Gettysburg and the museum which had an exhibition and video of the defining battle of the American Civil War. It also led to the first meeting of Mabel and a pen friend from Finlayville, Pennsylvania. She and Vaughn Chapman had been writing to one another for forty years since school days, but had never met personally. Vaughn and her husband travelled to Chambersburg to meet us and we found them a charming couple. Prior to the Chambersburg concert we sang at the morning service in the National Cathedral in Washington. It is a splendid building in the style of the ancient cathedrals of Canterbury and York. The Provost preached the sermon to a very large congregation which filled the nave.

Our repertoire for the tour included Schubert, *Mass in G major* and Mozart, *Ave verum corpus*, both accompanied by the string ensemble; Jacob Handl *Omnes de Saba venient*; Peter Phillips *Ascendit Deus*; Byrd *Ave verum corpus*; S S Wesley, *Blessed be the*

God and Father; Cedric Thorpe Davie *Come Holy Ghost*; Stanford *Te Deum in B flat*; Britten *Jubilate in C;* and Howells *Magnificat and Nunc Dimittis (Collegium Regale).* A few instrumental solos were contributed by various players.

The letters we received from various official sources and places are an indication of the appreciation and impact our performances made.

Circular Letter of Introduction provided by The Rotary Club of Edinburgh to the Rotary Clubs to be visited in the United States:

Dear President

Will you please accept the warmest greetings and best wishes from the President and members of the Rotary Club of Edinburgh.

A prominent member of our club for fifteen years, Rotarian Dennis Townhill is music master of the Cathedral Church of St Mary in Edinburgh. He devotes a great deal of his talent to the education of the young people in the Cathedral Music School and to the development of his choirs. This is a very extensive tour that he is undertaking and I know that he is looking forward very much to his American concerts and to taking part in the official bicentennial celebrations of American Independence.

I am glad he has been able to visit your Club and would hope that we would be able to welcome yourself or your members during a possible future visit to our lovely Edinburgh.

With renewed Rotary Greetings and Best Wishes
Yours sincerely
Jackson Rolland
President

Letter from Richmond Rotary Club:

July 13, 1976

Mr. Jackson Rolland, President
Rotary Club of Edinburgh

Dear President Jackson:

It was indeed an honor and a privilege to have a group of young talented musicians from St. Mary's Cathedral and the Music School present a program before our Club today. It is certainly an outstanding group and it is readily understandable that they are earning a very wide acclaim as noted in your letter to the now Past President, Arthur Weaver.

It was a delight to meet and visit with Dennis Townhill and to personally exchange Rotary greetings. His dynamic leadership as a choir master was certainly in evidence throughout the musical group.

We extend warmest greetings and thanks to the Rotary Club of Edinburgh, whose support and endorsement of the St. Mary's Choir has helped to make it possible for Rotarians in Richmond to enjoy an outstanding presentation.

Sincerely yours,
Paul H. Riley
President

Letter from the Jamestown Foundation:

July 12, 1976

D. Townhill, Esquire

Cathedral Church of St. Mary
Palmerston Place
Edinburgh EH12 5AW
Scotland

Dear Mr. Townhill

We were so pleased to receive from you the handsome color print of Louth Church from Westgate, which you left here at the Jamestown Festival Park as a memento of your visit on Saturday.

I am indeed sorry that I missed you, having been in Charlottesville to see your Queen that day.

We will hang the picture here and will be reminded of your choir's very well received tour in Virginia.

Yours sincerely,
Parke Rouse, Jr.

Letter to The Very Reverend Philip Crosfield, Provost of the Cathedral from Richard W Dirksen, Musician-in-residence, Washington Cathedral:

July 22, 1976

Dear Provost Crosfield:

Your kind note quickly arrived, and I pass on to your friends here your warm thanks. On behalf of the Dean, the Precentor and all our staff, your musicians made a beautiful service in God's praise last Sunday.

The cathedral was graced with their presence; your sermon was well received by all.

Cordially,
Richard W Dirksen
Musician-in-residence.

Letter to Philip Crosfield from The Reverend Donald H. Feick, Holy Trinity Episcopal Church, Chambersburg, PA:.

July 28, 1976

Dear Father Crosfield,

Just a note to tell you how much the people of Chambersburg enjoyed the concert given by your choir and Music School, on Sunday evening, July 18. It was a thrill and a distinct pleasure to have you with us that evening and we did so enjoy meeting the various members of your group. Please tell Dennis Townhill, The Director, that we felt the music was outstanding.

If you see Canon Hadfield, please give him my best regards.

With all good wishes to you and your family.

Sincerely,
(The Rev. Fr.) Donald H. Feick

Letter from Gerald R Ford, The White House, Washington:

August 10, 1976

Dear Dr. Crosfield:

I was delighted to learn that you and members of the St. Mary's Music School of Scotland visited the White House recently, and I want to thank you for bringing me a letter of greeting from the Lord Provost of Edinburgh as well as the book that tells about your Cathedral.

The warm wishes of friends from abroad have particular meaning during this Bicentennial year, and I hope that the special bond of friendship between our peoples will continue to grow and prosper for many years to come.

With my appreciation and best wishes,
Gerald R. Ford

The Very Reverend G. P. C. Crosfield
Provost
St. Mary's Cathedral
Edinburgh
Scotland

A letter from The City Chambers, Edinburgh:

6th September 1976

The Very Rev. Philip Crosfield,
Provost,
Cathedral Church of St. Mary The Virgin
EDINBURGH

Dear Provost,

The Lord Provost has received one or two very charming letters as a result of the visit of your Choristers to America. I enclose a photocopy of one which especially pleased the Lord Provost.

The Lord Provost hopes that you are now fully recovered.
Yours sincerely,
F.K.B. Murdoch,
Lord Provost's Secretary

CITY OF WILLIAMSBURG
WILLIAMSBURG, VIRGINIA

OFFICE OF THE MAYOR

August 31, 1976

Rt. Hon- John Millar, F.I.O.B.
The Lord Provost
City Chambers
Edinburgh, Scotland EH1 1PL

My Dear Lord Provost:
The Very Reverend Philip Crosfield, Provost of the Cathedral Church of St. Mary, Edinburgh, delivered your message during the intermission of the Choir's concert in Bruton Parish Church in July. The concert was excellent as was the participation by the Choir and orchestra in other services here in Williamsburg.

All those who came in contact with Mr. Crosfield and the members of the Choir and orchestra were most impressed with their professional excellence and pleasant company. They were outstanding representatives of your great city.

Thank you again for your letter and for sharing with us your outstanding musicians.

Sincerely yours
V. M. Geddy, Jr

The following year, with the help of some of the people I had met on the choir tour, I was able to arrange to give a series of recitals in Buffalo; Garden City, Long Island, NY; Richmond and Williamsburg, Virginia; St Louis, Missouri and Harrisburg, Pennsylvania. We had close connections in Buffalo for Charles Garton, a contemporary and friend at Lincoln School, was Professor of Classics at the University and a member of the congregation at St Paul's Cathedral where I played. Charles also arranged for me to give a lecture at the University. A good men and boys' choir was maintained at the Cathedral by Fred Burgomaster, and it was a pure coincidence that my visit took place during his last weekend as Director of Music. Fred had been appointed to a similar post at the Episcopal Cathedral in Indianapolis, where the music foundation was supported by a particularly large financial endowment. I was astonished to discover the yawning gap between the much larger payment and better facilities for church musicians in the USA to those in the UK. Similar variations exist in other professions too, and it was no surprise to be told by Charles Garton that it was just not financially worthwhile for him to consider moving back to Britain. Fred Burgomaster is an enthusiast for the music of Kenneth Leighton and he commissioned the setting *Missa Christi* for the one hundred and fiftieth anniversary of Christ Church Cathedral, Indianapolis, in 1988. It was one of the last of the composer's works to be written and performed before his death. Buffalo is very close to the Canadian border and it was a thrill to be taken to see Niagara Falls from both the American and Canadian sides.

My most vivid memory of Garden City, Long Island is the enormous volume of traffic on the journeys to and from the Cathedral of the Incarnation where I played. For my second visit to St Stephen's Church, Richmond and Bruton Church, Williamsburg, I felt as the Americans say, "right at home" and the organists, Granville Munson and Jock Darling, gave me a warm welcome. The music critic of the Richmond Times was not so warm in his comments on my performance of early English pieces on the splendid Aeolian-Skinner organ in St Stephen's. It was fair comment that the instrument was not as suitable for such music as the pieces by later composers in the programme. The report was more enthusiastic on the playing of pieces by Howells, Leighton, Mendelssohn and César Franck. It was good to see Jock Darling again in Williamsburg, and to spend a few days in that fascinating town. He also arranged for me to play in the Wren Chapel at the College of William and Mary. Jock was a scholarly musician, proud and knowledgeable of the history of Virginia's colonial past. He came over to Edinburgh in 1980 and gave a very good recital in St Mary's. I also greatly enjoyed playing in Christ Church Cathedral in St Louis, and the opportunity to see something of that great city. I was taken out for a sumptuous meal by Douglas Major, the organist, whom I had met in Washington Cathedral the previous year. I thought this was especially good of him as he was due to return to Washington the following morning to get married in the Cathedral there!

Our choir and orchestra tour in 1981 included many of the places we visited in 1976 with some notable variations. The string ensemble from the Music School was accompanied by Nigel Murray, now Director of Music. This enabled the players to make a more significant instrumental contribution to the programme we presented. Our journey did not go smoothly for we suffered long delays, and found ourselves stranded for over three hours in Reykjavik Airport in Iceland, waiting for a connection to New York. When the plane eventually arrived, we were told it had been overbooked and that nine passengers would need to stay overnight in Reykjavik. They were offered free hotel accommodation and a sightseeing tour as an incentive. To my horror, Nigel suggested that he and eight members of the orchestra were attracted by the offer! It was a potential nightmare scenario but fortunately I was able to dissuade them and the complete party of fifty-one embarked on the flight to New York. We arrived at John F Kennedy Airport very late, and very tired, with a bus journey to Arlington still to face. Our hope of some quiet sleep was shattered by the bus driver giving a commentary on the sights of New York, which excited the choristers but frustrated the adults. As the driver had to have a statutory period of rest we found ourselves eating breakfast at a roadside café at 3 o'clock in the morning! We finally arrived at our destination in Arlington about 7am on 4 July and unloaded our luggage in St Andrew's Church Hall. We had another delay until our hosts arrived to collect us. The choristers with inexhaustible energy filled the time playing games! It was remarkable that everyone assembled cheerfully the following morning for a rehearsal prior to singing at the Sunday service in St Andrew's. From Arlington we moved on to give concerts and sing for services in Richmond, Williamsburg and Virginia Beach as in 1976.

On that first visit to Williamsburg, Jock Darling had asked us to listen to one of his ex-trebles who he thought had a promising counter-tenor voice. Eric Ibler, our principal counter-tenor lay clerk, confirmed this and David Quittmeyer spent a year in Edinburgh singing with our choir and having voice lessons. By the time of our 1981 tour he had returned to the USA and volunteered to join us as an extra singer. We visited Jamestown again and were highly amused to see David in 17th-century costume joining in the "changing of the guard" ceremony in the compound of the reconstructed fort built by the first settlers! Charlottesville and Germantown were new venues where we had equally large and enthusiastic audiences. The arrangements in Germanstown were made for us by Anthony and Eileen Brooks, parents of one of our choristers, who had emigrated to the States. George Timberlake, Vicar of the Church of the Holy Spirit where we sang for the Sunday morning service on 19 July, kindly presented me with a full music edition of the American Episcopal Church Hymnal as a memento.

We sang at Evensong in Washington Cathedral on the same day and found the cantor was a very attractive woman priest! I have to say that it was something of an aural shock to hear the versicles sung an octave higher than usual although it is not uncommon nowadays in our own country. We also felt that our Chaplain, The Revd Allan Maclean, at that time a young and eligible bachelor, might be susceptible to her female charms! From Washington we travelled north to Princeton, New Jersey where we gave a recital in Trinity Episcopal Church at the invitation of the Director of Music James Litton. He had been appointed to a similar post at the famous church of St Bartholomew in New York, which had a renowned musical tradition. One of its former organists was Leonard Stokes, an Englishman who became world famous as the conductor, Leopold Stokowski. We performed in Trinity Church before John Bertalot, former organist of Blackburn Cathedral, arrived to succeed Jim Litton. By one of those unexpected freak coincidences, we met a young American opera singer whilst standing in line in the University cafeteria. She heard the members of our group talking and on finding that we were from St Mary's, Edinburgh, came to speak to me and Mabel. She had spent a period as resident singer at the Abbey on the Island of Iona at the same time as our daughter had been resident pianist!

An added bonus to our three-week tour was the opportunity for a full day's sightseeing in New York before we returned home from Kennedy Airport.

The last American tour during my time as Organist at St Mary's took place in 1984. The Lord Provost of Edinburgh told me that the city had recently "twinned" with San Diego, in southern California, and suggested that I should take the Cathedral choir and Music School orchestra to establish further links between the two cities. He offered to use his influence to persuade the sister city committee in San Diego to host us.

He was as good as his word, and we received an invitation to spend five days there. It was then a matter of finding other venues to make up a three-week tour. It was fortuitous that an American ordinand was studying at Edinburgh Theological College when we were planning the tour, and he was able to give us a personal introduction to the Dean of Trinity Episcopal Cathedral, Sacramento. Robert Ramsay, the Secretary of the Southern California branch of The Royal School of Church Music, was also enormously helpful in suggesting and finding other places for us to stay and perform. Happily, all, or almost all, of the arrangements were made and we set off from Edinburgh on 12 July, on the 7.10am flight for London where we transferred to the 11am jumbo jet which took us direct to Los Angeles. Peter Bonnington, a senior member of the firm of travel agents which had made the arrangements for all our tours, accompanied us as far as Los Angeles airport in order to ensure we made all our connections safely. He was particularly concerned that we should make the transfer to the bus which was to take us to San Diego. When we arrived, we understood his anxiety. The airport had undergone major reconstruction in preparation for the arrival of large numbers expected for the Olympic Games. The huge reception area was manned by armed security and customs officials. Every one of our party of fifty-one was individually questioned and had their luggage checked and examined. It was a very slow and tedious process. We discovered that the staff were undergoing training for the Olympic Games onrush which explained their meticulous care. Our bus was located and we eventually arrived safely in San Diego, after travelling continuously since leaving Edinburgh for over twenty-four hours. We had no time to recover as we were booked to give a concert the next evening, Friday 13 July! There was no point in being superstitious!

Our tour brochure gives details of our personnel, repertoire and itinerary.

The Choir of St Mary's Episcopal Cathedral and Instrumental Ensemble from St Mary's Music School, Edinburgh, Scotland Tour in California, U.S.A. - July 1984.

Personnel

The Very Revd G P C Crosfield, Provost of St Mary's Cathedral
Mrs S Crosfield
Dr Dennis Townhill, Choir Director
Mrs M Townhill
Nigel Murray, Instrumental Director
Mrs J Murray
Mrs L Lyall

The Instrumentalists

Paul Meikle	*Violin*	Malcolm Johnston	*Viola*
Gavin Rhind	*Violin*	Kitty Watson	*Viola*
Esther Geldard	*Violin*	Helen Duncan	*Cello*
Gillian Haggarty	*Violin*	Steven Osborne	*Cello/Piano*

154

Sarah-Jo Izzett	*Violin*	Catherine Smith	*Cello*
Andrea Jacobs	*Violin*	Carol Gould	*Double Bass*
Cluny Strachan	*Violin*	Ruth Binks	*Flute*
Julie Wilson	*Violin*	Celia Birkinshaw	*Bassoon*

The Choir

Susan Hamilton	*Head Chorister*		
Martin Wood	*Deputy Head Chorister*		
Donald MacBride	*Chorister*	Lindsay Allan	*Alto*
Kirsty MacGregor	*Chorister*	John Keen	*Alto*
Ethel-Jane Cormack	*Chorister*	Robert Marshall	*Alto*
Richard Townhill	*Chorister*	Peter Nardone	*Alto*
Mark Scott	*Chorister*	Martin Eastwood	*Tenor*
Neil Hamilton	*Chorister*	Gary Philbrick	*Tenor*
Daniel Stevenson	*Chorister*	Charles Walker	*Tenor*
Colin McKitterick	*Chorister*	Paul Crosfield	*Bass*
Gordon Adams	*Chorister*	Brian Flemming	*Bass*
Stuart Wood	*Chorister*	Colin Heggie	*Bass*
Katie McGlew	*Chorister*	Graeme Lyall	*Bass*
Alan Gould	*Chorister*	Peter Smyth	*Bass*
Jeremy Paton	*Chorister*	Simon Clarkson	*Organ Scholar*

MUSIC FOR CONCERTS AND SERVICES
to be selected from the following:-

Settings

William Byrd (1543-1623)	Mass for four voices
	Evening Canticles - The Second Service
Joseph Haydn (1732-1809)	"Heilig" Mass
Franz Schubert (1797-1828)	Mass in G major
Thomas Attwood Walmisley (1814-1856)	Evening Canticles in D minor
Charles Villiers Stanford (1852-1924)	Te Deum in B flat
Benjamin Britten (1913-1976)	Jubilate in C

Anthems and Miscellaneous Pieces

Anonymous (c 1250)	Alle Psallite cum luya
Anonymous (16th century)	Lord, for thy tender mercies sake
	Rejoice in the Lord alway
Christopher Tye (1497-1572)	O come ye servants of the Lord
William Byrd (1543-1623)	Ave verum corpus
Peter Philips (c.1560-1628)	Ascendit Deus
John Mundy (c.1585-1630)	Verse Anthem, Sing joyfully
Richard Ayleward (1626-1669)	Preces and Responses

Henry Purcell (1659-1695)	Verse Anthem, Rejoice in the Lord alway
Georg Frideric Handel (1685-1759)	Coronation Anthem, Zadok the Priest
William Boyce (1711-1779)	Verse Anthem, O where shall wisdom be found
Charles Hubert Parry (1848-1918)	Coronation Anthem, I was glad
Charles Villiers Stanford (1852-1924)	Beati quorum via
Edward Bairstow (1875-1946)	Lord, thou hast been our refuge
Herbert Howells (1892-1983)	Like as the hart
Cedric Thorpe Davie (1913-1983)	Come Holy Ghost, the Maker
Dennis Townhill (b. 1925)	Lo, God is here
John Rutter (b. 1946)	A Gaelic Blessing
J.S. Bach (1685-1750)	Aria from cantata 17 "Wer dank opfert"
Gustav Holst (1874-1934)	Song for Voice and Violin

Music for Organ

Alfred Hollins (1865-1942)	A Trumpet Minuet
Percy Whitlock (1903-1946)	Salix and Lantana from Plymouth Suite
Louis Vierne (1870-1937)	Final from Symphonie 1

Music for String Orchestra

Philip Telemann (1681-1767)	Don Quixote Suite
Edvard Grieg (1843-1907)	Holberg Suite
Gustav Holst (1874-1934)	St Paul's Suite
Samuel Barber (1910-1981)	Adagio

Chamber Music

Beethoven (1770-1827)	Serenade for Violin, Viola, Flute
Wieniawski (1835-1880)	Duet for two Violins
Kodaly (1882-1967)	Serenade for two Violins and Viola
	Duo for Violin and 'Cello
Shostakovich (1906-1975)	String Quartet 8
Handel (1685-1759)	Sonata IX for Flute and Bassoon

ITINERARY

Thursday, 12th July	Arrive in San Diego
Friday, 13th July	1930 hrs. Concert in The Fletcher Hills Presbyterian Church, El Cajon
Sunday, 15th July	1000 hrs. Service in St Paul's Episcopal Church, Sixth Ave. San Diego
	1900 hrs. Concert in the First Presbyterian Church, Date St San Diego

Tuesday, 17ᵗʰ July	2015 hrs. Concert in The Little Bridges Auditorium, Pomona College, Claremont
Wed, 18ᵗʰ July	1100 hrs. Concert in Plaza Garden Stage, Disneyland
Friday, 20ᵗʰ July	1930 hrs. Evensong and Concert in The Church of Our Saviour, San Gabriel
Sunday, 22ⁿᵈ July	1000 hrs. Service in St John's Episcopal Church, Ross
Tuesday, 24ᵗʰ July	1930 hrs. Concert in The First Presbyterian Church, San Anselmo
Wed, 25ᵗʰ July	2000 hrs. Concert in The Memorial Church, Stanford University
Saturday, 28ᵗʰ July	2000 hrs. Concert in Trinity Episcopal Cathedral, Capitol Ave. Sacramento
Sunday, 29ᵗʰ July	1015 hrs. Service in Trinity Episcopal Cathedral, Sacramento to mark the consecration of Samuel Seabury, the first Bishop of the American Episcopal Church
Monday 30ᵗʰ July	leave from San Francisco Airport.

ACKNOWLEDGMENTS OF DONATIONS

The British Council
The City of Edinburgh District Council
Ferranti plc
The General Synod of The Scottish Episcopal Church
The Rotary Club of Edinburgh Jubilee Charity Fund
The Royal Bank of Scotland
The Scottish Council of Social Service
The Scottish and Newcastle Breweries PLC
Those firms who have taken up advertising space in this brochure
and many individuals

San Diego is a beautiful city with stunning views of the ocean, and we were most generously welcomed by all the families who took us into their homes. Rotarians, Don and Dot Jenkinson hosted Mabel and me, and in our free time took us on a Harbor excursion and to lunch at Anthony's renowned seafood restaurant. We picnicked in Balbao Park prior to a performance of the musical, My Fair Lady, at the Open Air Theatre. The theatre is under the flight path of incoming aircraft and the performers literally "froze" in mid-sentence and gesture until the noise level had subsided and then resumed where they had left off! It was a very strange sensation, as were the American accents in this most "English" play. The San Diego Sister Society arranged a wonderful bus tour of the city, and a day at the world-famous zoo where the bright pink-coloured flamingos were especially memorable. The weather was glorious, the concerts and service went well, and we again enjoyed the American specialities of outdoor pot-luck meals. The one problem on my mind since our departure was the fact that I had no confirmation that the arrangements for "housing" at our next venue, Claremont, had been made. Anxious phone calls only partly allayed my fears but I was told that the accommodation would be sorted out when we arrived.

Reluctantly, we left San Diego on Monday 16 July and travelled by bus to the grounds of St Ambrose Episcopal Church in Claremont, where the Rector and members of the congregation met us and we were able to work out housing and our hosts for everyone. It was a great relief when it was all completed! Catherine and Alfred Focke were our personal hosts. It was a new experience to be invited to pick our own lemons and grapefruit from their orchard! They also took us for a picnic supper in the nearby mountains where the cool temperature was, as Mabel described it "sheer joy" after the heat of the day!

Pomona College, where we gave our concert, is one of the few residential campuses in the USA similar to the Oxbridge model in the UK. We also visited the new and remarkable museum established by Raymond Alf, containing examples of the earliest known forms of life (some three-and-a-half billion years old). The museum stands in the grounds of Webb private preparatory school which has its own outdoor swimming pool. The opportunity to have a refreshing swim was probably appreciated even more than the museum!

We were fortunate enough to receive an invitation to give a concert in one of the bandstands in Disneyland. In return, we were given free access to all of the rides and entertainments. Since our concert took place in the morning, we had a generous amount of time to enjoy the delights of the place and the Master of the Choristers was in seventh heaven! It was so clean and well-organised with virtually no litter and what there was, was immediately collected by attendants.

From Claremont, we moved to San Gabriel where Graeme and Lynda Lyall joined Mabel and me as guests of Bill and Suzie Bradley. The Olympic Games had begun and Bill Bradley, who was an official steward, proudly wore his green "bunny outfit" for our benefit! He and Suzie generously entertained about twenty of our group for dinner in their "back yard". We wondered if Bill had connections with "Budweiser" as all the standard lamp shades carried the company's name. Our planned engagement to perform in Santa Barbara fell through, and so we had to make a twelve hour bus journey from Claremont to San Anselmo in the San Francisco area. We had hoped to take the coastal scenic route but were told it was unsafe for buses so we travelled a straight and rather boring highway.

The day after our arrival in San Anselmo both choir and orchestra provided music for the morning service in St John's Church, Ross. The Provost was invited to be the celebrant and found, unexpectedly, that he was assisted at the altar by a husband and wife who were both ordained priests. I am unsure whether, at that time, he approved of women priests! After the service, the whole group were given a barbecue lunch in Skip and Betty Way's beautiful garden. The weather was quite cool, and whilst a good many of the younger ones enjoyed a swim in the large private pool, Mabel and I "chickened" out of it. We stayed with George and "Bobby" Klein, who took us for an outing in the beautiful Muir Woods which seemed to be filled with giant redwood trees. A free day enabled us to see something of the sights of San Francisco. Although we had no official engagement, we visited Grace Episcopal Cathedral and the choir sang an informal programme of *a capella* music. It was a wonderful day in which we took a cruise around the bay and sailed close to the prison island of Alcatraz. We spent some time on Pier 39 with its incredible number of shops and restaurants and spectacular bay views including the Golden Gate Bridge. We also managed a visit to Chinatown and a ride on the newly restored cable cars which travel up and down the steep gradients of the streets. A totally fantastic city!

Our concert in Stanford University was another memorable experience. The view of the campus from the Hoover Tower provides an impressive sight of the Spanish-style buildings with their bright orange-coloured roofs . The Tower is named after Herbert Hoover, former President of the United States of America and houses his extensive library of books.

The Memorial Church, where we gave our concert, was a large, oval-shaped building. The apse at the east end was covered with renaissance-style paintings whilst mosaics adorned much of the remainder. The instrumental items and choir *a capella* motets were performed from the chancel whilst Parry's *I was glad* and Bairstow's *Lord, Thou hast been our refuge* were sung from the west gallery. There were two large organs, one of them a new mechanical action "Classical" instrument. The original romantic organ was built in 1901 by the Los Angeles firm of Murray M. Harris. Like the major stained glass windows, another feature of the church, it survived the 1906 earthquake virtually unharmed. The instrument was completely rebuilt in 1925 with a new, four-manual E M Skinner console. In 1933, the Aeolian-Skinner Company added an eight foot Tuba Mirabilis, sixteen foot Posaune and seven-rank mixture, modelled on similar stops in Leeds Parish Church in England. The three-manual, forty stop Classical instrument, suitable for the Baroque repertoire was built by the American firm of Fisk.[11]

Our individual hosts were Walter and Elinor Baer, who had a small swimming pool and jacuzzi in their garden which we were able to enjoy. They took us out for two memorable meals during our stay with them. The first was for supper at the Golden Spike Restaurant on the campus, which had a model railway track round the whole seating area and the trains ran round us at elbow level! The second was to a superb fish restaurant called "Top of the Market". Greatly daring, I ordered lobster whilst Mabel chose salmon cooked over a kind of barbecue which she described as "out of this world". Walter also opted to have lobster - but when the waiter came to take the order, his wife said, "You will have salmon, dear!"

Nigel Murray and the orchestra returned to the UK on Friday 27 July whilst the rest of us travelled to Sacramento, our final venue. Sacramento is the State Capital and Trinity Cathedral is the cathedral of the Diocese of Northern California. The concert on the Saturday evening was described as "A Scottish Festival" sponsored by the St Andrew's Society of Sacramento and the Cathedral congregation. We shared the programme with the St Andrew's Society of Modesto Pipe Band, who were resplendent in full highland dress.

They processed into the Cathedral playing *Scotland the Brave* and contributed a number of other well-known Airs, whilst the choir sang a number of Scots songs. The

11.   Ref. Stanford Memorial Church (1980), Gail Stockholm.

second half was given over to church music ending with John Rutter's setting of *A Gaelic Blessing*. At the reception in the Cathedral House, there was a presentation of Highland Dancing, accompanied by the band. The whole evening could not have been more Scottish if we had been back home in Edinburgh! We sang at the morning service the next day in the Cathedral, at which the Provost preached. It was a special service to mark the consecration of Samuel Seabury, the first Bishop of the American Episcopal Church, in Aberdeen, two hundred years previously.

Thus the musical part of our tour was completed, but there were one or two special experiences which we treasure. To our surprise and delight, Vaughn and Bob Chapman flew some 3,000 miles from Pennsylvania to see us! We spent a lovely time together looking round Old Sacramento with its steam train and wooden buildings and shops. It is a fascinating reconstruction of the town in the time of the "Gold Rush". Mabel and I were hosted by Margaret Kelly and she, and her daughter Jeannie, took us for a drive to Sutter's Fort, Coloma, where the gold rush began. We saw the wooden shacks and rough conditions in which the "Forty-Niners" lived. In complete contrast, we drove through Cameron Park where each house not only had a garage for two cars but also a private aeroplane parked outside! I had a photo taken of myself standing by two of these planes as visible evidence of their existence and the owners' affluence - but not mine!

We left California to return to Edinburgh from San Francisco Airport on 30 July and arrived back the following day.

Chapter 14 - Organists and Organ Recitals - Television and Radio Broadcasts

"We hear your choir on our radio in New Zealand"

Building up a repertoire of music suitable for playing before and after services and performing in public recitals are part and parcel of the organist's profession, and I had begun to do this from an early stage in my career. Louth provided a modest platform, and Grimsby a wider audience where I organised regular series of recitals and began to broadcast for the BBC. It was not until I moved to Edinburgh that engagements as a solo performer began to escalate into an ever-increasing activity. Organ recitals in the UK have never attracted large audiences, generally speaking, but in recent years there has been an upsurge of interest. There are many reasons for this, not least the provision of new instruments in secular concert halls where the player may be seen performing and establish a rapport with the audience. Scholarly research into organ construction and design as well as performance practice have all led to more effective and authentic versions of the composer's intentions. Nowhere has this upsurge and veritable explosion of new organs been more marked than in Scotland where for centuries the organ had been regarded as a " kist o' whistles!"

In Edinburgh itself, notable instruments have been installed in the University Reid Concert Hall (Ahrend); Greyfriars Kirk (Peter Collins); St Andrew and St George and Palmerston Place Church (both Wells Kennedy); St Giles' Cathedral (Rieger) and the most recent in the Canongate Kirk (Frobenius). Many other instruments have had restoration work done on them and the organ in the City's principal concert venue, the Usher Hall, which has been virtually unplayable for over thirty years, will eventually be brought back into action.

An annual series of celebrity organ recitals was held before the advent of the new instruments and this brought some of the world's most distinguished players to the City. The recitals took place in St Giles' Cathedral, the McEwan Hall and St Mary's, and were organised by a committee chaired by Herrick Bunney. When I took over this responsibility, many of the visitors stayed with us, becoming good friends and widening our circle of contacts. After a few years this series was abandoned through financial loss caused by insufficient support. Nevertheless, recitals continued to be held in different venues and celebrities invited on an individual basis.

The list is much too long to quote in full, but there are some who deserve special mention. Only three weeks after our arrival in Edinburgh, Flor Peeters, the distinguished Belgian organist-composer, gave the re-opening recital on the restored instrument in Palmerston Place Church.

It was especially interesting to hear him play some of his own music including pieces which I had learnt and performed in Grimsby. *Toccata, Fugue and Hymne on Ave maris stella* is a particularly effective piece which I had included in an early broadcast programme from Grimsby. Legendary players such as Fernando Germani, Marcel Dupré and Jeanne Demessieux were heard towards the end of their careers. Indeed, I believe that Germani and Dupré were on their final recital tours. Dupré was suffering the increasing effects of arthritis in his finger joints, and I felt saddened that such a great performer was so obviously unable to control his playing. However, his technical lapses were entirely forgotten and forgiven in his wonderful improvisation at the end of his programme. Having myself spent many hours preparing the complete organ works of J S Bach for performance during the three weeks of four Edinburgh Festivals, and having been very dependent on the printed music, it was both chastening and humbling to learn that Germani played the works from memory!

Pierre Cochereau combined his post as organist of Notre Dame Cathedral in Paris with that of Directeur du Conservatoire in Nice, where he lived in the idyllic sounding Villa Paradisa. It was during our first visit to the Côte d'Azur in 1962 that I first met him and invited him to give a recital in St Mary's during the Cathedral's Festival programme of 1963. He accepted, and when the time came I met him at the airport and drove him into the City pointing out various features of interest on the way. He asked if he could have a look in the Cathedral before taking his luggage into the house. A lunch-time organ recital was being given by Francis Thomas, a former chorister and assistant organist. As we quietly walked round, the organ sound increased to a substantial forte and Pierre whispered, "Is that full organ?" I shook my head. Eventually the music reached a big climax and again he asked, "Is that full organ?". This time I nodded in the affirmative and he said, "Not as loud as the organ in Notre Dame!"

He told me that at the end of each financial year, the Cathedral Administrator asked him if any work or addition was needed on the organ so that surplus money could be used up, otherwise it would have been passed to the Government! No wonder the size and sound of the instrument grew! Hearing and watching the wide variety of great organists perform was like a series of free master classes, and I learnt a great deal especially of the interpretation of music by their own native composers. On this first visit to Edinburgh, Pierre included the *Trois Pièces* of César Franck and *Dieu parmi nous* by Olivier Messiaen. The treatment of and registration of these pieces was particularly interesting. Some years later, Jean Langlais played the *Trois Pièces* in St Mary's which did not markedly differ from Cochereau's version. He also played his own *Trois Paraphrases Grégorienne* - all new to me, and I was prompted to buy the music and to learn them. Both were brilliant improvisers, especially Cochereau, who seemed able to provide a twenty to thirty minute instant symphony from any submitted theme at the drop of a hat. I found, on the other hand, that his performance of Bach was overblown and too orchestral for my taste. His version of the "Great" *Prelude and Fugue in B minor* (S 544) included "soloing" the E minor entry of the fugue subject on the Tuba. Indeed, his "fortissimo" seemed to be full organ plus Tuba and "piano", full organ without Tuba!

I greatly regretted that I did not go to see him at Notre Dame when we were on holiday in Paris some years later just before he died. He invited me to give a recital in Notre Dame and when I asked him what sort of fee would be offered, he replied, "Oh, we do not pay a fee, c'est pour l'honneur et la gloire." Considering that we paid him £400 (a substantial amount in 1963) plus travel expenses and accommodation, his response was difficult to accept.

Few visiting organists played in Lincoln during my time there, as Gordon Slater mostly gave the three annual recitals himself on Bank Holiday Mondays after Easter, Whitsun and the beginning of August. I do remember a fine recital by Dr Ken Andrews which included a lovely performance of César Franck's *Pastorale in E major*. Another recitalist who also made a great impression upon me was William Hardwick, organist of St Ann's Church, Manchester. He was a very modest man and undemonstrative player with impeccable technique and control. His programme included the Saint-Saens *Rhapsody No 3 on Breton Folk-songs* and Gigout *Grand Choeur Dialogué* - two more pieces to add to my repertoire! Francis Jackson played in Grimsby, at my invitation, and he became the most frequent visitor to Edinburgh for one purpose or another. He and his wife, Priscilla, have been our good friends for over forty years and Francis a greatly admired composer and performer.

Among other outstanding organists brought to Edinburgh by the Celebrity Organ Recitals Committee were Allan Wicks (Canterbury Cathedral), Noel Rawsthorne (Liverpool Cathedral), Marilyn Mason (Michigan), Gillian Weir (London), Ralph Downes (Brompton Oratory, London), Jiri Ropek (Prague), Piet van Egmond (Netherlands), Joseph Bucher (Zurich), Anton Heiller (Vienna), Melville Cook (Hereford Cathedral), Peter Hurford (St Alban's Abbey), George Thalben-Ball (Temple Church, London) and Guy Bovet (Geneva).

Allan Wicks' programme in St Mary's during the Edinburgh Festival of 1962 was recorded by the BBC and included the first broadcast performance of the *Passacaglia and Fugue* by John Joubert. Gillian Weir's first visit coincided with the annual dinner of the Edinburgh Society of Organists in 1964. She had just won a prize at the St Alban's International Organ Competition and was due to play in the McEwan Hall on the day following the dinner. She had to practise during the night and so we gave her a house key to let herself in. It appears she arrived back in the early hours the next morning. When she eventually came down for a late breakfast she complained bitterly about the organ, saying she could not understand how anyone could expect her to play on such an instrument. I have to confess I felt some sympathy for her, as it was a strange mixture of pipework spread over a wide area behind the stage at the rear of the hall. It had also been subject to restoration and additions by several different organ builders and included stops by Robert Hope-Jones which sounded like motor horns! Peter Williams, a senior lecturer at the University Music Faculty, considered that the instrument should be preserved as an example of an interesting monstrosity! Ralph Downes, Designer and Curator of the new organ in the Royal Festival Hall, London had a profound influence upon organ design and performance in the 1960s. His recital in St Mary's was a model of clarity and thoughtful registration. His interpretation of Bach's *Prelude and Fugue in C major* (S 547) made a deep impression, especially the restrained version of the fugue. Jiri Ropek was a fine player who played in St Mary's in 1965 and 1972. I remember him more for his revelations of life in Czechoslovakia under communist rule. He told me that he was not allowed to bring his wife with him in order to ensure his return, and that he had to account for all his expenses and hand over the balance of his fees to the authorities in Prague. The variety and quantity of food in Britain astonished him, and he told us that fresh fruit such as apples, oranges and bananas were not readily available in eastern European countries. British players were by no means over-shadowed and although George Thalben-Ball was in his 80s, he was still superb. His command of the instrument was complete and his playing engendered a larger number of encores than anyone else I've ever heard.

Caleb Jarvis, Organist at St George's Hall, Liverpool, came to play in St Mary's in 1966 and this led to an invitation for me to play in Liverpool and a succession of bizarre events. I travelled by car from Edinburgh and was given directions to an hotel near the Hall. On arrival at the outskirts of the city, I was told to follow signs for the Mersey Tunnel, take the last exit before reaching the Tunnel and on no account, go through it. All was well until the last few hundred yards when I missed the exit and found myself irrevocably at the toll booths with a long line of cars behind me. When I apologetically told the attendant that I did not want to go through the Tunnel, he exploded angrily, "What the hell do you think you are doing? Come through the barrier and stop there (pointing to the right) and wait until I've got a break in the traffic." Eventually he was able to direct me down a slip road to the hotel with the parting shot, "And don't come back here again!"

At this time, practice had to be done through the night as the Hall was in use for the law courts during the day. The organ console was situated in a high gallery at one end of the Hall which was in darkness apart from the console lights. The magnificent organ built by "Father" Henry Willis in 1855, with four manuals, one hundred stops, including an unusually large number of mixtures, and a concave-radiating pedal board, is described in The British Organ as the first modern organ in the country. The Hall is very reverberant and so it was not surprising that after I had been practising for some time, I was startled to hear a very indistinct voice calling out. Eventually I deciphered this cavernous message from the caretaker asking, "Would you like a cup of tea?" It seemed a good opportunity for a break and I made my way down to his office below the ground floor. I fancy he wanted some company to relieve the tedium of the night-shift. He explained that prisoners were formerly kept in cells to await trial and offered to show me round, which he did, relating gruesome details of the crimes committed by some of them. He then took me up a flight of stairs enclosed in wire mesh. When we reached the top, he switched on an electric light and pointed across the room saying, "That's where the Judge sits!" He had placed me in the dock of the court-room! It has acted as a deterrent to wrong-doing ever since.

Many other British organists have been invited to play at St Mary's including Robert Munns, Andrew Seivewright (Carlisle Cathedral), Margaret Cobb (London), Bryan Hesford (at Brecon Cathedral when he came in 1963), Arthur Wills (Ely Cathedral), Nicholas Danby (Farm Street Roman Catholic Church, London), David Sanger, Patrick Russill (Brompton Oratory, London), Roy Massey (Birmingham and Hereford Cathedrals), Roger Fisher (Chester Cathedral), James Lancelot (Durham Cathedral), David Lumsden (New College, Oxford), George McPhee (Paisley Abbey) and Colin Walsh (Lincoln Cathedral)

My own recitals have extended throughout the UK from Shetland to Sussex, and happily many of the venues have been revisited a number of times. They include most of the Anglican cathedrals, City of London churches, churches large and small, civic halls such as those at Newcastle, Dundee, Coatbridge, Aberdeen, Perth, Glasgow, (Kelvingrove Art Gallery), Edinburgh (McEwan Hall), Liverpool (St George's Hall) and some university colleges. For a variety of reasons, not always musical, a few of these are particularly memorable. Aberdeen has a special place in my affections and the old pre-Reformation Cathedral of St Machar is not only a lovely building but also possesses a fine three-manual "Father" Willis organ. It was one of the first I played in Scotland after arriving in Edinburgh, by invitation of David Murray. Paisley Abbey was another early venue and another well restored pre-Reformation building. Its splendid organ has a good deal of pipe-work by Aristide Cavaillé-Coll, the famous 19th-century French builder, and ideal for playing music by Romantic composers. The Minister on this first visit was Dr Rogan who entertained me afterwards with generous measures of scotch whisky! The Abbey has always maintained a high standard of choral music in its services with a choir containing boys as well as adults. The present Organist is Dr George McPhee MBE, a colleague at the RSAMD and one of Scotland's most eminent church musicians. For many years, his choir and ours at St Mary's have enjoyed happy and regular joint services in each other's buildings.

One of my visits to Chester Cathedral turned out to become something of a nightmare. Mabel was with me on this occasion and we were locked in the empty building after Evensong for me to practise. Roger Fisher, the organist, arranged to collect us later in the evening. A most horrendous thunderstorm developed which not only set off car alarms throughout the city and cut off electricity supplies in many houses and buildings, but also set off the Cathedral security alarm. This made a very loud high-pitched noise. Unfortunately, we had no means of either communicating with anyone nor getting out of the building. We spent an uncomfortable couple of hours until Roger turned up at the time arranged to release us. None of us could understand why no one had responded earlier to the alarm. St Paul's Cathedral in London was not so traumatic, but finding the way to the exit alone at night through the vast crypt, created a certain amount of uncertainty and anxiety!

Roy Massey never allowed me to forget the occasion at Hereford when I played an entire programme for manuals only. Since I was just recovering from a hernia operation, there was no alternative short of cancelling the engagement. I did subsequently convince him that I was capable of also playing with my feet.

Before moving to Lincoln, Gordon Slater had been organist at Leicester Cathedral and it was an emotional and nostalgic experience to play there many years after his death and in the presence of his daughter and his son's widow. Nowadays, I frequently practice in St George's West Church of Scotland in Edinburgh where the famous blind organist/composer, Alfred Hollins, served for nearly fifty years, and I feel conscious of literally pedalling in his renowned footsteps!

St John's College, Cambridge, rates high on my list and not only for the generous hospitality of George and Nan Guest. The first time I played there, the pages were turned for me by Andrew Nethsinga, now organist at Truro Cathedral. To compound the nervous tension, I noticed that Richard Walker, one of my former assistants, was in the congregation /audience.

One of the extra perks of playing at St John's was to dine in Hall and afterwards take port with the Master of the College in his rooms. Ely Cathedral and the Grosvenor Chapel, London, posed problems of a different kind. At Ely, the organ was to be restored and at the time I was engaged to play, the instrument was not all functioning properly. In particular, four ranks of pipes on the Great manual sounded whether you wanted them or not. This involved radical changes in the way the whole programme was played. I managed as well as I could but felt disconcerted when I found that David Lumsden and Arthur Wills had been in the audience!

The recital at the Grosvenor Chapel proved even more potentially disastrous. My page-turner was to have been Colin Menzies, a former Edinburgh citizen, now working in London for the Church of England and a member of the congregation at Grosvenor Chapel. He did not manage to get to the church for the beginning of the recital and I had to recruit someone from the audience. A young lady volunteered who said she was an organist. The opening piece was the *Prelude and Fugue in D*, (S 532) by Bach which I played from a photo-copy of single sheets to save carrying a large and heavy volume. All was well until the fugue when the page-turner pulled a page away and also scattered others around the organ console! Fortunately, I knew the piece well enough to continue playing until she had rescued the sheets and replaced them on the music desk, but it was a hairy and scary few moments.

In common with other cathedrals, a good many radio and television programmes were broadcast from St Mary's. We had our share of regular broadcasts of Choral Evensong including first broadcasts of music written by various composers for the choir. In 1970, the BBC announced that it was to discontinue the weekly broadcast of the Service. This brought widespread protest including some from people of no religious affiliation or religious belief. Writing in "The Listener" of 4 December 1969, Marghanita Laski referred to "A beautiful Choral Evensong last week from the Scottish Episcopal Church (sic) of St Mary's Edinburgh." Happily the protests were successful and the broadcasts have continued.

On 14 January 1962 a service of Holy Communion was broadcast from the Cathedral in which the celebrant was our new Bishop, Kenneth Carey. The setting was Darke in F, and I asked the composer if he would provide us with music for some phrases in the Scottish rite which were not included in the English one. He did so, and I received an appreciative letter of the choir's singing after the broadcast. On Christmas Day 1962 we were invited to broadcast a service of Lessons and Carols on the BBC Home Service following the Queen's Christmas message. We took this as a great compliment, since the traditional service had been heard from King's College, Cambridge, the previous afternoon! This was repeated a number of times in subsequent years. The Radio Times of 1964 printed the whole service for the evening of Christmas Day with the following heading: "St Mary's Cathedral, with its choir school and notable choirmasters, consistently achieves a high standard of English Cathedral music. In recognition of this, tonight's Service of Carols from Edinburgh replaces the repeat broadcast from King's College, Cambridge."

Regular organ recitals continued on the various radio channels, the first from St Mary's was in April 1962. The programme was as follows: *Voluntary in C minor*, Maurice Greene; *A Maggot*, Thomas Arne; *Chorale Prelude, Ich ruf' zu dir* and *Prelude and Fugue in A minor* (S 543), J S Bach; *Mors et Resurrectio*, Jean Langlais.

At this time, the BBC tended to select the programme to be performed, no doubt with the particular instrument and building in mind and to prevent undue repetition. Usually about six weeks' advance notice was given and occasionally problems could arise. For a broadcast on 16 December 1965, I was requested to play the following: Bach, Four Preludes on *Allein Gott in der Höh sei Ehr* (S 715, 711,716, 717) and Prelude on *Ein feste Burg ist unser Gott*, (S 720), finishing with Reger, *Fantasia on Ein feste Burg*, Opus 27. Although I had never heard or played the Reger piece, I was horrified at its complexity and had to sweat blood and tears through many hours to learn it in time. I was more circumspect before accepting future programmes containing unknown pieces.

As previously mentioned in an earlier chapter, the composer, Kenneth Leighton, was Reid Professor of Music at Edinburgh University. He passed on copies of his organ and church music to me, often in manuscript photo-copies, before publication. I learnt the organ pieces as he gave them to me and he listened to my performances and helped me to get them better. I especially treasure the copy of his *Prelude, Scherzo and Passacaglia*, Opus 41which he inscribed after a recital in St Mary's - "With best wishes and warmest thanks for a magnificent performance. Kenneth Leighton 20/5/64". I was privileged to give the first concert performances of many of the pieces and also first broadcasts. The planned recording of his complete organ works was achieved during the week 12 to 17 February 1990, produced by Neil Collier on the Priory label in a 3 CD set. I was joined by Peter Backhouse for the duet setting of the Scottish Psalm Tune Martyrs, Opus 73.

In February 1966, we broadcast a programme in the series "Britain's Cathedrals and their Music", devised and produced by the distinguished composer Sebastian Forbes. Nineteen cathedrals were selected to take part and our programme was introduced by John Betjeman.

I was amused to receive a letter from a former pupil after a broadcast in June 1967, in which she said that she had listened to a "rather good recital of Bach organ music on the radio and that when she looked in the Radio Times she was astonished to discover that it was given by me!"

In the spring of 1969, I contributed two of six weekly broadcasts featuring some of the older organs still existing in Scotland, of which there are very few. The programmes were introduced by Ronald Calder, producer for BBC Scotland. The historic "Snetzler" organ in the Masonic Lodge in the Canongate, and the "Father" Willis instrument in the Song School, were allotted to me. The "Snetzler" organ is especially interesting as it is housed in a building considered to be the oldest in the world to be built and used continuously for masonic meetings. The earliest recorded minutes of the Lodge date from 1677 and its members have included many famous personalities such as the Earl of Roslin, Robert Burns, James Hogg, (the Ettrick Shepherd) and James Boswell, the biographer of Samuel Johnson. In 1754, the office bearers of the Lodge commissioned John Snetzler, the foremost organ builder of the period in London, to build a chamber organ for their chapel of St John. It was completed in 1757 at a cost of £70, transported by sea to the port of Leith and then by cart to the Canongate, where it was installed in an alcove in the chapel on 4 August of that year. It still stands there today with its original case, pipe-work, mechanism and hand-blowing lever. It has a single manual of $4^{1}/_{2}$ octaves compass from G below the Bass stave and 6 stops.

Original Specification

Stopped Diapason	8	Open Diapason	8
Flute	4	Principal4	
Sesquialtra	II (Lower half)	Cornet	II (Upper half)

The programmes were designed to demonstrate the tonal qualities and resources of the two instruments with appropriate music as listed below.

17 April 1969 Lodge Canongate Kilwinning No 2

Voluntaries in G major and A minor	John Stanley (1713-1786)
Three Fugues	Handel (1685-1759)
Voluntary on the Old 100th	Henry Purcell (1659-1695)

27 April 1969 The Song School

Prelude and Fugue in A minor	Charles Wesley (1757-1834)
Chorale Partita, "Christus der ist mein leben"	J Pachelbel (1653-1706)
Air and Gavotte	Samuel Wesley (1766-1837)
Andante in E minor	S S Wesley (1810-1876)
Allabreve in D	J S Bach (1685-1750)
Canzona in G minor	Buxtehude (1637-1707)

Fortunately, the members have preserved it faithfully without any alteration except that in 1912, a Salicional and Vox Celeste were added with a Swell box but happily these are on a separate soundboard outside the original case. As Lodge organist, I greatly enjoy playing on this beautiful instrument.

The last of this selection of radio broadcasts to come to mind is a programme of sonatas for violin and chamber organ played by Leonard Friedman and myself in St Mary's on 20 December 1975. Leonard was a wonderful violinist and a specialist in music of the Baroque period. He founded and directed the Scottish Baroque Ensemble, a small group of professional players, and we collaborated many times, notably in a series of Bach Cantatas in the Cathedral and in performances of the Bach Passions.

Leonard could be somewhat unpredictable and the "live" broadcast recital turned out to be a "hair-raising" experience for me. We rehearsed together beforehand and I carefully noted changes of pace, decoration and other musical details in my copy, only to find that in the performance, Leonard ignored many of these and seemed to improvise as he went along! The programme consisted of Sonata in A, Op. 5 No 2, Vivaldi (1678-1741); Sinfonia No 4 (1629) Montalbano; Sonata in A Op. 5 No 9, Corelli (1653-1713); Sonata No 15 in E, Handel (1685-1750).

I never imagined that I would be involved in the world of "pop" music, but in 1983 George Cochrane, a Melrose businessman, told me that he had written two songs and would like the choristers to record them. At the time there was a lot of publicity on the plight of refugees and the care and safety of children. The words of the two songs reflected these concerns. As George had no knowledge of musical notation, I had to transcribe the tunes from his sung version of them and add some vocal backing. A local "pop" musician devised synthesised accompaniments and the songs were recorded in his studios. It was certainly a new and different experience! *Tell Us* (Children's Anthem for Peace) and *Was that a tear Lord?* (Theme for the World's Refugees) were issued on a single in 1984, and adopted by the UK United Nations Association and The United Nations High Commissioner for Refugees. In 1986, the recording of *Tell Us* was re-issued as a commemorative song of the 13th Commonwealth Games which were held in Edinburgh that year. Additional backing was added including the skirl of the bagpipes, to give some distinctive Scottish flavour.

Despite a fair amount of publicity, the songs did not take off as well as George Cochrane had hoped, as the disc-jockeys considered they were religious rather than "pop". However, the choristers were featured singing *Tell Us* in Edinburgh's Botanic Garden on ITV's "Highway" programme with Sir Harry Secombe.

Of a number of other television appearances, two are of special interest. In September 1990 the BBC transmitted "Songs of Praise" from Lichfield Cathedral in which the choristers, pupils, staff and parents from the northern (sic) division of choir schools provided the congregation. It was something of a publicity exercise for the schools and cathedral music and HRH The Duchess of Kent attended and gave her support. The choristers robed and sat together in the choir whilst the remainder sat in the nave. The principal conductor was Jonathan Rees-Williams, at that time Organist at Lichfield and Philip Moore, Organist and Master of the Music, York Minster, relayed his beat to the congregation. Hazel White, one of our head choristers was selected for interview during the programme and together with Philip Allison, Headmaster of St Mary's Music School and myself, was presented to the Duchess after the recording.

Finally, in June 1991, we were invited to record two programmes in St Mary's for the American TV production, "Joy of Music", featuring the organist, Diane Bish. It is a regular series shown throughout the USA and as we were to discover, further afield as well. From time to time, the company travel to other countries and film in places and buildings of interest with good instruments. The choristers sang in both programmes, and in the first were joined by a string ensemble from the Music School. Diane Bish played the solo part in the *Benedictus* from Haydn's *Little Organ Mass* and accompanied Philip Ledger's charming carol *Stille, Stille*. She introduced the programmes, played several organ pieces and interviewed Nigel Murray and me on the work of the choir and the school. Some time later, I heard that we had been seen and heard in Canada and the Bahamas.

This prompted Leroy Thompson, an organist in the Bahamas, to write and invite me to give two recitals there in April 1994. It so happened that our daughter and her husband, Ian, had spent three years in Nassau, early in their married life, where Ian had an appointment with the Public Health Authority. We had a holiday with them during their stay, and I had no hesitation in accepting an invitation to revisit that idyllic part of the world!

On that occasion, the flight from the UK to Nassau had made a stop en route in Bermuda. This prompted me to write to Graham Garton, who was at that time Director of the Dunbarton School of Music on the island, to ask if he could arrange a recital for me there. We had been fellow choristers at Lincoln and he and his wife Barbara were good friends. He readily agreed and suggested that Mabel and I should spend a week with them which made the whole trip worthwhile. When it came to booking the flights I discovered that Bermuda was no longer an en route stop between the UK and Nassau! Consequently, we had to travel Glasgow - Gatwick - Bermuda, then Bermuda - New York - Miami - Nassau and for the return journey home, Nassau - Miami, Miami - London. It was a lot more hassle and more expensive but not worth changing plans.

We left Edinburgh on 5 April 1994 and as the recital in St John's Church, Pembroke did not take place until 10 April, preparation was leisurely and we had time to explore and enjoy Bermuda. We had a swim in the sea at Horseshoe Beach, reputed to be the most beautiful in the world; attended service in the Cathedral on the Sunday morning; were given a private tour round the Governor's residence and I managed to attend a Lodge where I sat with Sir Edwin Leather, former UK MP and retired Governor of Bermuda. We were fascinated by the old town of St George and the original colonial buildings, including St Peter's Church which is the oldest Anglican church in the western hemisphere. The recital was well attended and the programme of pieces by Handel, Stanley, Bach, Elgar, Bairstow, César Franck, Gigout and Kenneth Leighton was well received.

We left Bermuda for Nassau on 12 April where we had been booked into a luxurious hotel with its own outdoor swimming pool and private beach! The first recital was planned for 14 April in Holy Trinity Anglican Church where Leroy Thompson was organist. The second was to have taken place in Freeport, Grand Bahamas the following day but was cancelled as the electronic organ was no longer playable! It was disappointing, but we had the compensation of an extra free day in Nassau. The recital programme was the same as that for Bermuda and attracted a capacity audience. We also received a warm welcome and generous hospitality from members of The District Grand Lodge of the Bahamas who had prior notice of our visit.We reluctantly left Nassau on 16 April for Miami, where we were to transfer to a direct flight to London, Heathrow. Near disaster struck as our baggage tickets had been lost and the airline could not tell whether our luggage had been transferred from the Nassau flight. Mabel took this badly and vowed she would never travel abroad with me again! Fortunately, all was well and the luggage had been checked through to the UK and we collected it on arrival with a great feeling of relief.

Chapter 15 - The End of an Era (1990-1991)

"Thank God he's gone!"

Two major events marked the year 1990. The first was the retirement, at the end of June, of Philip Crosfield as Provost of St Mary's Cathedral. He had made a remarkable contribution to the life and witness of the church in general and in twenty-two years ministry at the Cathedral, the first two as Vice-Provost.

It was fortunate he remained in office long enough to carry through a number of significant ventures. In particular the development of the Music School and The Workshop project, neither of which would have succeeded but for his sense of vision, drive and determination. It was just recognition of his life's work that he was awarded the OBE in the Queen's Birthday Honours. A great farewell party was held in the nave of the Cathedral on Saturday 23 June, when tributes and presentations were made to Philip and to his wife, Sue. It was said that the Cathedral was transformed into the grandeur of a medieval banqueting hall with tables that groaned with delicacies fit for a royal occasion!

The second major event was the arrival and installation of a new Provost at the beginning of September. Graham Forbes moved back to his birthplace from Perth where he had been Provost of St Ninian's Cathedral for eight years. Fortunately and happily, he treasures and values the choral tradition of St Mary's and recognises its unique position in Scotland. As with Philip Crosfield, he was a great personal support and has worked hard to increase the financial resources necessary to maintain the music foundation of the Cathedral.

Both Provosts brought an added bonus from their families. Paul Crosfield and the three Forbes' boys sang in the choir although Duncan and Andrew Forbes could only attend during school holidays. I was highly flattered when I was told that the Forbes' boys thought I was real "cool"!

On a more personal note, I celebrated my 65th birthday on 29 May. To mark the occasion, a special performance of Bach's *B minor Mass* was arranged for the previous weekend. The London Festival Orchestra very kindly agreed to make a special visit to take part and the "obbligato" solos by Edward Beckett (flute), Richard Friedman (violin) and Ross Pople ('cello) were magical. Sarah Leonard (soprano), Katrine Townhill (mezzo-soprano), Neil Mackie (tenor) and Geoffrey Davidson (bass) were the vocal soloists whilst the Cathedral choir and my Scottish Cantata Singers made an excellent job of the chorus work. After the performance, John Wilbraham (principal trumpet) reminded me that it was twenty-nine years since he had last played in the Mass for me in Grimsby! Members of the Friends of Cathedral Music attended the performance as part of their spring regional gathering and a special programme was arranged for them on the Sunday in addition to the services. Nigel Murray conducted the strings of St Mary's Music School in a selection of pieces before and after the morning Eucharist, and the players accompanied Haydn's *Little Organ Mass* during the service. An unexpected surprise had been prepared by Tony Harvey, organiser of the FCM gathering. He produced an iced birthday cake suitably inscribed from the Friends which was cut after the service.

FCM Gathering at St Mary's Cathedral (1990)
Philip Crosfield, Nigel Murray, Dennis and Mabel Townhill, Tony Harvey.

After a buffet lunch in the Chapter House, a tour of the Music School was followed by a composite organ recital before Evensong given by Peter Backhouse and the two organ scholars, Iain Ogg and Martin Wood. The day was rounded off with a short talk on the music establishment by myself, preceded, of course, by tea and Scottish Shortbread!

The FCM was formed to support cathedral choral foundations and raise public awareness of the unique tradition of cathedral music in this country. St Mary's was one of the first foundations to receive generous grants from the FCM and has been enormously grateful for their support.

On Monday 28 May Mabel and I drove the three hundred miles to a mountainside cottage in Wales where we spent a few days holiday with Ian, Barbara and family. We returned home on Friday 1 June ready for a Diocesan Choirs Festival the next day. After the Sunday services, I set off to drive three hundred miles north to Thurso to adjudicate at the Caithness Festival the following Monday to Friday. I was back home on Saturday 9 June in time to enjoy an annual dinner in Perth, with the Scottish cathedral organists. The following evening, I conducted the choir with the LFO in their annual concert in the Cathedral Classics series and on 11 and 12 June adjudicated at the Livingston Musical Festival. Wednesday 13 June I travelled to Addington Palace, Croydon, for a farewell party for Vincent Waterhouse, retiring Secretary of the RSCM and attended the Council Meeting. It was a hectic few weeks but not much different from the normal schedule!

In October, I told the Provost that I wished to retire from my Cathedral appointment at the end of June, 1991. There was no specific retiring age in my contract but I had long

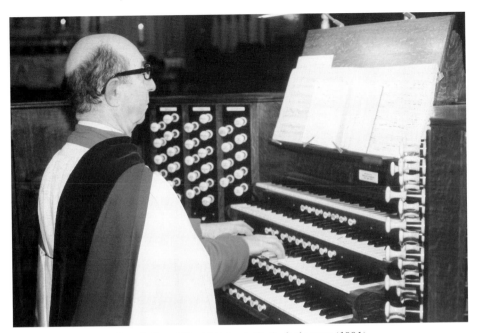

Dennis Townhill at St Mary's Cathedral organ (1991)

Photo by Peter Backhouse

felt that it was better to stop before it became difficult to maintain high standards. Nowadays, most Cathedrals set a retiring age of sixty or sixty-five and even shorter-term contracts of seven years. As with many colleagues of my generation and previously, there was no provision for an occupational retirement pension and if you were also in "tied" housing, the future could be very precarious. However, we had our own house and there were plenty of opportunities for professional work, providing I remained in good health. I felt sorry that this decision was made so soon after the new Provost's arrival, but I was able to support him through his first year and allow ample time for a successor to be found.

The year sped by and it seemed no time at all before June 1991 arrived, and the effective end of thirty years' service at St Mary's Cathedral. It was always a busy month and this one began with a concert by the London Festival Orchestra, on 9 June, in which I directed the choir and orchestra for the last time. The review in The Scotsman commented that "spirits couldn't fail to lift at the sound of the St Mary's trebles" and that "in Mozart's *Missa Brevis*, the choir produced some fine solo and ensemble singing." At a reception afterwards, the Chairman of British Gas, whose firm sponsored the Cathedral Classics series, presented me with a mounted red stag on behalf of the orchestra. It now stands proudly like a "Monarch of the Glen" on a bookcase in our sitting room. On 13 June I attended the RSCM Council meeting in London after which I moved north to adjudicate at the Upper Weardale Festival for the fourth time!

Choral Evensong was broadcast on Wednesday 19 June in which the music consisted of Introit: *Laudate Dominum*, Knut Nystedt; Leighton *Responses*; Canticles: *Stanford in C*; Anthem: *Save us, O Lord*, Bairstow. The organ voluntary was *Concert Overture in C minor* by Alfred Hollins, which prompted the distinguished organist David Liddle to write warmly congratulating me on my playing. I was very happy to inform him that it was Peter Backhouse who played the piece and who deserved all the credit.

On the 20 June I adjudicated the finals of the Saltire Society Scots Song Festival in Stirling, and three days later began my last week in charge of the music at St Mary's. Several events were arranged during the week, some known to me and some completely unexpected. I was asked to give a farewell recital lasting fifty-five minutes on the Wednesday evening and to invite members of our family. Afterwards, there would be a glass of wine and some presentations would be made. As the Provost said in the Cathedral News, "The precise details of what will happen then will remain a state secret until the night!" Typical of the clergy, he had plotted a series of surprises and we were overwhelmed by the generosity and diversity of it all. The week began with a splendid Evensong sung by the combined choirs of the seven Scottish Episcopal Cathedrals and my colleagues presented me with a handmade conductor's baton in a beautifully wrought engraved case signed by all the organists. During the day a band from the Scottish Association of Bellringers and the Cathedral rang a specially composed peal of 5030 Stedman Caters conducted by John Pladdys, and a quarter peal on the Wednesday. We were given a framed record of the peal and names of the ringers inscribed "to mark the retirement of Dr Dennis Townhill, Cathedral Organist and Master of the Choristers after thirty years."

After the recital on Wednesday 26 June, to an audience which filled the Cathedral, the Provost compèred a succession of happenings. Philip Crosfield gave a very warmhearted appreciation of my musical contribution to the life and witness of the Cathedral; the two head choristers handed me a cheque from donations from the congregation and various organisations; the two youngest choristers presented Mabel with a bouquet of flowers and then came a complete surprise. The robed choir processed from the back of the nave to the podium and, conducted by Peter Backhouse, sang a specially commissioned anthem composed by Francis Jackson. After the performance, Francis appeared, as it were out of the blue, and presented me with his inscribed manuscript score. It is a splendid setting for unaccompanied double choir of words by The Revd Fred Pratt Green who kindly also signed the copy. I later learned he had done this in the presence of Ronald Watson, Journal Editor of Norfolk Organists's Association. The evocative words are reproduced below:

When, in our music, God is glorified,
And adoration leaves no room for pride,
It is as though the whole creation cried
Alleluia.

How often making music we have found
A new dimension in the world of sound,
As worship moved us to a more profound
Alleluia.

So has the Church, in liturgy and song,
In faith and love, through centuries of wrong,
Borne witness to the truth in every tongue;
Alleluia.

Let every instrument be tuned for praise!
Let all rejoice - who have a voice to raise!
And may God give us faith to sing
Alleluia!

Reprinted by permission of Stainer & Bell Ltd.

I never did understand how Peter Backhouse and the choir managed secretly to rehearse the anthem over a period of some weeks without my knowledge. There were tales of "lookouts" being placed and choristers hiding behind trees!

At the end of the evening the Provost announced my appointment as Organist Emeritus, and that a brass plate had been screwed onto the organ case during my recital. No doubt to ensure I had not changed my mind. A framed copy was also given to us:

"In honour of Dr. Dennis Townhill D Mus, B Mus, FRCO, ADCM, FRSCM, LRAM, Organist and Master of the Choristers 1961- 1991 on his appointment as Organist Emeritus 26 June 1991."

The Provost said that previous organists were commemorated on wooden plaques but they were dead, and I wasn't yet!!

Sheila and Tony Beber presented us with a memory album and all present were invited to sign it, adding any comments they wished. I had told the choristers of my impending retirement and jokingly said that some people might say "Thank God he's going." A small probationer echoed this when he signed the book and added "Thank God he's gone."

The Bishop was the first to sign and the signatures are a permanent reminder of a memorable day. There was more to come, for the following evening we were taxied to the Balmoral Hotel where a dinner was given for us and the family, and many of those past and present who had been associated with us.

The services on the last Sunday of the choir year were beautifully sung and included the Valedictory for leaving choristers and the Old Choristers' reunion, followed by a buffet meal. Members of the choir and parents gave us a video player with recordings of the week's services and events as well as films of the Norway tour, television programmes and a framed colour photograph of the choir. Finally, at the end of the year prize-giving at the Music School, we were given a comprehensive book on church architecture signed by all the pupils. We felt that expressions of appreciation could not have been greater and we have been immensely blessed. The Provost described it as "The end of an era".

St Mary's Cathedral Choir (1991)

Photo by Peter Backhouse

At Buckingham Palace (1992)

Photo by Studio D, Blackpool

177

Chapter 16 - Unfinished Coda

"A final fling!"

Retirement from the Cathedral appointment released time for increased professional activity in a number of directions. More regular organ practice prompted a considerable number of organ recitals throughout the UK and an unexpected opportunity to play in eastern Europe.

The Rotary Club of Edinburgh was one of six from different countries to sponsor the new Rotary Club of Kiev, and members were invited to attend the Charter celebrations. In May 1992 Mabel and I joined the party of fourteen to spend five days in Kiev and two days in Vienna. The trip was a revelation, not least for the enormous contrast between the two cities. Kiev has imposing buildings but is grey, drab and poorly lit at night, whilst Vienna was so obviously affluent and alive. We received a warm welcome from the Kiev Rotarians who did all they could to make our visit enjoyable.

The night before the official Charter ceremony we were taken to a beautifully dressed production of Tchaikowsky's Sleeping Beauty ballet in the splendid Opera House. The auditorium was packed with many families and their children. We were told that it was very cheap for local people but we found our ticket prices were very expensive! We were accommodated on board a cruise liner moored on the river Dnieper, on which the Charter dinner was held. The Charter ceremony took place earlier in the day in the Palace of Culture, where we were entertained by groups of folk singers and dancers dressed in traditional costumes. One of our members, with business connections in Kiev, had suggested that I should be invited to give an organ recital as part of the celebrations. Many years previously Hans Heintze had told me of the great interest in organ music in the former USSR, and he was right.

The organ hall, a converted Roman Catholic church, was filled to capacity with an audience of over a thousand including those attending the Rotary ceremony. The reception of the programme was overwhelming and especially to the arrangement of the "Great Gate of Kiev" which I played as an encore.

During the afternoon whilst I was waiting to practise, I received a number of visitors including Vladimir Koshouba, the leading Ukrainian organist. He invited me to take part in an international organ festival that he was organising the following year.

Our party left Kiev for Vienna and we duly arrived at our luxurious hotel. It was beautiful weather, and the next morning we sat outside on the pavement sipping coffee and enjoying the colourful sight and scent of the flowers in the open-air market. The wide variety of fruit and vegetables and other goods displayed on the stalls reflected the general atmosphere of freedom and prosperity. We spent a day's sight-seeing in the city, including visits to St Stephen's Cathedral where both Haydn and Schubert sang as boys and to the house where Mozart lived, as well as a visit to his grave. In the evening we had a meal at an inn in the Vienna Woods, where we were entertained by musicians in national costume playing well-known pieces by Johann Strauss.

Following Vladimir Koshouba's invitation, I set off for a two-week recital tour in

Ukraine on 15 September 1993. In terms of the engagement, the British Council funded my return fare and I was provided with meals, accommodation and travel costs during the tour. Fees were paid in Ukrainian "coupons" but, as Hans Heintze had warned me, the money had to be spent within the country as there was no exchange rate and you were not allowed to take money out!

Koshouba met me on arrival in Kiev and took me by car to the Hotel Moscow, in the city centre, where the visiting players were accommodated. Armed guards were stationed at the entrance to the bedrooms and evidence of identity had to be produced. Room keys were handed out and collected by a formidable lady seated at a table and Vladimir warned me to keep my room door locked and not to allow anyone in! The following morning I was taken for a visit to a monastery where I bought a lovely ikon of Our Lady, was given a good lunch in a nearby restaurant and then put on a train at 4pm for a fifteen-and-a-half hour journey to Cernovci, near the Romanian border, for my first recital engagement. The train was old, the cabin door lock was broken and the shared toilet in the corridor was revolting. My anxiety was increased when I found I was sharing a four-berth cabin with three Moldavians. Fortunately, they were quietly behaved and spent most of the night playing cards whilst I lay on my bunk unable to sleep! It was with a feeling of great relief, when the train arrived in Cernovci at 7.30 the next morning, that I found Vasilij Koshman and Ostep Sauchuk waiting to meet me. They were the administrators of the Chamber Music Hall where I was to give the first of three recitals in the city and were a friendly pair who looked after me well.

The halls were converted churches and the organs were placed at the east end, where the altar would have stood, with players visible to the audience. The instruments were mostly by German or Czechoslovakian builders, mechanical action and none more than twenty years old.

Audiences were huge, often overflowing into standing as well. Multiple encores were insisted upon, bouquets of flowers were presented by members of the audience after individual pieces, and the reception could not have been warmer. I was transported around in a large, black Cadillac, driven by a chauffeur, and felt very important! I was somewhat nonplussed whenever we stopped to find people crowding around the car, peering in and shaking their fists at me. Apparently such luxurious cars were used by former communist party officials who were not popular! As I was in Cernovci over a weekend, I was able to attend church and started at a Ukrainian Orthodox service and then moved to Holy Trinity Cathedral. Both buildings were full of worshippers of all ages, and I was deeply moved by the reverence and devotion of the congregations. The Cathedral was surrounded by armed police for security as there was a bitter dispute between the Russian Orthodox Church and the now independent Ukrainian Orthodox Church, over ownership of the building. The next day I was shown round the city, including the University campus by Mikhail Onishchenko, a young graduate who spoke excellent English. He was aware of the difference between conditions in Ukraine and western countries and told me they were at least seventy years behind us. The weather was colder and there was a broken window in the train cabin on the return journey to Kiev, as a result of which I caught a bad cold and sore throat. At least it was less traumatic for I shared a two-berth cabin with a pleasant young businessman and we managed to converse in French!

I attended a meeting of Kiev Rotary Club the following evening, and enjoyed meeting again some of the members who had been present at the Charter celebrations. Unfortunately, I developed a bad nose-bleed which refused to stop, and was taken by ambulance to the hospital where it was dealt with. It was a lucky coincidence that the speaker at the club was the Minister of Health and I got priority treatment.

Vladimir Koshouba drove me to my next venue in Bila Cervca, a town some 100 kilometres south of Kiev. Here the converted church also served as an art gallery with paintings by Ukrainian artists hung round the walls, and I bought some as souvenirs. The concert was televised and afterwards we were given a meal at the home of the hall administrator. He and his wife, a careworn, sad-looking lady, were very welcoming and provided a simple wholesome supper. The house and contents were typically Victorian in style. There was no running hot water and the chemical lavatory was situated in a shed at the end of the garden path, lit by candle and without toilet paper.

Koshouba and I returned to Kiev, and I had a free day for sightseeing including a visit to Vladimir's home which he shared with his parents, wife Svetlana and their small daughter Victoria. Accommodation was limited to a bed-sitting room for the parents, a similar room for Vladimir and family which also did duty as a music room, a small kitchen and small shower room with toilet.

We left Kiev by an overnight train to Dniepropetrovsk, a large town in the south of the country on the banks of the river and a mere ten-hour journey. The coaches were much more luxurious and comfortable than before. To my astonishment, I found we were sharing a four-berth cabin with two very attractive young ladies named Olga and Tsenya! Vladimir was able to chat to them but they neither spoke nor understood English. Apparently Olga was visiting her family in Dniepropetrovsk and worked for a firm in Kiev which was one of the sponsors of the Organ Festival.

Dniepropetrovsk seemed to be a prosperous city with a plentiful variety of food. Our hotel was comfortable and well appointed, unlike the one in Cernovci which had no water available in the room, the light did not work and the samovar leaked!

The concert hall was a most attractive building standing in its own spacious grounds and with a good restaurant. My two recitals on successive evenings were played to full houses, standing ovations and multiple encores. The first was recorded for television and radio. Vladimir took me on a sightseeing tour the second day which included a visit to the indoor market. He bought large quantities of meat and cooking oil to take home as these were not readily available in Kiev. The weather had been dry and sunny throughout, so far, and on this particular day it was very hot and tiring for such a long period of walking around. Back in Kiev the next morning, after the overnight train journey, I was taken by Vladimir to the Military headquarters. His father had been a Colonel in the army and Vladimir had been brought up with the son of a fellow officer friend who was now in command of the Kiev headquarters. The reason for the visit was to obtain the services of a couple of soldiers to help reconstruct Vladimir's parents' old house. I soon learnt that in Ukraine who you knew was more important than what you knew.

A sauna had just been installed in the barracks for the exclusive use of the senior officers. We were invited to try it out and whilst I had never previously experienced a sauna, and was somewhat apprehensive, I accepted. Plunging in to the cold water of the pool after sitting naked in the very hot temperature of the "sweating room" was a daunting prospect. However, it was remarkably refreshing although I was glad there was no photographic record of the two of us clad only in woollen "bobble" hats. In the evening I attended the recital by Gisbert Ledekkekker from Holland, one of the other visiting players. He was stylish and technically accurate, but made no attempt to acknowledge the audience in any way.

I was booked to give two recitals in Kiev on the last two days of the tour and was now prepared for the usual reception. I was due to be collected from the hotel on the first evening by one of Vladimir's helpers but she failed to arrive! In some panic, I decided to take a taxi and hoped I could make myself understood. Fortunately, there was a taxi rank outside the hotel and I had some Ukrainian currency. The driver luckily spoke some English and we managed some discussion on the prospects for Dynamo Kiev football club who I noticed were playing that evening. The final day was busy with a radio interview, official lunch given for all visiting players by the Arts Committee of Ukraine and practice for the concert. There was one alarming moment during the concert when a strange wild-looking man walked towards the platform as I was acknowledging applause. He turned out to be a writer who had written a poem in my honour during the concert and which he presented to me.

So the tour came to an end and I look back with a mixed bag of memories, but most of all of the enormous goodwill and friendliness of the people I met and the great appreciation and enthusiasm of the audiences. I left Kiev on 29 September with many souvenirs bought with the fees. Whilst I received repeated invitations to return, for one reason or another, I have not done so. However, I did arrange a recital tour in Britain for Koshouba and also met a number of young Ukrainian businessmen for whom our Rotary Club provided professional experience in Edinburgh. We also sponsored holidays in Scotland for some of the children affected by the Chernobyl nuclear power disaster.

I had been examining for the Associated Board of the Royal Schools of Music throughout the UK since 1968, but had never pursued the possibility of an overseas tour, as I felt that I should not leave my Cathedral duties for the length of time a tour would involve. When that obstacle was removed I was able to accept the invitation to go to Hong Kong for nine weeks from 8 October to 11 December 1994. This proved a fascinating experience and a glimpse of a completely different culture from our own. Mabel accompanied me for the first fortnight and shared the excitement of the first sight of the former colony as the jumbo jet descended between a forest of skyscrapers to the airport. It seemed incredible that more than six million people could live in such a confined space. In the morning they emerged like a never ending stream of ants on to the streets and into the underground trains. Despite cramped living conditions it was impressive to see the children invariably smart and tidy in their school uniforms and wearing clean, freshly-ironed white shirts and blouses.

An incredible 39,000 candidates are examined annually in Hong Kong, the Associated Board's largest centre in the world, and I was one of a group of twenty-six examiners. My first three weeks were spent in Shatin in a splendid new hotel in Pak Hok Ting Street, from where I travelled by train to examine at The Twinkle Star Paradise Company in Tai Po, near the Chinese border. Susan Smith, a charming New Zealand examiner, was also staying in our hotel otherwise we were separated from the rest of our colleagues and our wives. This meant that Mabel was left to her own devices whilst we were away examining during the day and missed the social contacts with the others. However, overall she enjoyed her stay and we did have some free days together and outings including a trip round Hong Kong and Kowloon by Chinese sampan, a tour to Aberdeen Harbour, Victoria Peak by cable car giving spectacular views, and Stanley open-air market where you can buy nearly anything! We attended a concert by the Hong Kong Symphony Orchestra in the City Hall with Susan and Shirley Ip, a Chinese friend of hers. The following day, Shirley took us all out for lunch in a revolving restaurant at the top of one of the skyscrapers on Hong Kong Island, where we greatly enjoyed our first experience of Dim Sum, a varied selection of Chinese snacks. Mabel left for the return flight to the UK on 24 October and the next Sunday, I moved to Hong Kong Island for a three week spell of examining at Eddie's Piano Company studios in Taikooshing. I was sorry to leave the Royal Park Hotel and its luxurious accommodation and friendly staff but it was a great pleasure to meet up with some of the other examiners. Colin Tipple, also from Edinburgh, Peter Stevenson, former organist of Portsmouth Cathedral and Louis Carus, Principal of the Birmingham Conservatoire and formerly Head of Strings at the RSAMD, were all well-known to me and I found great cameraderie with new colleagues.

Hong Kong has a thriving cultural life with many concerts by international groups and solo artists in some splendid halls. These included piano recitals by Fou T'song, concerts by Moscow State Orchestra, English Chamber Orchestra and another by the Hong Kong Symphony Orchestra. I discovered that Laurie Gargan, one of my former students at the RSAMD, was playing trumpet in the Hong Kong Orchestra. We met after one of the concerts and he and one of his fellow trumpet players invited me to join them for a meal the following week, and go to the race meeting at the Happy Valley Course. Of all the unlikely places, they took me for traditional British fish-and-chips at Hong Kong's Harry Ramsden's restaurant. Even the waiters were from Yorkshire!

The race course was floodlit and the crowd of about 35,000 people generated a tremendous atmosphere. Although I lost $50, I have rarely spent such an exciting and enjoyable evening, aided and abetted by the enthusiastic, good humoured company of my two young companions.

The last three weeks were spent in Kowloon where I joined a large number of colleagues examining in the Tom Lee Studios in Austin Road. With papers to check and joint meals here and there with them, there was never a dull moment and the time flew by. I also managed to fit in visits to three Rotary Club meetings and some Masonic Lodges.

The main purpose of the tour was, of course, examining. Most of my candidates were for piano and all understood the stereotyped instructions given in English. The children were utterly disarming and very polite, although the standard of performance varied between very good and very poor. We had been told that the failure rate was likely to be much greater than in the UK. Some candidates entered for the same examination more than once in the same period on the grounds that pass or fail depended more on good fortune or a sympathetic examiner than good preparation! Whilst technical facility was sometimes considerable there was often little understanding of the difference in style between music by composers from different periods.

Family Concert at Inveraray Castle (1994)

FCOCA Executive (1996) with Dr Francis Jackson

Photo by Margaret Horner

I left Hong Kong with so many happy memories and great respect for the diligence and commitment of the Chinese. An invitation to return in 1996, regretfully had to be refused, and that signalled the end of my time as a Board examiner.

Invitations to adjudicate at competitive music festivals continued until I decided to "Call it a day" last year. By this time, I had judged at most Festivals in Scotland, many English ones and a good many in Northern Ireland, so that I felt I had had a good innings.

One highlight was to be invited to propose the toast to the British Federation of Festivals at the Conference dinner in Glasgow in 1994. I felt this was a rare honour considering I was an immigrant Englishman, a member of a minority non-conformist sect in Scotland and living in Edinburgh. When I mentioned that I had travelled from Edinburgh in the east to Glasgow in the west and that the "Wise Men" had likewise come from the east, a senior Glasgow Councillor growled, "Aye, and there's nae evidence they ever went back again!"

In the early 1960s, as mentioned earlier, I initiated an RSCM residential course for choristers in Edinburgh and directed it for fourteen years, continuing a commitment begun in Louth and Grimsby. It has been encouraging to see the work of the RSCM spreading to other denominations north of the border, and I have been proud to represent Scotland on the Council.

Family matters are largely a private affair, but it has been an increasing source of joy and pleasure to see our two children happily married and providing us with six splendid grandchildren. Not surprisingly, they are all musical and in the last fifteen years we have been able to give public concerts together and raise funds for many worthwhile causes. They allow the "old man" to join in with them and the younger ones do not hesitate to tell him how he should be playing his part! It is invidious to single out particular concerts but for sheer beauty of surroundings and ambience our two performances in the Armoury Hall at Inveraray Castle in 1994 and 1995 by invitation of Their Graces The Duke and Duchess of Argyll have a special place. They were in aid of the Crarae Gardens Trust, and followed the first concert for the Trust in Cumlodden Church the previous year. Nine members of the family took part and we provided a programme of music from Haydn to Horovitz. The instruments ranged from violin, viola, 'cellos, clarinet, trumpet, trombone, piano and a solo singer in various combinations!

Gratitude for the opportunities provided by my early years in Lincoln, as a Cathedral chorister, has remained strong and it has been an enormous pleasure to retain a connection with many of my contemporary fellow choristers. This prompted me to initiate a revival in 1969 of St Mary's Cathedral Old Choristers' Association and happily, it is continuing enthusiastically with Eric Ibler as Chairman and The Revd James Milne as Secretary. James is the first of my former choristers to become ordained. Since retirement, it has been possible to make a more positive contribution nationally through the Federation of Cathedral Old Choristers' Associations. Having served on the Executive Committee as Vice-Chairman from 1994, I succeeded Geoffrey Mitchell as Chairman in 1997 and am now well into the five-year term of office.

More could be written but reaching the millennium seems a good time to conclude this account of a privileged life of music making.

Laus Deo.

Appendix

Recordings

The number of our recordings is modest compared with other cathedrals and Collegiate churches and most are now unavailable. However, they have been well received and some have had circulation in many countries and extracts transmitted in broadcast programmes over many years.

We have been fortunate in having a number of eminent authorities write the notes on the words and music e.g. Bach-Leighton organ music - Professor Peter Williams; Songs of Praise - The Revd Dr Erik Routley; Child in the Manger - Elizabeth Poston; Gelineau Psalms - Dom Gregory Murray; Organ Works of Kenneth Leighton - Giles Easterbrook of Novello; Famous Hymns of Praise - Dr Donald Webster.

Listening to the recordings in retrospect, it is pleasing to hear the choir maintaining a consistent standard of performance. This was confirmed by a lay clerk of the late 1980s who told me he had bought a copy of the 1966 recording of "Music for Easter" and that "it was very good!" In an article for Choir and Organ in 1999, Simon Lindley comments "the music of St Mary's occupies a special place in the heart of any child of the Gelineau generation. The choir's treasured recording of Father Gelineau's psalmody gets right to the nub of this spiritual and musical utterance by a brilliant combination of simplicity and sophistication." The Roman Catholic origins of the settings prompted Alec Robertson of The Gramophone to write that "the recording is very good, as one would expect from the choir of St Mary's R C Cathedral in Edinburgh, which has achieved such a high reputation under Arthur Oldham (sic!) The recording is in every way excellent and makes delightful listening." We received an apology and correction in the next month's edition but we felt the reviewer might have read the cover more carefully! A few years later I received a letter from Mel Butler, lecturer in Church Music at the Eastman School of Music in Rochester, NY in the USA, telling me that he regularly used the recording for his classes. This had prompted him to ask if he might spend part of his sabbatical leave in Edinburgh to study choir training methods with me.

Although the complete organ works of Kenneth Leighton were recorded in 1990, it was not until 1995 that they were issued. It had been my hope that the recording would not only be a personal tribute but also help in some way to make the music more widely known. The initial pressing has sold out on both sides of the Atlantic and received high praise from a wide variety of reviews. The British Music Society critic commented, "this is a superb release - Dr Dennis Townhill possesses an intimate knowledge and understanding of the music - I do not think that his performances can be bettered and this set is likely to remain unsurpassed for years." Robert Lawrenson in Organists' Review says "Dr Townhill plays with consummate musicianship, assured technique and a grasp of the very heart and soul of Leighton's music," whilst the account in Tempo states "This set forms a fitting testament to the composer's memory and is a vital document of British

Dennis Townhill and Kenneth Leighton (1986)

Photo by Mrs J Leighton

organ music." Andrew Thomson, an Edinburgh music graduate and pupil of Kenneth Leighton, now an eminent author and journalist, sent me a copy of his generous review in Choir and Organ. He added a personal note "It's wonderful and I mean every word I have written. You have done Kenneth proud! Many congratulations". I treasure that.

1. 1965
    Bach and Leighton Organ Music   Waverley Records LLD 1033. SLLP 1034.
    Dennis Townhill
    J S Bach: Preludes for the Church Year from the Little
                                     Organ Book
    Advent   Nun Komm' der Heiden Heiland S 599
    Christmas   Vom Himmel hoch S 606
                                     In dulci jubilo S 608
    New Year's Eve   Das alte jahr vergangen ist S 614
    New Year's Day   In dir ist Freude S 615
    Feast of Purification   Mit fried' und freud S 616
    Passiontide   O Lamme Gottes unschuldig S 618
    Easter   Christ lag in Todesbanden S 625
                                     Erstanden ist der heil'ge Christ S 628
    Ascension   Heut' triumphiret Gottes Sohn S 630
    Whitsuntide   Komm Gott, Schöpfer heiliger Geist S 631 (a)
    Kenneth Leighton: Prelude, Scherzo and Passacaglia Opus 41

2. 1965
    Songs of Praise - Combined Cathedral Choirs of Carlisle, Newcastle and
    St Mary's Edinburgh - Alpha Records PHA 3009 SPHA 3010
    Dennis Townhill (Conductor) Andrew Seivewright and Colin Ross (Organists)
    (a) Praise, my soul the King of Heaven   (Goss)
    (b) Let all the world in every corner sing (Luckington)
    (c) O worship the King   (Hanover)
    (d) I to the hills will lift mine eyes   (French)
    (e) Praise to the Lord, the Almighty   (Lobe den Herren)
    (f) A safe stronghold   (Ein feste Burg)
    (g) Glorious things of thee are spoken   (Austria)
    (h) The King of love   (Dykes)
    (i) O, for a thousand tongues   (Richmond)
    (j) Jesu, the very thought of Thee   (St Botolph)
    (k) Come down, O Love divine   (Down Ampney)
    (l) Dear Lord and Father of mankind   (Repton)
    (m) The day Thou gavest   (St Clement)

3. 1966
    Music for Easter - EMI CLP 3525 CSD 3526
    Dennis Townhill (Conductor and Solo Organist) George Hay
    (Organ Accompaniments)

    (a) O Sons and Daughters let us sing   arr. Walford Davies
    (b) Chorale: Christ the Lord hath risen
    (c) Preludes on Christ ist erstanden   J S Bach S 627

(d)	Haec Dies	Byrd
(e)	Pascha nostrum	Byrd
(f)	Surgen Jesus	Philips
(g)	The strife is o'er (Vulpius)	arr. Henry Ley
(h)	This joyful Eastertide	arr. Charles Wood
(i)	The world itself (Piae Cantiones)	harm. Praetorius
(j)	We will be merry (trad. German)	harm. Michael Praetorius
(k)	An Easter Alleluya for organ	Gordon Slater
(l)	Cheer up, friends and neighbours (trad. French)	
		harm. Martin Shaw
(m)	Love is come again (Old French)	
(n)	Christ the Lord is risen (Old German)	harm. Geoffrey Shaw

4. 1969

Child in the Manger - MCA CKPS 1001
Dennis Townhill (Conductor and Solo Organist) Keith Griffiths (Organ Accompaniments) Sinfonia of Edinburgh (Leader Daphne Godson)

(a)	The Boys' Carol (Personent Hodie)	trans.and arr. Elizabeth Poston
(b)	Lullay myn lyking	R R Terry
(c)	Child in the Manger (Bunessan)	arr. Elizabeth Poston
(d)	Chorale Prelude on Wie schön leuchtet der Morgenstern	
		J Pachelbel
(e)	Cradle Song	Byrd
(f)	Dunbar's Carol	Elizabeth Poston
(g)	Hark! The Herald Angels sing	arr. David Willcocks
(h)	Patapan (trad Burgundian)	arr. Frank Spedding
(i)	Balulalow (trad Scots)	arr. Elizabeth Poston
(j)	Ecce novum gaudium (Old Scots)	harm. Kenneth Elliott
(k)	Chorale Prelude on In dulci jubilo	J S Bach S 751
(l)	Ane sang o' the birth of Christ (Old Scots)	
		arr. Kenneth Elliott
(m)	Torches	John Joubert
(n)	O come, all ye faithful	arr. David Willcocks

5. 1970

The Gelineau Psalms - MCA MKPS 2008
Dennis Townhill (Conductor) Richard Walker (Organ) Robert Jenner and Geoffrey Bolt (Trumpets) Andrew Shivas (Timpani) Andrew Fraser and Kenneth Blyth (Trebles) Harry Brashaw and Ronald Binnie (Tenors) Colin Fox (Baritone) arr. David Lord

(a) Psalm 95 O sing a new song to the Lord
(b) Psalm 114 I love the Lord

(c)   Psalm 5 To my words give ear
(d)   Psalm 99 Cry out with joy
(e)   Psalm 22 The Lord is my shepherd
(f)   Psalm 32 Ring out your joy to the Lord
(g)   Canticle of Simeon (Nunc Dimittis)
(h)   Psalm 144 I will give you glory
(i)   Psalm 80 Ring out your joy to God our strength
(j)   Psalm 83 How lovely is your dwelling place
(k)   Psalm 119 To the Lord in the hour of my distress
(l)   Psalm 150 Praise God in his Holy Place

6.   1975
     The Choir of St Mary's Cathedral - Criterion records CRS 253
     Dennis Townhill (Conductor) John Taylor (Cathedral Organ) Eric Ibler
     (Chamber Organ) Instrumentalists of St Mary's Music School

     (a)   Kyrie and Gloria from Mass in G major   Schubert
           Iain White (Treble) Colin Heggie (Counter Tenor) Tom Scratchley (Tenor)
           Peter Backhouse (Bass)
     (b)   Rejoice in the Lord alway   Purcell
           Colin Heggie (Counter Tenor) Peter McLean (Tenor)
           Charles Hetherington (Bass)
     (c)   Last Movement (Allegro) from Double Violin Concerto
                                                   J S Bach
           Kari Jones and Colin Harrison (Violins)
     (d)   Omnes de Saba venient   Jacob Handl
     (e)   O leave your sheep (trad. French)   arr. Kenneth Leighton
     (f)   Ecce novum gaudium(Old Scots)   harm. Kenneth Elliott
     (g)   Child in the Manger (Bunessan)   arr. Elizabeth Poston
     (h)   Christ the Lord hath risen (12th century)
     (i)   Come, Holy Ghost the Maker   Cedric Thorpe Davie
     (j)   Gloria tibi Domine   Byrd
     (k)   Alle Psallite cum luya   (Franconian Motet c. 1250)

7.   1977
     Music for St John Baptist Day - Criterion records C 257
     Dennis Townhill plays the Snetzler organ in Lodge Canongate Kilwinning,
     Edinburgh

     (a)   The Prince of Denmark's March   Jeremiah Clarke
     (b)   Voluntary on the Old 100th Psalm Tune   Henry Purcell
     (c)   Minuet from Berenice   Handel
     (d)   Dead March from Saul   Handel
     (e)   March from The Occasional Oratorio   Handel

(f)	Adagio and Trumpet Tune	John Stanley
(g)	Voluntary No 3 in E major	John Stanley
(h)	Concerto for Organ in F major (Cuckoo and Nightingale)
		Handel
(i)	Voluntary No 2 in A minor	John Stanley
(j)	Voluntary No 7 in E minor	John Stanley

8.   1979

Music for Christmas - Produced by Richard Hammerton
Dennis Townhill (Conductor and Solo Organist) Peter Backhouse
(Organ Accompaniments)

(a)	The Cathedral Bell tolling Midnight	
(b)	Processional: Hodie Christus natus est (Plainchant)	
(c)	Fantasia on In dulci jubilo	J S Bach S 729
(d)	Adam lay ybounden	Boris Ord
(e)	Ding dong merrily on high(Old French)	harm. C Wood
(f)	In the bleak midwinter	Harold Darke
	Sandy Sutherland (Tenor)	
(g)	The Angel Gabriel (Old Basque)	
(h)	Infant Holy (trad. Polish)	arr. Edmund Rubbra
(i)	Paean	Kenneth Leighton
(j)	Chorale In dulci jubilo	J S Bach
(k)	Jerusalem, rejoice for joy	E Poston
(l)	Chorale Prelude on Wie schön leuchtet der Morgenstern	
		J Pachelbel
(m)	The Three Kings	Peter Cornelius
	Nigel Waugh (Baritone)	
(n)	Chorale Prelude on Es ist ein' Ros' entsprungen	
		Brahms
(o)	O leave your sheep	arr. Kenneth Leighton
(p)	Recessional Hodie Christus natus est (Plainchant)	

9.   1984

The Choristers Auld Reekie Records Gala 1A & 1B
Tell Us
The Children's Anthem for Peace   Susan Hamilton   (Treble)
Was that a tear, Lord?   Theme for the World's Refugees

10.   1987

19th and 20th Century Organ Music Priory PRC 223
Dennis Townhill (Organ)

| (a) | Sonata No1 in F minor | Mendelssohn |

(b)   A Trumpet Minuet   Hollins
(c)   Allegretto grazioso   Hollins
(d)   Grand Choeur No1 in G minor   Hollins
(e)   Three Preludes on Scottish Psalm Tunes Robin Orr
      (1) Martyrs   (2) Selma   (3) Balfour
(f)   Five Preludes on Scottish Psalm Tunes   Frederick Rimmer
(1)   Culross No 1 (2) Abbey (3) Elgin (4) Soldau (5) Culross No 2
(g)   Veni Redemptor - A Celebration Op 93   Kenneth Leighton

11.   1988
      Three Edinburgh Organs Priory PRC 250
      Dennis Townhill (Organ)
      Lodge Canongate Kilwinning - Johan Snetzler 1757

      (a)   Voluntary No 2 in A minor   J Stanley
      (b)   Voluntary No 7 in E minor   J Stanley
      (c)   Voluntary No 10 in G minor   J Stanley
      (d)   Voluntary No 1 in A major   J Stanley

      The Song School, St Mary's Cathedral - Henry Willis 1887
      (e)   Partita Christus der ist mein leben   J Pachelbel
      (f)   Prelude and Fugue in A minor   C Wesley
      (g)   Two Pieces No 6 and No 7   S Wesley
      (h)   Andante in E minor   S S Wesley

      St Mary's Church, Bellevue - T C Lewis 1882

      (i)   Sonata No 6 in D minor   Mendelssohn
      (j)   March in G major   Henry Smart

12.   1988
      My beloved spake - Priory PRCD 251
      The Choir of St Mary's Cathedral with the Orchestra of St Mary's
      Music School
      Dennis Townhill (Conductor) Peter Backhouse (Organ)

      (a)   My beloved spake   H Purcell
            Robert Marshall (Alto) Sam King (Tenor) Christopher Bevan and
            Colin Heggie (Basses) George Hlawiczka (Violin Obbligato)
            Sandy Bartai ('Cello Continuo) Peter Backhouse (Chamber Organ)
      (b)   Chacony in G minor for strings   H Purcell
            directed by Nigel Murray
      (c)   Save us, O Lord   E C Bairstow

(d)	Lord, Thou hast been our refuge	E C Bairstow
(e)	Benedicite in G major	Francis Jackson
(f)	Te Deum in D major	Francis Jackson
(g)	I heard a voice from Heaven	Dennis Townhill
	Kate McGlew (Treble)	
(h)	Lo, God is here	Dennis Townhill
(i)	Awake, my glory	Kenneth Leighton
	Stuart Wood (Treble)	
(j)	What love is this of thine?	Kenneth Leighton
	Jeremy Paton (Treble)	
	Christopher Bevan (Baritone)	

13.   1990

The Complete Organ Works of Kenneth Leighton Priory 3 CD Set PRCD 326
Dennis Townhill (Organ)

(a)	Prelude, Scherzo and Passacaglia (Opus 41)	1963
(b)	Elegy	1965
(c)	Fanfare	1966
(d)	Paean	1966
(e)	Et Resurrexit - Theme, Fantasy and Fugue (Opus 49)	1966
(f)	Festival Fanfare	1968
(g)	Improvisation - In memoriam Maurice de Sausmarez	1969
(h)	Chorale Prelude on Rockingham	1975
(i)	Six Fantasies on Hymn Tunes (Opus 72)	1975
	(1) Helmsley (2) Aus der Tiefe (3) Lumetto (4) St Columba	
	(5)Veni Emmanuel (6) Hanover	
(j)	Martyrs - Dialogues on a Scottish Psalm Tune (Opus 73)	1976
	(for organ duet) with Peter Backhouse	
(k)	Ode	1977
(l)	Missa de Gloria - Dublin Festival Mass (Opus 82)	1980
	(1) Kyrie (2) Gloria (3) Credo (4) Sanctus and Benedictus	
	(5) Agnus Dei (6) Ite, Missa est	
(m)	Veni Redemptor: A Celebration (Opus 93)	1985
(n)	Veni Creator Spiritus - Prelude	1987

14.   1991

Famous Hymns of Praise Priory PRCD 376
Dennis Townhill (Conductor) Peter Backhouse (Organ)

(a)	Come, thou long expected Jesus	J Stainer
(b)	My song is love unknown	J Ireland
(c)	We sing the praise of Him	S Nicholson

(d)	Come down, O Love Divine	R Vaughan Williams
	Graham Kirk (Treble)	
(e)	Come, Holy Ghost - Plainsong	
	Robert Marshall (Tenor)	
(f)	Holy, Holy, Holy	J B Dykes
(g)	The God of Abraham Praise	Hebrew Melody
(h)	All creatures of our God and King	17th Century
	Descant : Christopher Gower	
(i)	Alleluia, sing to Jesus	R H Pritchard
	Descant: Dennis Townhill	
(j)	All my hope on God is founded	H Howells
	Descant: Dennis Townhill	
(k)	Angel voices ever singing	E G Monk
(l)	Be Thou my vision (trad. Irish)	
	Descant: Dennis Townhill	
(m)	City of God	T Haweis
	Descant: Alan Gray	
(n)	Eternal Father, strong to save	J B Dykes
(o)	Glorious things of thee are spoken	C Taylor
(p)	O praise ye the Lord	C H H Parry
(q)	O worship the King	W Croft
	Descant: Alan Gray	
(r)	Praise, my soul	J Goss
	Mark Wood (Treble)	
	Descant: Dennis Townhill	
(s)	Through all the changing scenes of life	G Smart
(t)	God is love	C H H Parry
(u)	Praise to the Holiest in the height	J B Dykes
(v)	Dear Lord and Father	C H H Parry
	Agnes Bradley and	
	Mark Wood (Trebles)	
	Robert Marshall (Tenor)	
(w)	The day Thou gavest	C Scholefield

Acknowledgements

Grateful acknowledgement is made for information obtained from the following:

1. A Short History of Lincoln (1979), by Sir Francis Hill, published by Lincoln Civic Trust
2. The Pictorial History of Lincoln Cathedral, by Colin Dunlop, published by Pitkin Pictorials, Ltd.
3. St James' Church, Louth (1989), published by Jarrold Printing, Norwich.
4. The Buildings of Scotland - Edinburgh (1984), by John Gifford, Colin McWilliam and David Walker, published by Penguin Books.
5. Music and the Reformation in England (1967), by Peter le Huray, published by Herbert Jenkins.
6. Songs and Stones (1996), by Philip Crosfield, published by St Mary's Cathedral, Palmerston Place, Edinburgh.
7. Old Coates House (1989), by Ishbel Gray with contributions by Allan Maclean, published by St Mary's Cathedral, Palmerston Place, Edinburgh.
8. Some Notes on the Mural Paintings in the Song School of St Mary's Cathedral (1995), by Margaret C Campbell, published by NJA Data Design.
9. St Mary's Music School - 25 Years (1998), compiled and edited by Sally Wyllie, published by St Mary's Music School, Edinburgh.
10. A Seminary of Learning (1994), by Edward Luscombe, published by The Scottish Episcopal Church.
11. Stanford Memorial Chapel, published by Stanford University, USA.

Photographs have been identified and acknowledged where known.

Index

Abbott, Eric, 34.
Addington Palace, 60, 172.
Allison, Miss, 11.
Allison, Philip, 95.
Allt, Greenhouse, 60.
Andrews, H Ken, 30, 48, 163.
Associated Board, 21, 40, 44, 134, 182.

Bach, J S, 14, 21, 25, 29, 32, 40, 41, 43,
  51, 54, 57, 72, 73, 91, 110, 113, 114,
  131, 167, 171.
Backhouse, Peter, 83, 110, 112, 116, 142,
  172, 174.
Bailey, Bill, 26.
Bairstow, E C, 21, 29.
Baker, Janet, 51.
Ball, E C (Ted), 44.
Beavans, Peggy, 41.
Beethoven, 27, 43.
Belford, Fred, 85.
Bennett, G J, 12, 71.
Bentley, G B, 34.
Bermuda, 170.
Betjeman, John, 167.
Beverley Minster, 51.
Bottomley, Herbert, 32.
Brahms, 21, 27, 55, 72, 110, 131.
Brewer, Sydney, 22.
Brigg Fair, 33.
Brigg Choral Society, 33, 40, 41.
Brigg Girls' High School, 32, 41.
Brigg Music Festival, 33.
British Broadcasting Corporation, 54, 87,
  111, 117, 166, 167.
British Federation of Festivals, 185.
Britten, Benjamin, 32, 51, 52, 112, 134.
Brompton Holy Trinity, 60.
Brown, Wilfred, 14, 58.
Broxholme, Geoff, 22.
Bruckner, 77.
Buckingham Palace, 177.
Bullock, Ernest, 30.

Bunney, Herrick, 111, 118, 161.
Burton, Humphrey, 39, 44, 59.
Burton Parish Church, 28, 75.
Buxtehude, 134.
Byram-Wigfield, Timothy, 81.
Byrd, William, 11, 21, 30.
Byres, John, 68.

Cathedrals
  Aberdeen St Machar, 96, 165.
  Birmingham, 20, 50, 58.
  Canterbury, 110.
  Carlisle, 48, 107.
  Chester, 50, 165.
  Coventry, 122.
  Dundee, 76.
  Durham, 67, 81, 107.
  Ely, 166.
  Hereford, 101, 165.
  Leicester, 165.
  Lichfield, 169.
  Liverpool Anglican, 163.
  London St Paul's, 67, 72, 108, 165.
  Manchester, 81, 82.
  Newcastle, 44, 107.
  Peterborough, 42, 55.
  St Edmundsbury, 121.
  Salisbury, 121.
  Wakefield, 118.
  Winchester, 42, 81, 82.
Camden, Archie, 57, 58.
Campbell, George, 75.
Canongate, 63, 167.
Carey, Kenneth, 75, 79.
Chapel Royal, 66.
Chapman, Vaughn, 147, 160.
Clinton, Gordon, 14, 112.
Cochereau, Pierre, 162.
Collinson, T H, 67, 68, 72, 81, 109.
Copenhagen, 130.
Corelli, 52.
Coxon, Carolyn, 95, 121.

Cromwell, Oliver, 77.
Crosfield, G P C, 80, 93, 109, 130, 171, 174.
Crowe, James, 82.
Cullington, Donald, 82.
Czerny, 28.

Dams, C T H, 28, 59.
Davie, C Thorpe, 119.
Davies, Robert, 91.
Davis, Andrew, 130.
Deering, Richard, 77.
Delius, 33, 101.
Dexter, Harold, 39, 44, 47, 49.
Dickens, Charles, 26.
Dorward, David, 72, 115.
Dickson, Elizabeth, 93.
Dickson, Hester, 93.
Dickson, Joan, 93.
Doig, John, 94.
Dowden, John, 67.
Dunlop, Colin, 71, 75, 79.
Duruflé, Maurice, 72.
Dvorak, 21.
Dwane, Eddie, 26.

Edinburgh 61, 63, 73.
    Chamber Orchestra, 72.
    International Festival, 112, 114, 117.
    Old St Paul's Church, 67.
    St Giles' Cathedral, 67, 109, 118.
    St John's Church, 66, 71, 79.
    St Mary's Episcopal Cathedral, 16, 24, 59, 166.
        Centenary Celebrations, 108 (ff).
        Choir, 66, 70, 113.
        Choir School, 24, 68.
        Clergy, 75, 79 (ff).
        Organists, 81, 82, 83, 84, 104, 161 (ff).
        "Royal" occasions, 103, 104.
        Song School, 66, 85, 91, 95.
    St Mary's Music School, 93 (ff), 110, 113, 146.

St Mary's Roman Catholic Cathedral, 109, 187.
    Theological College, 73, 102.

Edmonstone, A F, 90.
Edwards, John, 40.
Ellingworth, Dorothy, 35.
Ellingworth, Harris, 22, 35.
Ellingworth, Mrs Mabel, 35.
Ellingworth, Tony, 35.
Elliott, Kenneth, 71.
Elsmere, E C H, 28.
Elsmere, Miss, 28.
Elwes, Gervase, 33.
Esam, Gerald, 23.

Fauré, 73, 116.
Federation of Cathedral Old Choristers' Associations, 75, 111, 185.
Fellowes, E H, 30.
Ferguson, R, 94.
Ferrier, Kathleen, 14.
Finch, Norman, 55, 110.
Fisher, Geoffrey, 48, 89.
Fisher, Roger, 165.
Flatt, Roy, 73.
Fletcher, Peter, 44.
Forbes, Graham, 75, 171.
Forster, Peter, 75.
Foskett, Reginald, 59, 79.
Foskett, Daphne, 79.
Fountain, George, 19.
Fox, Douglas, 32.
France, 127.
    Côte dAzur, 127.
    Nice, 127.
    Paris, 128, 162.
Franck, César, 27, 132, 140.
Franklin, G F, 29.
Freeman, Jack, 18.
Freeman, "Bill", 18, 19, 112.
Freeman, Michael, 17, 35, 37.
Freemasonry, 55, 170.

Jackson, Priscilla, 60, 163.
Jacobson, Maurice, 33.
Jeffcoat, Richard, 98.
Jeffcoat, Rupert, 98, 113.
Johnson, Robert, 71.
Johnson, Ronald, 105.
Jones, Kari, 101.
Jones, Louise, 101.
Joubert, John, 163.
Joyce, Robert, 48.

Keith, John, 68.
Kellie, Edward, 66.
Kidd, Robert, 71.
Kilbrandon, Lord, 64.
Kimpton, Geoffrey, 22.
Kimpton, Norah, 21.
King Charles I, 66, 110.
King, Geoffrey, 72, 97.
Knight, Gerald, 48.
Kodaly, Zoltan, 51.

Lambeth Palace, 48.
Landale, Susan, 104, 128.
Langdon, Jack, 64.
Langdon, Ralph, 64.
Langlais, Jean, 162.
Ledger, Philip, 134, 169.
Leighton, Kenneth, 72, 107, 108, 115,
    116-118, 130, 167, 187.
Ley, H G, 48.
Lincoln 7, 35, 75.
    Cathedral, 11, 13, 18.
    Cathedral Choir, 12, 22.
    Cathedral Clergy, 34.
    Cathedral Song School, 11.
    City Football Ground, 34.
    City School, 22.
    Competitive Festival, 21, 33.
    Imp, 13.
    Lincoln School, 11, 14, 18, 24, 75.
    Lincoln Theological College, 20, 34.
    Musical Society, 14.
    Orchestral Society, 14.

South Park High School, 21.
St Mary-le-Wigford, 20, 28.
St Mary Magdalen, 28.
St Michael-on-the-Mount, 20.
St Peter-at-Gowts, 10, 37.
St Peter-at-Gowts Primary School, 11.
St Peter-at-Gowts Youth Fellowship,
    34, 35.
Lloyd Webber, Andrew, 54, 114.
Lloyd Webber, Julian, 54.
Lloyd Webber, William, 54.
Lochgilphead, 73.
Lodge Canongate, Kilwinning, 167.
Louth 20, 37.
    Choral Society, 39, 40, 57.
    Grammar School, 37, 39, 40, 145.
    Louth Music Club, 43.
    Louth Orchestral Society, 40.
    Louth Parish Church, 37, 41, 149.
    Parish Church Choir, 42.
    Parish Church Clergy, 39.
Lumsden, David, 44, 109, 166.
Lythgoe, Clive, 51.

Maksymiuk, Jerzy, 102.
Manchester Camerata, 52.
Mansfield, 41, 59.
Market Rasen, 32, 50.
Markham, Gervase, 45, 59.
Marriner, Neville, 27, 43.
Marsden, Lisle, 55.
Martineau, George, 93.
Massey, Roy, 50, 164, 165.
Mathias, William, 72.
Maxwell Davies, Peter, 102.
McKenzie Report, 93.
McKie, William, 59.
McLeod, John, 72, 115.
Meanwell, Rebecca, 9.
Mendelssohn, 71, 72, 99, 132.
Menuhin, Yehudi, 12, 93, 96, 112.
Messiaen, 162.
Messiah, 14.
Methodist Church, 22, 51, 54.

Milford, T R, 34.
Missin, Russell, 44.
Moiseiwitch, 32.
Moss, Basil, 34.
Mountney, Frederick, 32.
Mozart, 27, 71, 116, 173, 179.
Munns, Robert, 44, 60.
Murray, David, 96, 165.
Murray, Nigel, 95, 152, 171.

Nassau, 169.
Naylor, Peter, 72.
Newark, 26, 56.
Newman, Sydney, 59, 93.
Nicholas, Michael, 50, 57.
Nolan, Michael, 94.
Norman and Beard, 37.
Northampton, 48.
Northcote, Sydney, 33.
Norway 133, 141.
    Aamodt, Thorlief, 134.
    Bergen, 133, 142.
    Kristiansand, 133.
    Stavanger, 133.
    Sangolt, Roald, 141.
    Stord, 141.
Nye, Sharon, 94.

Oakeley, Herbert, 86.
Ogdon, John, 50.
Old Coates House, 68, 95.
Ormiston, Forbes, 59.
Orr, Robin, 107.
Osborne, Steven, 101.
Owens, Matthew, 82.
Oxford,
    Christ Church, 48, 81.
    New College, 30.

Palestrina, 68.
Panton, Kathrein, 75.
Parry, C H H, 21.
Parsons, Eric, 81.
Pattison, George, 75.

Pears, Peter, 32.
Peebles, David, 71.
Phillips, John, 26, 33.
Philomusica of London, 57.
Pini, Carl, 57.
Pollard, E M, 11.
Polwarth, Jean, 96.
Porter, George, 37.
Poston, Elizabeth, 52, 187.
Procter, Norma, 14.
Purcell, Henry, 68, 144.

Race, Steve, 27.
Ramsay, Ivor, 79.
Raphael, Roger, 93.
Redshaw, Alec, 51, 110.
Richardson, Enid, 19.
Richardson, Rupert, 19.
Riches, Kenneth, 52.
Rimmer, Frederick, 107.
Robson, Stanley, 45.
Rodger, Patrick, 79-81, 109.
Rose, Andrew, 77.
Rose Music Shop, 20.
Rotary, 43, 55, 64, 104, 147, 179.
Routley, Erik, 48, 187.
Royal Academy of Music, 19.
Royal College of Music, 27.
Royal College of Organists, 29, 48.
Royal School of Church Music, 42, 48,
    59, 60, 111, 117, 172, 185.
Royal Scottish Academy of Music and
    Drama, 30, 63, 93, 109.
Rushworth and Dreaper, 90.

Sanders, John, 50.
Schubert, 27, 71, 116, 179.
Schütz, 73.
Scotland, Jack, 89.
Scott, George Gilbert, 67, 110.
Scott, John Oldrid, 85, 86.
Scottish Baroque Ensemble, 91.
Scunthorpe, 50.
Seiber, Matyas, 72.